Reminiscences of
Rear Admiral Kemp Tolley
U.S. Navy (Retired)
Volume II

U.S. Naval Institute
Annapolis, Maryland
1984

Preface to Volume II

In this second and concluding volume devoted to his life story, Rear Admiral Tolley continues to spin the sort of tales that make for pleasurable reading. Interspersed with the narrative are a series of strong opinions on a variety of subjects, for Admiral Tolley is a man of conviction. Probably the most striking are his opinions on President Franklin D. Roosevelt and the controversy surrounding the Japanese attack on Pearl Harbor in 1941. At the time, Tolley was skipper of the barely armed schooner Lanikai which had been hastily made a commissioned U.S. Navy ship. In Tolley's account, he and the other crew members were to be sacrificial bait in an attempt to lure the Japanese into starting hostilities. They were saved from such a fate when the Japanese fleet struck at Pearl Harbor instead. Even so, the Lanikai was not yet out of peril, and Tolley provides a fascinating account of her escape from the Philippines to Australia.

The first volume of this history provides ample evidence that Tolley had an unconventional career as a junior officer, marked by sporadic and ultimately successful efforts to learn the Russian language. That training was put to good use when Tolley spent a fair portion of World War II as assistant naval attache in Moscow, and in this narrative he provides a good deal of insight into the frustrations and amusing sidelights of trying to deal with the Soviets. While in Russia, Tolley married a Russian, and it took a great deal of effort to get her out of the country--another very convincing demonstration that little was easy where the Soviets were involved.

Late in the war, the unconventional officer moved into a billet that was quite conventional for one of his rank. He was navigator of the fast battleship North Carolina during the closing months of the war against Japan. Afterward he was an intelligence officer in Washington, and later at the Armed Forces Staff College, for he had demonstrated a great talent for intelligence collection in previous tours of duty.

During the late 1940s and early 1950s, Tolley developed yet another specialty to go with intelligence and foreign languages--this time in amphibious warfare. Assignment after assignment took him to the "gator navy": as commanding officer of the attack transport Vermilion, Commander LST Squadron Two, operations officer on the staff of Commander Amphibious Group Two, and Commander Amphibious Squadron Five. The amphibs have long been considered a neglected part of the Navy, but that is certainly not the case here; in Tolley's description of his various duties, the men and ships of the amphibious force get their due.

To round out the telling of his naval story, Admiral Tolley provides an account of his years in Japan. The man who might have been killed by the Japanese on board the Lanikai wound up instead as commander of the former Imperial Japanese Navy base in Yokosuka, a splendid support facility for U.S. Seventh Fleet by the time Tolley arrived in the mid-1950s. The diplomatic talents he had demonstrated in Russia were to serve him in good

Preface--Page 3

stead in his development of a marvelous rapport with the Japanese. He succeeded as a goodwill ambassador to such an extent that the Japanese did not want him to leave when it came time for him to retire from active duty in the Navy.

Probably something of the same feeling will come to a reader at the end of this second volume. The story has been such fun that one is inclined to wish that the admiral's account would not end.

                                            Paul Stillwell
                                            Director of Oral History
                                            U.S. Naval Institute
                                            March 1984

REAR ADMIRAL KEMP TOLLEY
U. S. Navy Retired

Kemp Tolley was born in Manila, Philippine Islands, on 29 April 1908, son of the late Mrs. Oscar Kemp (Beulah Passano) Tolley of Baltimore, Maryland, and the late Lieutenant Colonel O. K. Tolley, USA, of Harford County Maryland. He attended Baltimore Polytechnic Institute prior to his appointment to the U. S. Naval Academy, Annapolis, Maryland, on 16 June 1925 as a Midshipman from Maryland. There he was a member of the gym team and rifle team all four years. Graduated and commissioned ensign on 6 June 1929, he was subsequently promoted to the rank of rear admiral at the time of his retirement from active duty in June 1959.

After graduation from the Naval Academy in June 1929, he spent the summer with the Navy Rifle Team at Wakefield, Massachusetts, and at Camp Perry, Ohio, then for seven months served on board the USS Florida, a unit of Battleship Division Two, Scouting Fleet, as a junior watch and division officer, anti-aircraft division. He remained at sea until June 1934, with successive service as communication watch officer, staff of the Commander in Chief, U. S. Fleet, in USS Texas; in the USS Canopus, flagship and tender for Submarine Squadron Five, Asiatic Fleet, as watch and division officer, deck; communication watch officer on the staff of Commander in Chief, Asiatic Fleet, in USS Houston; and as communication officer in the USS Mindanao, and aide to Commander South China Patrol.

During the period May 1934 until June 1936, he was on duty under instruction in the Russian language at Shanghai, China; Harbin, Mancuria; and Riga, Latvia, and on independent intelligence duty in Eastern Europe. Then he was assigned to the USS Wyoming as watch and division, and turret officer, until March 1937, during which that battleship was a unit of the Training Squadron, Atlantic Fleet. He next served as aide to the Commander South China Patrol, in USS Mindanao, during the early part of the Sino-Japanese War in 1937, and until July 1938. Following that, he was executive officer of the USS Tutuila, a gunboat on the upper Yangtze until November 1939, after which he was again on duty in Shanghai for eight months in an intelligence capacity.

In July 1940 he was detached for return to the United States and from September of that year he was first an instructor in French at the Naval Academy, then instructor of the first and only Naval Reserve midshipman battalion to be trained at the Naval Academy. Again assigned to Asiatic duty, he served four months as executive officer of the Yangtze gunboat USS Wake, and at Manila in early December 1941, commissioned and assumed command of the yacht USS Lanikai, a two-masted 76-foot schooner with a largely Filipino crew. The ship's original mission of fomenting an incident aborted by Pearl Harbor, Tolley sailed her through the Japanese blockade, arriving in Australia three months and 4,000 miles later. For this service he was awarded the Bronze Star with combat V, with the following citation:

> For meritorious service as Commanding Officer of the U.S.S. LANIKAI from 8 December 1941 to 27 April 1942. Commanding an auxiliary schooner converted to a camouflaged radio picket vessel, Captain (then Lieutenant)

Tolley participated in the early phases of the defense of the Philippines, carrying out courier, patrol, and intelligence duties. Later, he volunteered to run the Japanese air and surface blockade to join the Allied Forces in the Netherlands East Indies where he served with distinction with the American-Dutch-British-Australian Forces until waters in that area became untenable. Refusing passage on a larger vessel he again ran the Japanese blockade, sailing his small ship to Fremantle, Australia. By his outstanding professional skill and dangers, Captain Tolley upheld the highest traditions of the United States Naval Service.

From May 1942 until May 1944 he served as assistant naval attache at Moscow, USSR. For service there, he received a letter of commendation, with ribbon, from the Secretary of the Navy, as follows:

> For exceptionally meritorious services as Intelligence Officer and Interpreter to the U. S. Military Mission to the Union of Soviet Socialist Republics from 12 June 1942 to 25 May 1944. His keen observation and brilliant reportorial interpretatings, together with his capacity to handle delicate and difficult liaison problems were of outstanding importance to the maintenance of Allies relations and to the support of the war effort.

The last year of the World War II hostilities he spent as navigator of the battleship USS North Carolina, in the Pacific area with Task Group 38.5 of the Third Fleet, and later operating with Task Force 58. In that capacity the then Commander Tolley participated in the Leyte operation (Luzon, Formosa, China Coast, and Nansei Shoto attacks) in January 1945; assault and occupation of Iwo Jima in February-March 1945; Fifth and Third Fleet raids in support of the Okinawa Gunto operations, during which Tolley was wounded by shell fragments; and Third Fleet operations against Japan, July-August 1945.

He returned to the United States in September 1945 and, reporting for duty to the Navy Department, Washington, D. C., was assigned the Special Branch, Naval Operations until May 1947. He assumed command, in June, of the attack cargo ship USS <u>Vermilion</u> and remained in command until September 1948, during which period that vessel participated in European occupation operations from 1 March to 1 May 1948. He served as Commander LST Squadron Two from September 1948 to August 1949, then had a three year tour as Director of the Intelligence Division at the Armed Forces Staff College, Norfolk, Virginia.

Duty from July 1952 until December 1954 as operations officer on the staff of Commander Amphibious Group Two, preceded his command of Amphibious Squadron Five, which on its deployment to the Far East became Amphibious Group, Western Pacific until June 1956. In August of that year he reported to Commander Fleet Activities, Yokosuka, Japan, as Chief of Staff and Aide, and on 19 June 1958, he was designated Commander Fleet Activities, Yokosuka. On termination of that duty in June 1959, Tolley was decorated by the Emperor of Japan with the Order of the Sacred Treasure, Third Class, for his efforts in promoting Japanese-American friendship and cooperation.

In addition to the Bronze Star, Rear Admiral Tolley holds the Commendation Ribbon, Purple Heart (for wounds received at Okinawa); the Army Unit Citation Badge; Yangtze Service Medal; Navy Expeditionary Medal; China Service Medal; American Defense Service Medal; Asiatic-Pacific Campaign Medal with one silver and two bronze stars (seven operations); European-African Middle East Campaign Medal; World War II Victory Medal; Navy Occupation Service Medal (Europe clasp); National Defense Service Medal;

and the Philippine Defense, Liberation (with star), Independence Ribbon, and Philippine Unit Citation. Also, the Japanese Order of the Sacred Treasure.

Admiral Tolley's residence is Monkton, Maryland. He was married to Vlada Gritsenko of Moscow, USSR, in Moscow on 15 November 1943. They have two daughters, Neena and Lynn. Since retirement, he has written close to one hundred articles for various periodicals, and three books, a trilogy on his life: Yangtze Patrol, Cruise of the Lanikai, and Caviar and Commissars. For some years he has been Historian of the Yangtze River Patrol Association and publisher of its quarterly magazine, The Yangtze Patroller.

DECLARATION OF TRUST

The undersigned does hereby appoint and designate as his (her) Trustee herein, the Secretary-Treasurer and Publisher of the United States Naval Institute to perform and discharge the following duties, powers, and privileges in connection with the possession and use of a certain taped interview between the undersigned and the Oral History Department of the United States Naval Institute.

1. Classification of Transcript.

   (X)a. If classified OPEN, the transcript(s) may be read or the recording(s) audited by the qualified personnel upon presentation of proper credentials, as determined by the Secretary-Treasurer of the U.S. Naval Institute.

   ( )b. If classified PERMISSION REQUIRED TO CITE OR QUOTE, the user will be required to obtain permission in writing from the interviewee prior to quoting or citing from either the transcript(s) or the recording(s).

   ( )c. If classified PERMISSION REQUIRED, permission must be obtained in writing from the interviewee before the transcribed interview(s) can be examined or the tape recording(s) audited.

   ( )d. If classified CLOSED, the transcribed interview(s) and the tape recording(s) will be sealed until a time specified by the interviewee. This may be until the death of the interviewee or for any specified number of years.

2. It is expressly understood that in giving this authorization, I am in no way precluded from placing such restrictions as I may desire upon use of the interview at any time during my lifetime, nor does this authorization in any way affect my rights to the copyright of my literary expressions that may be contained in the interview.

Witness my hand and seal this 31st day of August 1981

I hereby accept and consent to the foregoing Declaration of Trust and the powers therein conferred upon me as Trustee:

10 Sept. 1981

Tolley #4 -485-

Interview No. 4 with Rear-Admiral Kemp Tolley, U.S. Navy (Retired)

Place: At his residence in Monkton, Maryland

Date: Thursday, 25 September 1975

Subject: Biography

By: John T. Mason, Jr.

Q: We begin Chapter 4 today. Last time you had brought us to the point where you arrived in Manila and the war was about to break out and you are about to be given command of the LANIKAI. Will you take over at that point?

Adm. T.: The story that I will probably tell you now has been covered in the book Cruise of the Lanikai which includes the story of the hegira of the ship itself from Manila to Australia and the raison d'etre of the ship in the beginning. However, the fact that the book was published has brought in some comment and also there are some items that I wasn't able to use in the book as I would have been blasted by the serious historians because this is all hearsay or undocumented material but it might be useful to add it in here for historial purposes because I might not have any suitable vehicle ever to put this before the people who might be interested.

One of the items that I knew about at the time of writing the book, but didn't put in it, was the undocumented proof that Roosevelt knew about the proposed Japanese attack on Pearl Harbor before it happened.

The story is this: Admiral Kimmel's lawyer was named Edward Hanify and he in turn had a lawyer friend whose name was Taliaferro (lawyers are in cahoots behind your back and you never quite know who is your friend and who is scratching whose back). In any case, Taliaferro was the lawyer for Roosevelt's son-in-law, Curtis Dall, and after Pearl Harbor Dall, in a burst of confidence, told his friend --Lawyer Taliaferro --that he had been in the White House early in December, which presumably would have been about the first or second; he was already estranged from his wife but he had visiting rights with the kids and the kids were living in the White House at that time. He had dropped in to see the President, with whom he was on good terms still, and the President expressed the following: "We will get our incident but we will take some losses; there might be 19 or 20 planes." And, when he was saying this, Roosevelt was rubbing his hands together in the characteristic gesture that he did when he was pleased with something. Of course Taliaferro was on good terms with Hanify and he told this to Hanify and Hanify said, "For God's sake go back and get this thing in writing, nail it down somehow because this is absolutely essential to our case, to make it clear to Admiral Kimmel in some respects." Well, it happened that Taliaferro had exactly the same idea so when Dall told him this he had said, "Would you make a deposition to that effect?" And Dall had said, "Sure." Taliaferro told Hanify that and Hanify said, "Rush back and get the deposition before he changes his mind," but he was too late as Dall said, "Sorry, I just don't dare because this would estrange me from my family forever, I can't do it." Dall is of course still alive and very active, in fact he is executive director or whatever the head man is at LIBERTY LOBBY. I have never met him personally but we have corresponded and he has suggested that I come over and see him some time. The chances of getting anything out of him now are rather minor, I would say. He has written a book, a small one, called My Exploited Father-in-law, F.D.R. The book doesn't reveal too much but it has some veiled references in there that make it fairly evident to anyone who knows the background to the whole thing, that there was far more than met the eye in the joint Congressional investigation of Pearl Harbor. Obviously, he is reluctant to reveal these things and I am sure he knows it. Of course, that was another blind alley and we can't do a thing about it because we have no documentary proof and I strongly doubt that Dall would talk because it would make him look almost like a perjurer due to the fact that he didn't speak up when the time was ripe--at the time of the investigation--to save a man, certainly not crucified so long and so tightly to the cross as Kimmel was.

Another interesting clue which opens up a whole new ballgame as far as George Marshall is concerned: Just the other day I saw an article in the paper--a long feature piece--"Who is one of the greatest men of the generation?" Of course the subject of the article was George Marshall. There are two schools of thought on George Marshall and the majority school is that he was a magnificent fellow--that he was essential in bringing the United States out of the morass of the war, both as Secretary of State and of course his previous duty as Chief of Staff of the Army which he whipped together in record shape, got it over on the other side, marvelously equipped and so forth--all these things are said to be the work of George Marshall. Of course, the so-called Marshall Plan was largely the work of George Kennan, but you don't hear George Kennan's name batted around - Marshall is given the credit for making it up and ramming it through. What appears to be more like an honest assessment of the guy is that he was a marvelously loyal subordinate of FDR's. Of course, any military man, when he gets an order, is supposed to give a cheery "Aye, aye, Sir", and regardless of what he thinks or what advice he had given prior to that, once the decision is made he is expected to go on and do it without quibble, question, equivocation, or in any sense not putting his full shoulder behind the order. Obviously that was Marshall's main proclivity and undoubtedly his main value as far as Roosevelt was concerned. Stark was different. Stark would give him the cheery "Aye, aye, Sir" and all that but he had nothing like the strength of personality that Marshall had and he created not a patch of the awe on his subordinates that Marshall did--they were all scared to death of Marshall but nobody was ever scared stiff of "Betty" Stark, they thought he was a nice, old man. He was a bright man but I don't think anybody would dispute the fact that he was not a strong man. So, what we conclude then was that Marshall was given more or less carte blanche, although FDR had a Chief of Staff in the form of Admiral Leahy an official White House Chief of Staff, his real chief of staff and his real alter-ego, other than in the purely political world, was George Marshall; of course the political guy was Harry Hopkins.

The many small things that pop up, for example, in the joint investigation of Congress into Pearl Harbor, there are at least four that I can think of, instances on Marshall's part where he either intentionally lied, under oath, or his memory was so bad that it almost suggested that he was talking himself out of the situation which he knew but didn't want to be associated with. He was questioned by some very clever lawyers and there were occasions where he made flat statements that such and such was the case-- that he had or had not seen certain documents and then they would produce the documents with his initials on--so the inference is that he initialed stuff without knowledge what he was initialing or he had a very bad memory or he was simply prevaricating--that he knew he had seen it but didn't want to be associated with it. Of course, the most famous situation of all--the so-called lapse of memory on where he was on the night prior to Pearl Harbor. This, of course, was not all that long afterward, it was in 1945 and 1946 that this investigation went on--that after all was only four years after the date of one of the most momentous incidents in all history, certainly all contemporary history, and how a man cannot remember where he was is rather expressive at least.

Now one of the readers of my book was a man named Stahlman, who was the owner and editor of one of the premier newspapers in Tennessee. During the war, in fact long before the war, he had been in the publishing business, he was a professional newspaper man and publisher, as was Colonel Knox, the Secretary of the Navy. They had been friends, so Stahlman got into the Navy and was a commander and was more or less closely associated with Knox and was one of the few people who was able to walk into Knox's office when he felt like it without an appointment. Shortly after Pearl Harbor, Knox told him, and Stahlman told me, that he, Knox, had been at the White House the night prior to Pearl Harbor along with Betty Stark, Hopkins, Stimson and one or two others and that they had sat around and conferred and waited, in effect, for something to happen during the wee hours of 7 December. Now, of course, we all know that Admiral Stark was at the theatre the night before Pearl Harbor, that Roosevelt tried to get in touch with him and when he found he was at the theatre he deferred and said "I don't want to have him paged because that will cause a flap. Everybody in Washington knows who Stark is." He didn't want to startle people so he left word for Stark to call him back when he got home. Now we don't know the content of that conversation, we have never even heard hints on it but one suggests, under the circumstances, that it was a call to get the hell over to the White House on the double, and that is where Marshall was according to Knox--at the White House. It seems pretty far fetched to imagine that Marshall could not remember where he was when, according to Secretary Knox, the whole crowd was there waiting tensely for either the attack on Pearl Harbor or an attack somewhere--they knew it would be coming somewhere as they had absolutely, positive information from daily overflights of the Japanese fleet on its way to Malaya. But the question is did they or did they not know about Pearl that far in advance? Now the Dall thing ties in to suggest that if the attack on Pearl was known but they didn't expect it to be anything like the force it was. The fact that Roosevelt told Dahl there would be 19 or 20 planes, that we would take some damage but we would get our incident suggest that they were desperately hoping that this 'small' incident would take place. Of course Roosevelt's faith in the Navy was such that probably they would be able to repulse it or if the damage was slight that it would be worth it. Another thing it suggests is that in the days prior to Pearl Harbor early in the month, he had promised Lord Halifax, the British Ambassador who had been importuning Roosevelt for weeks as to what his attitude would be if the Japanese attack came in the Far East and not the United States, to let him know what the United States attitude would be. Well all Roosevelt could tell him was that constitutionally the United States could not make war without Congress's declaring such--things were a little different in those days. So, around the first or second of December he assured Halifax that we could look with favor upon any conceivable aid which we would give the British in such a contingency. Then when Halifax came around again on the third or fourth, Roosevelt said, "When I said aid I meant armed aid but we will know in a few days whether we can do this or not. Now the few days of course would have been about the time it either took LANIKAI to get on station or (this of course Roosevelt had set up himself), or he expected the attack to materialize on Pearl Harbor--what else could have prompted him to make that statement?

So, also corroborated by Admiral Richardson's book, On the Treadmill to Pearl Harbor, in his closing chapters which by the way got by the Navy censorship in the form of Department of Naval History only by a squeak and only because Admiral Radford was so adamant that those last chapters should go in. Admiral Richardson, who had been Commander in Chief of the Pacific Fleet before he was fired in January of 1941 and replaced by Admiral Kimmel, had protested about having the fleet out there due to the exposed position and apparently that was one of the basic reasons he had been fired; there was another reason of course, that he had told the President in October of 1940 that the high command of the Navy had no confidence in the political leadership, which of course was a tremendously impertinent thing for a commander in chief to tell a President. Those things are in Richardson's book; and also the fact that he felt, although he had no proof, that Marshall had been designated as the only one who could send the warning to Pearl Harbor, and that this was corroborative by the fact that Stark, on the morning of Pearl Harbor (before it happened of course in Washington--this was 9 or ten o'clock in the morning and that was still 4 or 5 o'clock at Pearl) that the intercepted messages between Tokyo and Washington addressed to the Japanese Ambassador made it apparent that something was about to happen and that that something was most likely to happen at Washington time of 1 o'clock which would be 7:30 a.m. Pearl time (Zone plus 10:30 at that time). Stark demurred, he picked up the telephone then put it back down again by which he could make a direct scrambler phone call to Kimmel. The inference from that is that Marshall was indeed the one designated as the sole authority who could warn Pearl. The night before, Secretary Knox, having read the original 13 parts of the communication to the Ambassador, but not the executive part, the last part which said when to deliver the message, which was the key thing, Secretary Knox had sent a message personally warning Kimmel and when Knox got out there after Pearl Harbor, the first thing he did was to ask Kimmel, "Didn't you get my warning message that something was about to happen that would possibly involved Pearl Harbor?" Kimmel said, "No, I didn't get any message." Somebody killed the message. Obviously cabinet officer's messages are not loosely trifled with so all these things tie in and unfortunately none of it can be documented; all we have is the word of individuals who are either the party of the first part or party of the second part, on pretty fair corroboration from other sources. But again, undocumented and obviously you cannot base a book on rumor, at least not a serious history or something that purports to change something that has already been pretty well accepted as history without some sort of documentation. I don't think we will ever get our hands on it--it probably doesn't exist and it never did. Roosevelt was well known for either having given verbal instructions or using small memos which corroborated or gave the go-ahead on something he had already directed verbally so that there wasn't any piece of paper where the entire story was laid down on some of these actions of tremendous import.

For example: When Roosevelt directed that the three small ships be set up to be sent off the Indo-Chinese coast to "Report on Japanese moves", the whole thing being obviously a crack-brained scheme if, on the face of it, that were the real reason, he didn't put a thing in writing--there is absolutely nothing in writing in Roosevelt's hand; he called Stark over and described to him what he wanted done, Stark rushed back and told these specific details to his assistant Chief of Naval Operations, Royal Ingersoll and Admiral Ingersoll spent the afternoon being absolutely sure that he had gotten the proper gist of what the President wanted done and concurrently was making absolutely sure that it would be apparent to anybody who ever read the message that it was not Stark's idea but specifically the President's idea and that, he accomplished. Furthermore when Ingersoll (who I would say was without a doubt the most honest witness who ever appeared before the Joint Congressional Committee of Investigation) was questioned on this movement of the three small ships, he made it perfectly clear under repeated questioning from different angles, that it was solely Roosevelt's idea and that the Navy would <u>not</u> have done it both for reasons of practicality and for reasons of squandering manpower and that the ships could serve no useful purpose for the spurious reasons for which Roosevelt had it set up. All the complement of the three ships would probably have been no more than one hundred men--no it would have been more than that because ISABEL had at that time a crew of 125 and the other two ships, small chartered crafts such as the LANIKAI, would probably have had 20 apiece, so let us say they had a total complement of 150 men.

Q: The third ship, I take it, was never designated.

Adm. T.: The third ship was procured, it was a yacht about half the size of the LANIKAI and it lay alongside the dock at Cavite being outfitted and its name was the MOLLY MOORE. Subsequently she was taken up the Pasig River and burned before the Japanese occupied the city.

Those are some supplemental thoughts to be thrown in which were not in the <u>Cruise of the Lanikai</u>.

Admiral Standley had been Chief of Naval Operations in the mid-1930s and he was a strong and loyal supporter of President Roosevelt in all of the things he was doing which, from Standley's point of view, were all to the good because they were building up the Navy. There were several reasons for Roosevelt's enthusiasm about that, obviously the first one was that he loved the Navy and wanted to see it strong. Secondly he felt sure that he would manage somehow to get the country into war against the Nazis eventually and for that they would need a Navy. And, thirdly, it was a make-work proposition because the earlier shipbuilding to augment the Navy, the new cruisers particularly, were all built with work-relief funds, not Navy appropriations and it was a means of creating jobs for the vast numbers of unemployed; the unemployed rolls of course continued to be extremely high until we actually got into the war--which some people claim was one of the reasons why Roosevelt was so keen to support the British because by that means they could establish a large war industry and actually there were a lot of industrialists that had to be strongly coaxed and bribed--in the sense that they were guaranteed orders--to set up these factories. A great many of the industrialists of that time felt that the possibility of a British collapse was excellent, and, having built all these factories and spent all this money and capabilities, then what happens after the requirement for the arms is no longer there after the British have fallen? As far as Roosevelt was comcerned, it was necessary to do everything he could buck up the British by sending more and more supplies, by building up our own forces so that we could give evidence of our ability to come to their aid if the situation got too desperate.

I've gotten off the track a little, what we started off with was Standley. Actually Standley was a strong proponent of all these things and he was a loyal supporter of Roosevelt. In 1941, after Pearl Harbor, Roosevelt obviously knew that he had to have somebody who, presumably, would be on his side and would be far enough divorced from the current naval activities so as not to have any concurrent loyalties other than that to the Navy as a whole, so Standley was an obvious choice to be sent out to Pearl Harbor to view the damage and to make a preliminary assessment as to where the fault lay. I don't know whether he went out concurrently with Secretary Knox or separately, but in any case it was just a few days after Pearl Harbor that he went out. He came back and reported and his report is a matter of record. Then he was chosen on what you might almost call a drum-head court martial, the so-called Roberts Commission, and Justice Roberts being the chief member of the Investigating Committee of course had a tremendous amount of power and he was pretty much in Roosevelt's hand. He was a Republican, Justice Owen Roberts; he was a loyal supporter of FDR and he was trusted fully on this particular assignment. The constitution of that committee was such that it was pretty well stacked against any favorable decision as far as Kimmel was concerned. And, presumably, FDR felt that Admiral Standley would be a tame duck; but he wasn't. By the time he had gotten this commission under way and he had heard some of the testimony, he had changed his views considerably and, in a subsequent interview with Admiral Standley (this is all down on paper), he was disgusted with the whole procedure which he felt was ramrodded through-- Kimmel had no chance to testify with benefit of counsel. Of course, at that stage of the game, the fact that we were intercepting and decoding Japanese messages was not then known, nor was it used by the people on the court--this information was closely held until after the war--the fact that we even were breaking the Japanese code. They didn't know that on this commission and as a result they couldn't even infer that there could possibly be any complicity or any shortcomings at all on the Washington end. The whole thing could be classed otherwise as 100% culpability on the part of the people in Pearl. Admiral Standley wrote a minority opinion, and he also said in this interview (of which I have a copy) that the proceedings were run in such a slipshod way and they had two court reporters who were utterly incompetent, so that when he would try to review the evidence given the day before he could make nothing of it--items would be left out, others would be substituted, and the whole thing was a farce, so he wrote a minority opinion. When the report was in, somehow the minority opinion got lost; when Standley later checked up on it he found his minority opinion was not amongst those present. Of course by the time he got to Moscow he had had time to ruminate and sort of review the 'bidding'.

Q: Admiral Standley's appointment to Moscow came after that?

Adm. T.: After the smoke had cleared away from the Roberts Investigation he was appointed Ambassador to Moscow and he was there when I got there. We have skipped some intervening items so we will go back to the end of our cruise on the LANIKAI, and how I got to Moscow.

When LANIKAI got to West Australia there was no Asiatic Fleet left; out of the whole Asiatic Fleet of 2 cruisers, 12 destroyers, 28 submarines and 28 or 30 PBY flying boats; there then remained about 6 destroyers, all of the submarines except one had managed to get away, all the PBYs were gone, both cruisers--one had been sunk and the other so badly disabled she had to be sent back to the United States, so in effect the Asiatic Fleet had disappeared. What personnel had managed to escape was clustered in Perth, Western Australia. The place was absolutely undefended. There were no ground troops, no Australian Air Force of any consequence on that coast--the place was wide open. Things were so disorganized at that stage of the game that what little forces we had over there, and personnel, were not being made use of in any obvious respect. The commander of the area was Vice Admiral William Glassford who had been the former commander of a task force in the bob-tailed Asiatic fleet and actually there was nothing for what remained of the Navy there to do. Naturally enough, I felt this just like all the rest of us did. One day while I was lying alongside the dock Commander Creighton, who had been naval observer at Singapore, came down; he is an old friend of mine, we had been in ONI for quite some

time back and I think related before how I went to see Creighton and how I sent letters back directed to him, so he and I were on very good terms. He said "What in the world is a person with your capabilities in speaking the Russian language and with your intelligence experience doing in a back-wash like this, just lying around on a schooner. I said "My views are exactly 100% along those same lines, captain, but I would have been there too if circumstances had been a little different." Actually to get around to the beginning of all this, I had been a French prof at the Naval Academy in 1940--got there in 1940 and left in the spring of

1941--and I lived in an apartment in the Officers' Club and it was a pretty bare existence--most of the eligible young ladies in Annapolis had been led to the altar at graduation practically at the age of consent and there was nobody to associate with for a bachelor of thirty, so I was anxious to get out. But while there I used to fling some parties in the place and I thought first of all that this 'Bundles for Britain' party was such an asinine travesty on anything to really benefit the war, it was one of these 'do-gooder' propositions that had been gotten together by a lot of ladies who had nothing better to do, but aside from that fact, I lived in the club and they would have the party there about once a week and keep me awake until about 3:00 A.M. Just for funzies I had quite a few lapel buttons left that I had gotten in Shanghai (people wore over there to identify themselves) and they were Nazi buttons and Italian Fascist buttons and American flags and all those little things and I used to drop down to these Bundles for Britain parties wearing a Nazi button and nobody ever noticed me except one Russian assistant to old Daddy Weems. He didn't say a word about it. I used to talk Russian to him and call him Comrade, which incensed him enormously. But apparently the word got back to somebody and I learned later through friends at ONI, that they thought I was on the wrong side, that I was—in fact they weren't quite sure what side I was on because I had Nazi flags and Soviet flags hanging up in my room and some of the officers had gone over there, including Admiral VonHeimburg (he was then Commander VonHeimburg). Just for fun I had painted a picture—I am not much of a painter but I had exposed a negative with a projector, on the wall, and filled it in with chalk. So one time I had an elderly commander up there at one of these parties, the flags were on the wall—they were a permanent fixture—and this thing that I had painted on the wall was about five or six feet wide and four or five feet high, somebody commented on it and I said, "It is a very convenient thing because sometimes these walls seem to be closing in on me and that picture of the Yangtze River and the gunboat on it, of course my own home I feel safe there so I just pass out through that scene on the wall." Apparently the old boy who was there I guess didn't have a sense of humor and he told somebody later, "You know that guy Tolley has the most peculiar ideas, I wonder if he is all right?" There are people like that in the Navy with absolutely no sense of humor.

Q: Why did you run the risk though, with the Nazi buttons and that sort of thing?

Adm. T.: I didn't give a damn.

Q: You knew the possible implications?

Adm. T.: Of course I did, I was just baiting people, that's the way I was. I felt you never get to the bottom of anything until you stir up people's emotions and make them talk and then you can present your side or pretend it's your side but take their side and then switch. It's just part of the game that I used to like to play. In fact I still do, I like to bait people because otherwise you never get into any meaningful discussion.

Q: I know you do that, you like to be the devil's advocate, but you also know the way the Intelligence Organization work and how they stamp a person indelibly.

Adm. T.: Perhaps, but in this case as I have mentioned previously, I was planning to go back to China, marry my fiancee, settle down in China; of course in those days par for the course was Lieutenant Commander and Commander. It was very different unless you were one of the nose-to-the grindstone types or had particularly high attributes in gunnery or some special area of activity in the Navy but just a common, ordinary sailor like I was had no potential of ever expecting to be an admiral--that was the general feeling in those days. So, I didn't give a damn, to tell you the truth.

In June 1941, when the Nazis attacked the Russians the obvious thing seemed to me to be to get the hell over to the Soviet Union where I would be useful. I immediately jumped on my horse and went over to Washington to the detail office for lieutenants and asked about going out there. Of course you would never have known there was a war going on in Washington at that time. Certainly not in the Navy Department. They had all the leisure in the world. I sat around for half an hour I guess and talked to the two or three lieutenants in the detail section about going out and they let me off on different things. They said, "You know we have had people go out there for a third cruise and it is sort of like the guy going down for the third time, sometimes it is fatal. We have had two or three of them do that and they went off the rails. Tell you the truth all we want to do is have a little bull session with you and find out whether you seem normal or not. That's why we have been taking so long sitting around chatting about extraneous matters." And they said, "You seem perfectly O.K. to us, you're on your way." That sounded good to me. Before that, before even the Russians attacked, I saw this thing coming on. I had gone over to ONI early in the Spring, long before that and by that time VonHeimburg was in ONI as one of the factotums, so I naturally approached him as an old friend. I don't know what his desk was but he was in a position of influence and of course the German desk in those days controlled the Russian area, the Middle European area in which Russia was included; we had no naval attaché in Russia when I had been a language student in Riga, Latvia--I had been attached to the embassy in Berlin. We had no chance to get into the Soviet Union as they wouldn't allow us to come in as language students. In any case, VonHeimburg, recollecting no doubt the activity in the Tolley apartment, had demurred on sending me over there. Naturally when I went back to the detail office and walked right in to the guys and they said "Sure, you are on your way to the Far East," I thought well, going out to China is one thing and going to Russia is quite another. I am still not in Russia, but at least I can have the good luck to get off at Shanghai and stay there. But the chances are extremely small. The only ships we had in China were the river gunboats, the outside fleet didn't go up to China any more. The fact perhaps that I was a bachelor was behind my having been ordered to the USS WAKE at Shanghai, which happened to be there which was a great windfall for me. Actually, as it turned out, I didn't stay in China long, as we know the developments came along and I was soon on my way to Manila.

To get back again to Creighton; Creighton sent a message to Washington straight away; he said, "We'll get you en route to Russia where you belong. Meanwhile for want of something better to do, they decided the LANIKAI would be just the thing to go up the Australian coast for about a thousand miles and check the possible landing places or base areas for patrol seaplanes--Exmouth Gulf and Shark Bay. Shark Bay was the real place, Exmouth Gulf was too far north and too exposed; they thought Shark Bay might have some estuaries that would be ideal. Nobody knew anything about it, including the Australians. So up goes the LANIKAI and we spent about three or four weeks up there reconnoitering the place and of course we found no Japanese infiltrators, as we expected we might find they had been put ashore there to observe our aircraft movements. So, when we were on our way back we stopped at Geraldton, about 100 miles north of Perth and there was message there for me to get out to the airfield as there was a plane waiting there to take me down to Perth. From there

I went to Albany in southwest Australia and got aboard the tanker TRINITY and the TRINITY took 30 days to get to Abadan, Iraq--they went practically straight west until it was more or less due south of Iraq and then it turned north, the theory being that the Indian Ocean was hunting ground for Japanese and German submarines.

Q: Whose flag was she flying?

Adm. T.: The TRINITY was a tanker, one of the two naval tankers for the Asiatic Fleet. She was on her way up to Iraq for a load of oil to bring back to West Australia. So after this 30-day uneventful cruise, sighting absolutely nothing all the way, we finally got to Abadan and found it in the throes of a superior flap too, because German infiltrators had just tried to engineer a coup to take over Iraq. You may recall that Persia had been whacked up as it had been in 1907, the first time with the north part in the hands of the Russians, (Soviets in 1940 or 1941) and the British in the south, the theory being to circumvent any hanky-panky on the part of the Shah of Iran (the father of the present Shah) who was considered to be pro-German. Iraq was at that time hanging on the ropes too. So, Abadan was a very active place with lots of British troops around who had been flown in, Indian troops who were there to protect the only entrance we had for the southern flow of Lend-Lease; we had a very large military mission in Iran at that time, and they were sending military supplies (this was now in May 1942) and tremendous caravans of military supplies would go from the rail head above Teheran into the USSR, truckloads of war material and the trucks themselves. So it was a very important place. I stayed there about three or four days in Abadan and then went up to Teheran. Of course Abadan was as hot as the hinges of hell in the summertime and it was already at the point where you could scarcely stand it. Just as an indication of the way the Navy sometimes found itself running things--the British, as usual in a place like that, were there in superior numbers and a superior rank although 99% of the activity as far as the supply business was concerned was American, it was all American Lend-Lease coming through there but the British were holding the throttle valve so to speak, at the mouth of the Gulf, the mouth of the Euphrates River. I was very much surprised, among other things, to find there one of the Yangtze River gunboats, it was the CICALA and had come all the way around from China. It was one of the peripatetic flat-iron monitor type gunboats which had been built in 1917 for service on the Euphrates and on the Dvina River in North Russia and it finally wound up in China and served there for practically a generation. Some had been interned on the Yangtze River and this particular one had made her way back around to the Euphrates again where she had originally been intended to go. Anyway I got up to Teheran. I had no civilian clothes. In fact, I was wearing an Australian Army uniform because that was the only thing available in Western Australia. All the blue had long since been taken by the so-called refugees, those refugees being the former Asiatic Fleet. In fact Admiral Glassford himself was wearing a navy cut uniform made of Royal Australian Air Force sky blue and he suggested to some of his officers that they do likewise. He was rather a flamboyant type, very pro-British himself and liked to ape the British even to the extent sometimes of wearing patent leather chin-strap and high white hose with his shorts, which Americans rarely did. So the Royal Australian Air Force sky blue uniforms suited him very well. Anyway I turned up in Teheran in this Australian Army uniform with horse pants and kangaroo skin boots and with the intention of getting some civilian clothes. I had been informed on arrival that it was the intention to send me out to Vladivostok and for that purpose I would have to have civilian clothes. The Russians had allowed us to establish a naval observer out there, stationed in the consulate general as a member of the consulate general but not as a naval officer because the Japanese were also established there in a consulate general and they would have been extremely suspicious had they seen an American naval officer in uniform in those parts. Probably in effect, they would have demanded the same rights, which obviously the Russians were neither eager nor willing to do. So that is why the civilian clothes. Anyway, having just about gotten myself organized to go out and get some civilian clothes, I got a message from the American Embassy in Teheran to get cracking with the mail. I went around to the embassy to see about this and there was a gentleman there by the name of Minor, Second Secretary I guess, as I recall, so Mr. Minor was very nasty about the whole thing and he said "Haven't you heard there is a war going on? You're sitting around here on your fat backside in Teheran when you should be up there carrying on where you are supposed to be." I refrained from making any remarks about my foreknowledge about what kind of war was going on and after all one takes orders from the State Department under those circumstances, so I grabbed the mail bags and up I got to Kuibyshev --which was then the provisional capital of the Soviet Union. They had moved it from Moscow when the Germans were at the gates in December of 1941.

Q: Was it that easy to get transportation?

Adm. T.: The planes were flying regularly. Some of these were supply planes. They were Russian aircraft out of Teheran; my particular one as I recall, had two British Embassy mail couriers aboard and the rest were Russian civilians or military of one type or another.

Q: And you were in Australian uniform?

Adm. T.: I was in Australian uniform which, of course, didn't make any particular difference because I don't suppose they knew the difference between an Australian and an American anyway. But I had a perfectly good American passport so that was good enough to get me past the various frontier guards. We landed in Stalingrad, which was just a fueling stop, so then on to Kuibyshev. I stayed there about ten days after I got there on May 24, and by that time the pressure on Moscow had eased to the point that the legations and embassies had started to move back. I first met Admiral Standley there; he was established in a make-shift embassy--an old school house.

Q: He was replacing whom?

Adm. T.: Lawrence Steinhardt had been the previous Ambassador and he had moved on to Turkey, Ankara. Admiral Standley was more or less isolated from everything. The Russian government was scattered all over hell's half acre. Some of it had remained in Moscow. There was very little, if anything, that could be contacted in Kuibyshev--it was largely a mass of refugees. Food was scarce; some of the members of the embassy staff had mild cases of scurvy. The only thing to eat they had was an occasional meat ball and the British type of sausage which was about 90% cornmeal, the occasional cabbage and potato and that was about it. The Russians were in far worse shape than we were because all they had was black bread alone. One of my old friends turned up there. He was an ex-Asiatic Fleet sailor--George Roullard. He was an assistant naval attaché and George and I were walking up the cobble stone street one day and down, some distance from us, came a very vivid picture in a red sweater. The red sweather was pretty well filled and the fact that it was a cobble stone street and rather rough walking rather enhanced the bounce quality of the stuffing for the sweater and I was very much intrigued; this was the first interesting female I had seen in the Soviet Union. Most of them were just shapeless bundles of dark colored rags and gray faces. But this one was rather gay looking and when we got abeam I was dumbfounded to discover that George was a great friend and we stopped and chatted. She was at the time working for the American Embassy as a translator in the American Naval Attaché's office. About a year and a half later she became Mrs. Tolley.

Q: You met her in Kuibyshev?

Adm. T.: Yes. She had a rather interesting background--When the Lend-Lease was first started when the Russians were first attacked by the Germans, Harriman from the United States and Lord Beaverbrook from Britain went over to make preliminary arrangements for Lend-Lease and they needed translators, which the Russians were short of and we had none. So two former students of the Moscow University from the English language section there, the two students, one that I just spoke of, the young lady called Vlada, and a young man, had been school mates there and they had also been in England together where their fathers had been stationed on duty for the Soviet government, and they were bi-lingual, speaking English and Russian with equal facility. They had been attached to Harriman and Beaverbrook as interpreters and after they left, the embassy had been beefed up considerably and they desperately needed interpreters so they had both been taken on by the US Embassy, the boy as just general handy man and errand runner and interpreter for the embassy and Vlada as interpreter for the naval attaché. There was a considerable amount of paper work as the Russians are great on documents and everything has to be properly stamped and authenticated and so forth. It requires the correct phraseology, so she was very useful. I was very much intrigued by Admiral Standley's attitude. I had never met him before and of course I didn't know his background--the fact that he had been involved in the Pearl Harbor investigation and had seen the place and all that. He is a very close-mouthed man, he never revealed any of these things and I was very intrigued at the time at his very deep interest in my little escapade. So he said, "Having heard you tell this, I would like you to sit down and write this all down on paper."

Q: You mean the LANIKAI?

Adm. T.: The LANIKAI episode, and what my thoughts were on it.

Q: Did you have thoughts then similar to those you have now?

Adm. T.: They were just commencing to burgeon; the whole thing seemed so incredibly naive--that they would send ships out like that on reconnaisance that there just had to be something behind it--particularly when the staff in Surabaja had made every indication in veiled conversations that there was far more to it than met the eye. The reason I knew about that was, when the LANIKAI got to Surabaja we thought, at least I did, (way in the back seat as far as knowledge of the situation was concerned having been at sea and utterly incommunicado for a month) that the Pacific Fleet probably would be on their way out, that this was the end of the retreat, and the Indies would be the bastion and then we would advance from there back on up. So, I was prepared to stay there and be reassigned and start to fight the war again. Meanwhile the LANIKAI had no particular naval service she could perform so I was temporarily detached and sent up to the staff of the Commander of Southwest Pacific as communications watch officer and as such was able to read all the back files, all the correspondence about what was going on and I read myself into the war and you would agree that by my wildest imagination couldn't have believed existed-- the fact that there was an utter and complete debacle, that the Pacific Fleet was no more, in effect, and that there was, from my point of view, a whole new ballgame, and a whole new re-think. Well, among the other dispatches that I read there was the one from Roosevelt directing the three small ships affair.

Naturally enough, both Adair and myself were very much interested in this. Adair had been the flag lieutenant who had never really been employed as such, but he was also a fellow communications watch officer and all the staff had lived in a house in the suburbs that Admiral Glassford had set up as shore headquarters in connection with the Dutch--it was a joint headquarters, Dutch/American. After the port had been so vigorously bombed, it was a beautiful view and all that, but it was far more salubrious and healthful to be back in the suburbs and that is where we lived with practically all the members of the staff--the original members. And, there was much informal discussion about this and that and whenever it seemed expedient, I, as one of the very junior members of the group, brought up the LANIKAI situation; there were always veiled hints as to what they thought it was all about and whether they knew anything more or not I still don't know, but it certainly put me in a position, when I talked to Admiral Standley, to suggest that there was more to it than just what superfically met the eye. Of course, had I known his background, I would have understood his deep curiosity about the whole thing. From this end of the telescope, looking back, why was Standley there in the first place? Somebody wrote a book on the Russians in general, I have forgotten where I read it or when but it was written way back in the nineteenth century, and the suggestion then was that the Russians being a military oriented people and one to which the army was one of the chief props of the regime and the pride of the country and the vehicle by which Russian power would be extended all over Europe, which most Russians secretly and rather hopefully considered to be the future for them-- even then--the military had a glow about it that didn't exist in most countries and this guy knew that--he had been to Russia--and he suggested that the most effective ambassador would be a military man. Now whether somebody read that and took the advice or whether other people had the same view I don't know, but we have a succession of military ambassadors and Standley was one of them and General Bedell Smith was another and there was one more, Admiral Kirk. This I think is a pretty good score for one country, you have had a lot of Naval ambassadors in various places but that is about the best score that I know of for any one country having military ambassadors. So it seemed more or less logical I guess that he should be sent over there. On the other hand, again, somebody way back made the remark that there are two reasons for sending an ambassador to a remote place--one is because the action there demands it, the other is that they want to get him out of the way. Now after the Roberts Investigation, even not having known at that time that the Japanese intercepts existed, obviously Standley felt that it was a frame-up as far as Kimmel and Short were concerned, at Pearl. There is no doubt about it, in his subsequent writing, in the interview (a copy of which I have); I talked to the old gentleman in California in 1953 or 1954; his responses and his whole attitude at that stage had mellowed to the point that he felt free to say what he thought and what he thought was that Kimmel and Short had had a marvelous framing job done on them. Obviously he must have thought that in the beginning, and obviously Roosevelt knew that, because he was expecting a complete and unanimous whitewash by the Robert Commission--that was fairly obvious from the way it was set up and the people chosen-- so when Standley turned up with the minority report (which was mysteriously missing from the files afterward) it seemed probable (just reconstructing the crime so to speak) that the logical thing to do would be to get Standley out of town-- send him some place where he couldn't be got at by newspaper reporters or somebody who might fight out the opposition view.

Q: That perhaps was the implication of my question some time back asking if he was named ambassador to Russia after the Roberts Commission had reported.

Adm. T.: Oh yes, he was. And, it is such a logical thing. Now logical things don't necessarily mean that they are true things. I have been interested in this for a long time so I wrote to an old friend of mine in the State Department, Loy Henderson. Loy Henderson had been in the Russian business for many, many years and probably knew more about Russia than anybody except possibly George Kennan. Loy Henderson had suffered the same fate that is suggested as to why ambassadors are sent aboard--in other words, to get them out of the way where they can't do any harm. Loy Henderson had been chief of the Russian, or the Eastern European Section in the State Department which includes Russia; and he had laid down the facts of life as far as Russian abilities to prevaricate, to make difficulties in negotiations, and to the utter necessity to hold a complete check on almost everything that is connected with dealings with them but that wasn't Roosevelt's idea; Roosevelt felt that the approach to the Russians should be utterly open-handed, to trust them completely and, in connection with that he had had in the White

House as a military aide in the mid thirties, an army officer by the name of Philip Faymonville. Philip Faymonville had had a remarkable career just after WW1--in the period of the Russian revolution; he had been in Russia and had ridden a motorcycle into all sorts of remote places in the Far East and he had had a lot of personal and pretty hairy experiences out there and he was a bachelor and had no attachments anywhere except his love for adventure and his love for the Army and he had plenty of money, which was a requisite in those days for a military attaché because allowances were so piddling that the normal salaried naval or Army officer couldn't make out on it in any of the bigger capitals; so you found that many of the military attachés in those days were perennial military attachés--professional military attachés--they would repeat in one capital after another and they were all wealthy men. I met three or four of those in pre-war Europe-- Gilmor in Warsaw, Chase in Vienna, I have forgotten the guy's name in Turkey, but these were all wealthy men, and so was Faymonville and Major Shipp and Reagon was a wealthy man--he was a bachelor, professional attaché in Italy and heavens knows where else. Well, Faymonville was one of those and he was a professional you might say--pro-Communist, pro-Soviet, pro-Red--there is no doubt about that during his whole career; he finally wound up in California where he underwent either some actual trials or some confrontations with anti-Communist groups and he was indelibly identified and branded as, if not a member of the Communist party, he was quacking like a duck and walking like a duck as the saying goes. Anyway, Faymonville was a great favorite at the White House and he was a White House aide for some time. Then he went to the Soviet Union in the mid thirties as military attaché and he was the only one, we had no naval attaché; he was there for some time. In fact he came out to Vladivostok in 1937 to meet the USS AUGUSTA when she went up there on the first courtesy visit that an American naval vessel had ever made to the Soviet Union up to that time. Then he went back to the Unites States for some duty or other and then at about the time of the war he was back again as a spot Brigadier General as Chief of the Military Supply Mission (United States Military Supply Mission). So, that was the type that Roosevelt wanted. Henderson, who was a straight talker, who pulled no punches as far as his experiences with the Russians was concerned, was in effect, sent to Siberia--he was sent as Minister to Iraq, Baghdad. Now Baghdad was I suppose, just about as solid as insulation from contact with anybody that he might manage to influence in an anti-Soviet manner than if he had been sent to the middle of Africa. And, in fact, Henderson's dispatches at that time (they are all on record in the Red Books that the State Department puts out--thirty years after the fact, after the event) and Henderson absolutely called the turn then as to what has since happened in the Middle East. He wrote dispatches back, having talked to the Prime Minister of Iraq and to the King that they then had, and said, "If we continue to play footsie with the Jews in Israel, and to deny what the Arabs consider to be their side of the question, we will wind up with a most ungodly cans of worms." That was Henderson's repeated theme song for the whole year and a half that he was in Iraq. I stopped there to see him on the way out from Russia in May of 1944 and flew over from Teheran for the express purpose of stopping to see him and see what he had to say. I am sure he was glad to see me because the second front had just started then about the time I left Moscow, a few days afterward, and he was extremely interested in what the reaction had been in Moscow and the American Embassy. We had a long revealing chat, at least it was revealing from my point of view. Henderson is now living in Washington in retirement and we are in frequent correspondence with each other on various items--mostly on Russia. I asked him one time whether he thought Standley had been sent over there to put him on ice, get him out of reach, and he said he had no evidence of it, anything of that nature was always done on an informal, personal, no-writing plane as far as Roosevelt was concerned. They never knew his reasons and as far as he knew there was nothing whatsoever behind it, or any mysterious reason why he might have been sent there. So, who knows; Standley wouldn't say, possibly he wouldn't know but again we fall back in innuendo and what seems to be a logical explanation, because when anything needed to be done in the way of really solid diplomatic discussion with Stalin, Roosevelt never did it through the Ambassador. He sent some special envoy over--he would send Harriman or Willkie or General Hurley or Major General Follett Bradley (a Naval Academy graduate in 1910 and Major General in the Air Force). On several of those occasions Standley would not even be invited to go to the Kremlin for the conference between Stalin and the envoy--let us say Harriman--and presumably, maybe they did and maybe that didn't fill the old man in on what went on when they came away. But the more he stayed there the more disgusted he got at the treatment he was receiving. In other words, he was completely by-passed as far as I know, in practically everything. He was simply there, that was all. At one stage of the game he got so disgusted with the fact that the Russians were making absolutely no recognition of the fact of receipt of Lend-Lease. Now it is actually true that Lend-Lease constituted only about 10% of the total war material that the Russians used, but, that 10% was frequently in essential parts--it is just like the bearings in a wheel, without the bearings the automobile won't run although the rest of it might be O.K. In our case, the Lend-Lease material constituted items that were in desperately short supply and were of a vital type and they may or may not have swung the balance. In any case it probably saved a great many Russian lives at the cost of a great many American lives--the losses on the convoy run to Murmansk for example. Standley was so annoyed at the fact that there was no recognition of the extent of the quantity and the quality of the Lend-Lease to the Soviet Union that he called a press conference one day, purely on his own-- that I know--it was strictly on his own, and said "This may be a bombshell, it may end my career as Ambassador here but I want you to know certain things that you should pass on-- what my sentiments are and what I feel. I hope you will break this thing so that the Russians will be forced to make some concessions for what we are contributing. Heretofore there has been absolutely no public note of appreciation in Russian publicity on American help and I think it is absolutely a scandalous situation and somebody has to do something about it." The press correspondents were all on his side because they had desperately tried to go to the front. They were trying desperately to find something to justify their existence in Moscow. For example *Time* Magazine--we got it about a month late over there in the dip pouch--and there was this blurb in the front one time that said, "The marvelous coverage on the war in the East--the Russian/German war--is due to our correspondent Walter Graebner's three months at the front with the Russian armies." Of course we all sat back and had a big belly laugh and poor old Walter was very uncomfortable because the only front he had ever seen was the front row of the ballet. So the correspondents were 100% on Standley's side. They felt that not only were we being short-changed on publicity but we were being shortchanged on every-thing else--certainly the little reciprocity as far as news gathering was concerned. So they gleefully printed all this stuff and it hit the United States like a bomb and I am sure it discomfited Roosevelt and Company enormously but, by golly, it jarred loose public admission in the newspapers and on the radio in the USSR what the USA help consisted of. From that time on, old Standley was doomed, he didn't last much longer after that. He was pretty well disgusted and he was ready to go. These things I know perfectly well because we all ate in the mess together; we lived at Spasso House which was the Embassy and was the residency of the Ambassador and that is where we all ate until after Standley left and after Harriman came. The unfortunate part of the whole deal over there was the can of worms-- in respect to the military representation. The naval attaché was Captain Jack Harlan Duncan, who for seven or eight years had been Standley's personal aide when he was on active duty. He had been sent over there 50% as an old friend and 50% as somebody they just had to grab right quick and send over there when the war broke out. Duncan was then a captain who had been promoted to four stripes, along with more or less a group promotion due to the accelerated rate of promotions at that stage of the game, almost without selection. He may even had been spotted up to that rank for the job. The military attaché was Colonel Michela who was a 1925 graduate of West Point, and Faymonville was the Chief of the American Military Mission. Faymonville and Michela (who was there early in the game, so was Duncan and neither Michela nor Duncan was on speaking terms with Faymonville,) because Faymonville never consulted with any of them as far as the applicability of Russian requests. The Soviets would request certain types and quantities of material and normally, you would think that Faymonville as chief of the mission would so consult. He had no naval personnel on his staff; he had four civilian assistants, that was it. You would normally suspect, or think, that in staff cooperation he would ask naval advice on whether this was a suitable request and how it fitted in with our requirements at home, if we were normally suited to supply this or share it, or if something else might not be substituted that would be of a more suitable nature--that never happened. As I say, they didn't speak to each other. On those occasions when the Russians would need some professional help, which obviously Faymonville couldn't give, not being a Naval officer, Duncan and I, as interpreter, would go over to the liaison officer and we would discuss these matters and if Duncan would suggest something that might be more suitable or more available or better allocation to the war effort, or something like that, we would find that the Russians had gone directly to Faymonville and he would get it for them, or the word came back, deviously, from the Russians that if there was any trouble at all, all they had to do would be to appeal directly to Mrs. Roosevelt, and then there would be no problem. They could get anything they wanted--so don't be difficult. The only time I ever saw Duncan put the squeeze on these people was on one occasion when we were called over and they were inquiring about the availability of a bow casting for a cruiser (a large single piece of high quality steel) and apparently they were not able to provide it themselves--at that time Leningrad was wholly invested with the Germans and the yard at Nikolaev on the Black Sea was in German hands completely, Molotovsk was in the north and was being bombed from time to time and was working at very low capacity so presumably they didn't have any place to make it and they wanted this bow casting. Duncan said, "Well, I am not sure whether I understand exactly what you want. It would be very useful if I could go look at the cruiser and take several of my officers along, case the place, see what you need and then we will see what can be done about it." And they said, "Well Captain Duncan, the situation is very difficult. Actually the Navy yards are all invested with Germans, there is no place you could go." So Duncan said, "That's great, that's the best news I have had in a long time. Then you won't need that bow casting for your cruiser; you ain't got the cruiser." Well, we had another vodka and a piece of chocolate; it seems a strange mixture, but that's what they served and it is very good, by the way; off we went home and the next day we were called back again and they said "Which Navy yard would you like to go to? Would you like to go to Molotovsk or Komsomolsk," to get as far in the guts of the country as we could. So, out we go to Komsomolsk. It was fifteen days on the train and quite an adventure. None of us had ever done anything like that before and we were warned we had to carry our rations on our backs and we were given a liaison officer, a charming young man named Steve Tarasoff, who had studied English in the United States and had some bad experiences; he had lived in a boarding house whose proprietress was a real ogress, according to his description, who refused to give him part of the money back for the rent when he left in the middle of the month. He had been thrown in the pokey at Havre de Grace for some minor motor car violation and at that time he couldn't speak English, so he was in 'durance vile' for a day or two before the Embassy managed to find out where he was and spring him; so his views of American were mixed as you might imagine. But, he was awfully good to us and he came down to the train, the platform was absolutely swarming with these mobs of people. Duncan and I were equipped for a month's round trip in the way of rations and we had boxes and bales and cartons, sterno stoves, powdered coffee, you name it we had it. Steve Tarasoff turned up with what looked like two five-gallon Standard Oil tins, (that you see out in the Far East) and we said, "What's in the cans, Steve?" One was full of vodka and the other was full of sweetened condensed milk. We thought that was rather odd rations for a trip across the USSR but we considered he knew what he was doing. Steve and I were established in one coupe in this old original wagon lits car, which I presume had been confiscated from the French in the Revolution. It was a very comfortable thing with coupes, a little washroom between each one and rugs on the floor and all that, and Duncan had another one. We used Duncan's place for the dining hall, cooked and ate in there, and in general sort of camped out; the dining car served soup if you were so charitable as to call the stuff soup; but it then became apparent as to the value of that five-gallon can of vodka and condensed milk. All the way across Russia the train ran at about 15 or 20 miles an hour and stopped about every hour I guess, for water and to give the passengers a rest from the rattling, jolting and everybody would make a rush for the hot water boiler at the station--each station had a tap over which was the word Kipiatok which means boiling water and everybody would dash out with tin car or tea kettle and get boiling water in order to come back and make tea on the train. While at the stops our friend Steve would go ashore with his little container of vodka and another container of condensed milk and he would come back with 4 or 5 hard boiled eggs and half a chicken and a bunch of onions and a few boiled potatoes in their skins, some garlic or a glass full of berries of some kind--in other words it was a trading operation all across. Of course our rations complemented all this. We eventually arrived at Komsomolsk, having spent about three days in Khabarovsk to sort of rehabilitate ourselves. Duncan was sick, that's the reason we stayed in Khabarovsk, the fact that Duncan was flat out with the flu. I was the object of enormous curiosity on the streets. Nobody had ever seen a foreigner in those parts before, in uniform; they hadn't the foggiest idea of what I was, what side I was on. I was walking down the street one day in the company of the mayor of the town and Steve and some little kid tagging along with his mother; he was about six or seven years old, grabbed his mother's skirt and said, having taken one look at me, "My God Mama, there goes a Fritz!" I looked like I had been captured, I suppose, with these two characters on each side, these Russians. Then we went up to Komsomolsk. First though, one little more incident in the park, Steve and I were out sitting on a bench in a local park one day.

Q: This is in Khabarovsk?

Adm. T.: Still in Khabarovsk. It is an old, old city and it looks like something out of the Middle Ages almost, the baroque character of the buildings and the general beat-up and run-down condition of the streets and everything else. You see the Russians in general don't own, except in the country in special instances, they don't own their own buildings, they don't give a damn what happens to them, they fall apart, the cornices fall off, they need paint, the glass in the window frames is cracked and so forth-- nobody cares because it is not theirs.

Q: Who owns them?

Adm. T.: The government owns them, or the factory or office for which they work, owns them. In the case of the factory-owned quarters they are allocated out just like quarters are in the case of the military on the base.

Well, we were sitting on the park bench and, as usual, a bunch of kids collected--anywhere from 10 to 15 I guess-

and when they found out I was an American they were entranced. Shoulder boards had just been introduced in the Soviet Union-- the kind they had had back before the Revolution, and they were rather gay as they are much more decorative than our Navy shoulder boards. Of course Steve had his on but I still had my Australian Army job and it just had little cloth flaps up there. They were making fun of what poor shoulder boards I had and here the Russians were having these beautiful shoulder boards. They said, "By the way, where did I come from?" "America." "Oh, they knew all about American and said, "You know a lot of people around here try to get there, two or three of them tried to run away but they got caught." Then old Steve said, "Shhh, go away, go away, get out of here you kids." This conversation went on, of course when you get out in that neck of the woods nobody is inhibited like they are around Moscow, particularly with some creature from outer space like that. They wanted to spill the beans and kids are like that anyway. It was an enormous embarrassment for poor Steve the things these kids said and a very amusing piece of instruction for me.

Anyway, we finally got up to Komsomolsk and found they had a light cruiser on the ways, three destroyers, six or eight patrol vessels--quite an array and quite a large establishment too. It was one of these things we had never been told about and hadn't the foggiest idea it existed. It was one of these things turned up by a canny Irishman like Duncan. Of course one of the drawbacks that we all suffered was the tremendous respect that the Russians have for rank. They are probably the most rank-conscious people in the world.

Q: There for a long time they tried to abolish rank, didn't they?

Adm. T.: Up until 1937 they had what I suppose you would call post rank. When a man was between duties let us say, or unassigned at the moment, he had no marks at all on his collar, and you couldn't tell what he was. When we first established relations in the Soviet Union in 1933, they sent two naval persons, officers, to Washington as prospective naval attaché and assistant, and they called on the Director of Naval Intelligence and the first thing they did was to rush up to the doorkeeper who was a sergeant major in the Marine Corps (their full regimentals are beautiful, you know, with red stripes down the pants and this gold stuff on his sleeve) and they rushed up and pumped him by the hand and said, "Ve are so happy to meet you Coptain," and the sergeant cooled him off and said, "Excuse me, I am just the doorman. The Captain is inside." So, they finally got the two squired into the boss's office and over coffee and whatnot chatted about what they were going to do, and the director said, "By the way Sir, what is your rank, I don't see any marks on your collar." They were sort of monastic uniforms, a high button collar and a single row of gold buttons up the front. No marks at all on it. No shoulder marks, no collar insignia. "By the way, what is your rank?" The name of the number one guy was Oras. He had been a warrant officer in the Imperial Navy, I found out later; and Oras said, "What is the usual rank of naval attachés in Washington?" The director said, "Well, some of the big navies like the British and the German and the Japanese and Italian and so forth have captains, and the lesser Navies like the Brazilian, the Portuguese, the Turks, they would be commanders. So old Oras churned that around and in his head a while and he said, "I'm a Vice Admiral and my assistant is a Rear Admiral." The director was right well shook by that because the senior attaché in Washington was a captain. The senior American naval officer in Washington was of course a full admiral but there wasn't a single Vice Admiral in all of Washington. All the rest of them were rears. There were only two other Vice Admirals in the whole US Navy—no there were three, one in the Atlantic and two in the Pacific and all three of them at sea. Well of course that was too hot a potato for the director so he passed that to State. Who was then Secretary of State?

Q: Hull.

Adm. T.: Yes I guess it was. Well what made this doubly embarrassing was that Oras having established himself as a Vice Admiral, he was then named dean of the corps by virtue of his rank—Dean of the Corps of Naval Military Attaches in Washington. What could they do? Suppose they walk him back to captain, which he should have been, then he would lose the deanship which would be a horrible loss of face, it would be insupportable. Finally they got together with Ambassador Troyanovsky and Troyanovsky said, "Well we have absolutely no interest in rank or protocol of that sort," (lying like a trooper of course) and he said, "Let's fix it this way, we'll make ours a junior rear admiral in Washington and the number two guy we will kick back to commander and on the list of dignitaries in Washington—the dip list—he will be known as mister."

Q: In other words, they could make what they wanted out of it?

Adm. T.: They could screw it around to suit their fancy. So that's the way Mister Rear Admiral Oras spent the next year. Well, he was found down in the engine room of a yacht on which he had been invited for a cruise on the Potomac haranging the crew on the virtues of Communism--that was too much and they decided he had better go home and that was the end of Oras in Washington.

Meanwhile, our attaché, who had gone over with Bullitt to Moscow, was a captain in the Marine Corps by the name of Nimmer (who just died three weeks ago). Nimmer had seen the handwriting on the wall when he was aboard the USS PITTSBURGH out in China in 1932 or 1933 and had studied Russian, got permission to go up to Harbin, so he was ready for Moscow although there was some doubt if Moscow was ready for him at the time. He, as Naval attaché, was accompanied by a captain in the Army Air Corps named White and White subsequently became Chief of Staff of the Air Force many, many years later. White had gone over as Bullitt's airplane pilot, part of the agreement was that Bullitt should have his own airplane over there, have his own pilot and fly where he wanted to in Russia. But the airplane never got off the ground except to fly out of Russia, though on rare occasions he was allowed to go over to Sweden. Both White and Nimmer were withdrawn about a year after they got there. The bloom was very soon off the rose as recognition and the arrangements for restitution or reparations for American siezed property during the Revolution and war debts and all that sort of stuff. They got nowhere on that.

Q: They still haven't.

Adm. T.: And they still haven't. The new Ambassador Bullitt (of course he had gone over a starry-eyed liberal, he was right in Roosevelt's camp, 100%), he had gone over there with the greatest of hopes and of course everything turned sour, bitter in his mouth and he would meet Comrade (Foreign trade) Rosengotz at a party and Rosengotz would make some sneering remark or ignore him altogether. Of course the business men who rushed over there got nowhere because the Soviets did all their buying through their own agents in New York, AMTORG, or through ARKOS in London, and they weren't interested in fiddling around with some individual business man selling a suitcase full of socks. They wanted to buy a shipload of this or that and they didn't want to fool around with American salesmen in doing it. So, they recalled the two

Tolley #4 -541-

attachés and before they left, Nimmer and White went around and they finally got an audience with Voroshilov who was the Minister of War, one of the early mainstays of old Joe Stalin--a big shot, about as big as you could get to in those days. Voroshilov claimed that he was sorry that Nimmer and White had gotten nowhere as they claimed, as far as making contacts and getting around was concerned, and he regretted that they felt they wanted to leave and he of course would have to reciprocate and withdraw the Soviet Embassy attachés in Washington--but they didn't, they stayed, the Soviets did, ours came home. Faymonville was the first one to go back and that was largely on Roosevelt's hopes to maintain friendly relations because he felt Faymonville was a marvelously astutue guy, he spoke French and Russian and played the piano beautifully and was an urbane diplomatic type that could charm the birds out of the trees.

Q: Yet he was a Communist.

Adm. T.: Obviously, that is why Roosevelt thought he would just be the man to go over there because he was sympathetic toward the Russians and he felt that they would trust him. I had an interesting contretemps vis-a-vis old Faymonville; I had nothing against him, of course this feud that was going on upstairs between him, Duncan and Michela, struck me as being childish--they were all over there trying to fight the same war--Faymonville was an extremely polite guy, unctuous and a colonel. I was then a spot commander, I had been spotted up from lieutenant commander to commander and I'll tell you about that later. One time Tommy Thompson himself who became an ambassador, he was then second secretary, and he had a birthday party. We had a dacha out in the country to which we used to repair to sort of refresh ourselves and get away from the city atmosphere. It was an old country house with a garden, croquet grounds, and a little river in the back with a rowboat, a charming place. Amongst those present at the birthday party were half a dozen people from the ballet, who were allowed to associate with us, and Major General Follett Bradley who was over there on a special mission to Moscow to try to get Lend-Lease airplanes flown in by Alaska and over Siberia, on which he never got to first base; and there were three or four secretaries from other embassies and some smaller fry such as myself and some of the other assistant attachés and Faymonville. Of course everybody was pleasantly loaded with vodka. Faymonville was playing the piano and singing Russian songs and I just offhandedly remarked to Bradley, who was a dour, humorless kind of a guy (he really thought pretty well of himself) and I said, "You know that's the kind of a guy who would make a good ambassador, General Faymonville. Look at the way he performs, he is just absolutely wow as a diplomat." I went on drinking vodka and Bradley went on doing whatever he was doing. The next day I got called in by Duncan and he said, "Young man, what is this I hear from the embassy that you have recommended that Admiral Standley be replaced by General Faymonville? There are people very excited about this." I was dumbfounded, I didn't know what he was talking about; I was nursing a hangover anyway and not feeling too good. Then it became apparent what had happened--that Bradley had taken my offhand remark as a recommendation to make Faymonville ambassador to the Soviet Union. Naturally enough I was speechless, almost, and he said, "You have just got to remember young man that you are not in the wardroom of a destroyer, you are in an embassy now and you keep your trap shut on matters that don't concern you." He had a hangover himself I suppose. So that was one of my early lessons in what not to do at a diplomatic party, and how things can be misconstrued and screwed around.

To get back to this rank thing. As I said, the Russians were enormously rank conscious, and in the Navy they have

Captain, First Rank and Captain, Second Rank, and Captain Third Rank. The business of rank equivalents is a complicated one with the Soviets versus the United States. First of all they don't have any brigadier general; they jump from colonel to major general and the major general wears one star on his epaulets, in the Soviet Union. The captain, first rank, has solid gold epaulets which are in the same appearance category as flag officers; the captain, second rank, the equivalent is four stripes although the designation of it is not actually four stripes but it is far less glittering and less impressive rank insignia than that of captain, first rank; the one below captain, second rank, or the same general category, is less magnificient; so normally, the captain, second rank--the guy with the four stripes with the rather modest insignia would command a cruiser or some major ship. The captain, first rank, might command a battleship you might say, or a unit of several ships; actually I heard recently from friends in the Soviet Union that atomic submarines are being skippered in some cases by rear admirals. Of course, that has nothing to do with what the situation was when we were there. The difficulty we were laboring under was that my boss, with four stripes, was considered in effect a commander--not a captain but a commander because their equivalent of a captain, first rank, was in effect, a commodore. So, the recommendation was that everybody was upped. When I first went there I had just made lieutenant commander, had been promoted in April and I was spotted up to commander--the youngest one in the US Navy at that time--as soon as I got to the Soviet Union for reasons of prestige alone. If I gave a party at my apartment, on the rare occasions when Soviet Naval officers were invited and would come, nobody above the rank of commander--nobody wearing more than three stripes--would come unless I indicated in advance that my boss would be there, the captain. Now when he was advanced to rear admiral of course that put him in an entirely different league--it was roughly you might say, the difference between a minister in a country and an ambassador. The minister can demand an audience or ask for an audience with a cabinet minister but had the head of State and an ambassador can. In the case of a captain naval attache, he could request an audience with the commander in chief of the Soviet navy, who was a full admiral, but the chances were small that he would ever get there. Now if you were a rear admiral, he could ask or even demand an audience with the commander in chief and get it, so Duncan was spotted up to rear admiral for that purpose. The same sort of situation existed in Abadan, when I first got there, my ship the TRINITY was greeted by a lieutenant junior grade in the US Navy and he was, I estimate, 35 or 40 years old at the time and he was an eminent Boston scholar who had been what we used to call a bone digger; he was an archaeologist and had been on digs in Asia Minor for many years and knew the area intimately so he had been sent there as being an entirely appropriate one--but as lieutenant junior grade and as a result he was outranked by every conceivable guy including practically the skipper of the Iranian pilot boats. So, as soon as I got to Moscow I mentioned this to Duncan and (thinking about his own rank too) he immediately recommended that this fellow be promoted to lieutenant commander, which he was, bingo, just like that. The ability to do these things was there but nobody ever thought of it.

Q: Does the rule of common sense ever pertain? You speak of men of insufficient rank coming to see the head of the Russian Navy and having very little opportunity to succeed, but in case of need, in case of some problem that should be solved, does the rule of common sense pertain?

Adm. T.: The rule of common sense is one that you have to use considerable effort and ingenuity to apply; what you need is the rule of protocol in circumstances that you find in foreign capitals which is the standard procedure that you know will work. If you consider that a country is sufficiently important to merit that type of confrontation then you need to send a man of that rank there, it is as simple as that. It is just like in the old days. If it was a small country you sent a minister. We didn't give a damn who he saw or didn't see but if it was worth our while to be sure that we got to the top we sent an ambassador. Now, of course, there are no ministers at all that I know of, they are all ambassadors. It is a matter of what the other country thinks is your interest in them and the degree of importance in which you rate their structure, and they view you accordingly.

To get back however to how we got into Russia so easily, when I first arrived there I was greeted with something akin to incredulity, because they had all had the devil's own time from four to six weeks to get a visa. I had popped into Teheran and had my visa in two days and the explanation for that I can only surmise--I am full of surmises this morning and all sorts of back-stairs guesses on how things happened--but many years before that, relatively a good many years, 1938, I was in Hong Kong and there was a group of aviators from the 28th bombardment squadron--American mercenaries and Germans and Swiss, and who knows whatnot, flying for the Chinese Air Force and they had just gone over and bombed Formosa and had a pretty narrow squeak and as soon as they had done this the Japs had come over and bombed hell out of the airfields from which they had come and that was the end of the effort. I don't think they did much damage. It was purely a morale booster. So they were down in Hong Kong celebrating and glad to be out of it all; they had been paid relatively large sums for their efforts. Amongst those present, how he got into the shebang I don't know, was a fellow by the name of Wahamaki--he was a Finn--but it developed that he was a Finnish Communist and he made no bones about it and of course he was fairly safe in Hong Kong and the rest of China, being a Communist was not too bad in those days because the Soviets were the only ones who were materially helping the Chinese at that time. In 1938 for example, I was in Hankow, where a German military mission under von Falkenhausen, and right across the street was a Soviet military aviation mission under a Soviet general whose name I have forgotten, and they had their planes there, the short, stubby little I-15s and I-16s, monoplanes that their four machine guns shot through the propellors (when the propellors were not there) something that the Americans said was impossible--two machine guns O.K. but four impossible--but the Russians had done it and they

were being very successful. They were hot little jobs
like some of these little racers that they had used in international speed contests and they were giving the Japs a very
bad time but some of them got shot down. I used to go see
these guys in the hospital and talk to them. They were just
fresh out of the Soviet Union and just absolutely like from
outer space as far as understanding what it was all about.
But, in any case, the fact that they were present in China
had cooled off the violent anti-Communist campaign that
Chiang had started in 1927 and more or less carried on since
that time until the war against Japan started in July of 1937.
So, Wahamaki presumably was over there on some secret and
clandestine mission. I was very much impressed with the guy
chiefly because he was the strongest man I ever saw. He was
a relatively small guy but he could hold his chair out by
the back slat straight out, with one arm; try it some time.
Anyway, Wahamaki warmed up to me too. We both had had a few
whiskies by that time, and I told him that I spoke a certain
amount of Russian and was interested in the Soviet Union and
he said, "You know if you ever want to get anywhere with
those guys you have got to get in their confidence because
they are extremely suspicious of everybody not openly professing to admire their system or their country, in general

not just to be neutral because from their point of view to be neutral is to be anti. There is no middle ground. And I will tell you how you start this, when you go back up to Canton go around and have your picture taken in something that looks like a Soviet uniform and here is the place to go and have it done." So, I was a subscriber to the Soviet military newspaper Red Star, chiefly to keep myself in trim on reading Russian and the military roster; I had a picture of a Soviet military uniform and I went up to Canton and I think for about a dollar and a half or two bucks I had a Chinese tailor sew me a jacket together and here is the picture. The uniform that I had made for this picture led me to have made some other simple Russian blouses and we used these things at parties. We made the interesting discovery in Chungking and international places like that where there are a lot of foreigners--they were all different nationalities, they didn't speak each other's language too well, the common language was English--but if we got our shirt and tie off and our jacket and put one of these Russian shirts tied around the middle, they immediately dropped a lot of their inhibitions and the party proceeded along very gay lines. I was pretty well equipped with these shirts because in China it is extremely cheap to have anything hand-tailored and in Chungking I thought

"Well," remembering Wahanaki's advice, "Why don't I try this a little more stiffly up here?" There was a Russian--Soviet--embassy in Chungking and they were pretty much under the leper's cloak you might say, as far as the rest of the nations were concerned; this was in 1938-39 and they had just signed a pact with Hitler and the war was already on and that made them absolutely shit as far as the British were concerned and the French, because they were playing footsie with Hitler. Then along came 1940 and they laid into the Finns and that made them persona non grata with almost everybody, so the American assistant military attaché and I thought "Well this is a stupid thing to do; after all we are not fighting the war out there with our bare hands against anybody; the object of the drill is to get information." So he and I put on our frock coats and went over and made a call on the Soviet Embassy without saying a word to the ambassador or anybody-- old Captain Mathias--he spoke Chinese and the Russians spoke Chinese and I spoke Russian and they spoke Russian so we had rather a cool reception, they wondered I am sure what the hell we were doing there. But it was the beginning of a rather interesting association. I won't go so far as to say friendship. At the Fourth of July party, 1939 I think it was, we mixed a huge tub of punch. We got a full-sized fifty-gallon barrel, filled it about half full with tea and added one case of bourbon that we had up there, a few bottles of rum, in fact everything we had available, in the way of extra booze, and three or four pails full of Szechwan orange juice (the best in the world) and on top of it of course a big lump of ice was swimming. This is one of the rare occasions when the missionaries came out of the woodwork for the Fourth of July. So, they all swarmed down from the hills and it was a hot, hot, hot July, a completely cloudless day; they were all sweating (this was held in the Officers' Club up on the bank), all of the foreign colony was there. Now the missionaries made the gross tactical error of considering that this stuff in the barrel was tea. It looked like tea and it tasted like tea so in no time at all they were ready to sing hymns and join in the jollity and throw darts and it was one of the biggest days in the whole year. We also invited the Russians over. The second secretary arrived. The ambassador checked in sick, and somebody else checked in sick, but the military attaché, an old sergeant by the name of Ivanov, now a brigadier general, came over and two of the Soviet military attachés; they had a marvelous time. Ivanov after about t first half hour, very gruffly and unpolitely, asked for his boat. He had had enough. But the two younger guys stayed on until almost the next morning—the party lasted from noon of the Fourth of July until three the next morning—until the punch ran out. From then on we were pretty close friends so I thought, "Well if Wahamaki thought it was a good idea to go over to this (what obviously must have been a Russian letter box) to get my photo taken in Canton, why not lay it on thick over here?" So I had this photo taken here—the one I have just shown you—and gave a copy of it to Major Sigitov, one of the attachés, and obviously it wound up in my dossier in Moscow eventually. So whether that is why I got the quick visa or not, I don't know, but it certainly was a unique case.

Q: Well, you arrived in Kuybyshev and you met Standley; can you resume the story there?

Adm. T.: I have already said we went back up to Moscow and were ensconced in the Spasso House. The regular American Chancery was a very ornate and rather an elaborate building down on Mokovaya Square, which is cheek by jowl with Red Square and the view across Mokovaya Square includes the Lenin Museum, the Moscow Hotel, a long stretch of the Kremlin wall, and the former Czar's riding stables, and through the crack betwen the Lenin Library and the Kremlin Tower you can actually see a good hunk of Red Square. So it was a magnificient location. Unfortunately it was also a target for German bombers and several bombs had dropped in the vicinity and the whole area down there was heated from the steam plant somewhere that supplied the Kremlin and all these larger buildings; the bombings had broken the pipes, so, during that horrible winter of 1941 when the whole show was hanging on the ropes--the year of Stalingrad and so forth--we felt then that the whole place would fall. The steam had been cut off and the water pipes had frozen so Mokovaya and everything else down there was uninhabitable through water damage and no pipes, no heat, no nothing, so we all lived in Spasso House. It had this huge reception hall with a chandelier in the middle which must have weighed a ton; the dome of the reception hall was like the dome of a cathedral and it was the main room.

Q: This had been somebody's mansion?

Adm. T.: This was the family home probably of the Spassos-- one of the richest sugar barons in imperial Russia, and of course like everything else in the way of private property, it had been confiscated by the government, and it was made the American Embassy when Bullitt was over there. In fact I had been in Spasso before; I had come across the Trans-Siberian in 1935 on my way home to the United States; where by the way, I never got, as my orders were changed in Paris sending me back to duty in Europe for another year. Anyway, I got off in Moscow. Of course, tourists didn't exist in those days in the sense that they do now--30,000 to 50,000 Americans go over every year--in those days I dare say there weren't a dozen. There simply were no accommodations: there were a few European tourists but practically no Americans. The Embassy was very small, they had an Ambassador who was Bullitt of course; George Kennan had been there as second secretary but he had a perennial case of ulcers so he was down in Australia trying to get something decent to eat; and there were three or four other secretaries and that was it. Faymonville was off on a trip somewhere. I suppose you have seen in the newspapers--back in the old days--"As Reported by a Traveler"; you don't see that any more because there is a correspondent in every nook and cranny in the world. Naturally enough I checked into the embassy and my presence was reported to the ambassador and he wanted to see the traveler from the Far East. He wanted to know what was going on out there--he invited me over for a cocktail. So this awestruck young lieutenant went into this huge mausoleum, dimly lighted, and walked over in one corner which had been made more or less habitable for a tete-a-tete and we sat there and had a martini or two and Bullitt wanted to know what was going on in China. I said, "To the best of my knowledge things were approaching a climax, it might not be tomorrow but it was coming and that Chiang Kai-shek would have to make a deal with the Communists and form a united front otherwise there would simply be no hope against the Japanese." He said, "Oh! Nobody believes that!" in a very disgusted way and made it perfectly clear that that was the end of the seance and I was free to go anytime.

Well, about three months later Chiang Kai-shek went up the Sian to meet with Chang Hsueh-liang, the son of the old war lord of Manchuria, Chang Tso lin, and the idea of course was to make some kind of a deal with Chang Hsueh-liang who was Communistically inclined in that he realized that the only conceivable way to make any sort of showing against the Japs was to stop the business of the civil war in China and turn around with one front--one single face. Chang Hsueh-liang wasn't a Communist himself but he commanded a very sizable force that had been in Manchuria and had been run out of there in 1932 when the Japanese started to occupy Manchuria and by 1934 they had all of Manchuria and Chang Hsueh-liang and his troops had been chased out and they were up in Northwest China--up in the hills, the boondocks, Sian. Chiang Kai-shek was not exactly jailed, but he was put in quarters from which he couldn't get out. He saw the handwriting on the wall. This was a little more than he had counted on; he went up there to treat as equals and he was being, in effect, intimidated. The house where he was staying was surrounded and guarded so the old boy said, "The hell with this, I don't intend to be intimidated," so he jumped out of the window in the dark in his nightshirt, sprained his back, lost his false teeth, and in general, was in a sorry plight when he was picked up; threatened to kill himself and all that. But, to make a long story short, he made a deal with the Communists-- just as I told Bullitt would be done. We'll get back to Bullitt later on but one more thing about Bullitt and his inability to reason or to accept anybody else's reasoning, theories, or ideas if they were in contravention to his own-- just about the time France was falling (he was Ambassador to France) his military attaché went to him and said, "Mr. Ambassador, it is useless for us to attempt to marshal American opinion and supplies, to get anything over here to help these fellows, because they have had it. It is the end and they are about to collapse and there will be no more France," and Mr. Bullitt said, "That is not what my French friends tell me," and he went right ahead with the process. He was that kind of a guy, he was a man of fixed notions. He had gone over first of all to the Soviet Union in 1918-19 during the Paris Peace Conference. He was a young liberal at that time, I think from Harvard.

Q: He hailed from Philadelphia.

Adm. T.: And, apparently was viewed with considerable favor by Wilson as being a suitable one to send over there, but he got nowhere. He came back and told Wilson that the thing to do was to recognize the Sovet Union and accept it as a fait accompli, that the French, the British, the Dutch and the Belgians and so forth were equally interested in protecting their concessions over there to the point of intervening and completely alienating the Russian people as a whole against any chance of the restitution of the old regime, plus queering them with the rest of the world at large. Of course, Bullitt's advice was wholly unacceptable to Wilson and he went into a complete eclipse until Roosevelt and his liberalism came along. He and Bullitt were, you might say, contemporaries political-wise and money-wise and he was just the man for ambassador--that's why he went over there.

Now, to get back to this trip through Moscow in 1935 or 1936. My impressions then were what they had always been; that, in many respects, they were rather an undisciplined, savage lot; when they had the chance. The train trip across Russia had been a nightmare in some respects in that the food is atrocious (I didn't have the perspicacity to equip myself with a can of alcohol and a can of condensed milk, in those days, so I was on the Russian economy), and the train was pretty well loaded with soldiers, either going back to duty or from duty, on leave, and they all had a little money and they all congregated in the dining car and, when they found out I could speak some Russian, they were all over me like a blanket--such hospitality you never saw-- and I was forced to drink a lot of this stuff they called beer in those days. So by the time I got to Poland the reaction had set in and I was actually ready to go to a hospital, after drinking all this slop and eating all this garbage. It had been quite an experience but not one that I was inclined to repeat. When I got to Warsaw I stayed there about a week to recuperate and then scooted straight down to Greece to lie out in the sunshine. We are really jumping around on various things.

To get back to Bullitt again, and the war and the origin

of the war, and mentioning again that Roosevelt never did anything in writing if he could avoid it, the same was true of his machinations (if you want to call it that) in getting the war in Europe itself started. Of course, he was very pro-Jewish in the sense that he felt it was an outrage the way the Jews were being treated in Germany. He had tremendous Jewish influence brought to bear on him here, largely under the influence of people like Morganthau and even more so perhaps in an advisory way from his assistant, Harry Dexter White who was a Lithuanian Jew who, as time went on after the war, was convicted of being a dyed-in-the wool Communist, and Sam Rosenman, who wrote his speeches, and Felix Frankfurter and of course (those two fellows weren't Jews, they were card-carrying Communists in all but the actual fact) Laughlin Currie who was his adviser on China, and Owen Lattimore who was the other end of the line which misinformed Roosevelt in Washington about the situation in China. Currie and Lattimore are both Communists, in fact Currie, when the investigation got a little too hot and the wind was blowing down his neck, took it on the lam for South America where he still is as far as I know.

Q: Weren't they connected with the Johns Hopkins University?

Adm. T.: Lattimore, I think was a lecturer at Johns Hopkins. In fact he was invited over to Goucher College about two years ago to lecture on the Far East. I was invited down to listen and after the thing was over I was asked to come over to meet him, which I did with much interest. I was introduced as Admiral Tolley and he said, "Well, you probably belong to the group which is not too favorable toward what my views have been in the past," and I said, "I might as well tell you the truth, Dr. Lattimore, there were a lot of us who would, at one time or another, have liked to have seen you shot, but that doesn't by any means prevent us from sitting down and having a friendly chat," which we did for about half an hour.

Anyway, to get back to Roosevelt and his proclivity for not putting things on paper, he was desperately keen, there is no doubt about it in spite of all the apologists say, to do something to stop Hitler, which was a fairly reasonable attitude to take. After all he had in effect been given a free rein at Munich, and it looked like he was about to have the same thing happen to him in Poland--that if Poland succumbed without a struggle he would be, by all odds, the most powerful guy in Europe and impossible to stop. The Russians saw that at the time, the Russians, the French and the British were closeted in staff consultations to try to come to some sort of an agreement and the Russians were willing to furnish troops but Poland refused to allow them passage, so did Czechoslovakia, and the French and the British had no trust in the Soviets anyway so their importunities and whatnot, (this is at Munich by the way, not in the Polish crisis) so the whole thing was brushed off and as a result the Russians took a very dim view of any sincere thoughts on the part of the French and British for any sort of mutual action with them. What they thought, and rightly so, was that the French and the British would be delighted to see the Germans and the Soviets beat each other's brains out, if that could be cleverly arranged. Well, as far as Roosevelt was concerned he felt there was a strong possibility that the Poles would succumb just as the Czechs had at Munich--this was in 1938-- when the Polish invasion was started. In 1939, of course at this period Bullitt was in France as ambassador, and we had pretty good insight on what happened there because in the embassy in London there was a young American code clerk named Tyler Kent and Tyler Kent had the idea, from the conversations going back and forth between Churchill and Roosevelt (by private cable) that there was no doubt that the two were conniving to set up sort of a holy alliance, obviously aimed at Hitler, but naturally at that stage of the game Roosevelt had to be extremely cagey about it because:

a - Churchill was still First Lord of the Admirality--he wasn't yet Prime Minister and certainly Roosevelt had no vote of confidence of the American people to go along with any such idea. There are different schools of thought on what Roosevelt's motives were in this respect, in that the traffic that was carried on between Churchill and himself, wholly informal, Churchill was known as the Former Naval Person (a very poor means of covering his identity--wholly transparent) and they communicated in the "Gray" code, it was called gray because that was the color of it. It was actually a commercial code which was used to shorten telegrams in that one group in the code would represent a short sentence and cut cable tolls; but also the groups could be enciphered or otherwise screwed around, so it had a certain degree of security. However, it was well known that the gray code was absolutely public property--that everybody in the commercial world had a copy for the reason I have stated before. There are some people who theorized that Churchill and Roosevelt wanted the Germans to know that this was going on--to alert the Germans to the fact that they had better play this thing close to the belly-button or they could expect a powerful coalition. That is one theory.

b - The other theory is that maybe they were just plain careless or, it might be that they wanted to keep this dark secret between the two thus using in effect a private code rather than use the normal channels through the embassy codes that one would expect people to do in diplomacy.

Tyler Kent saw the handwriting on the wall-that we were being pulled into this thing. So he abstracted what he considered to be sufficiently damning or incriminating documents amongst those available--amongst tens of hundreds of exchanges of telegrams--and kept them for evidence in case the situation ever developed where it would be useful to prove his theory. At the same time he was closely allied with a White Russian group, and particularly with the daughter of a former White Russian admiral. I won't term it as a Fascist group, it was simply a rightist outfit that felt that it was international jury or international basic policy on the part of these two would-be world leaders that was leading the United States down the garden path and the fact that they may or may not have passed any of this information to Hitler is immaterial because, as I mentioned before, Churchill and Roosevelt would have welcomed the possibility that Hitler had seen some of these things. In any case, they weren't quite sure what Tyler Kent had got or to what extent he had passed them on, or to what other things he had done, so the Americans turned him over to the British justice and he was convicted of the British State Secrets Act and thrown in the pokey for two years.

Q: How was he apprehended in the first place?

Adm. T.: The mechanics of the discovery, how the thing was split I don't know but the British are pretty well known for their ability to crack down on matters of that type--they have very secret intelligence outfits, they blow their case through defectors from time to time, but, they also have been known for the last couple hundred years, to be pretty clever at intelligence. In any case, they got him, they jailed him; he had two sympathizers, young Americans, who felt that he had been railroaded, first of all, he was an American turned over to the British because the Americans apparently under those circumstances had nothing to nail him on and they didn't think they had sufficient evidence to hold him down. These two Americans decided they would go back to the United States and publicize his case and see what could be done about it. One of them turned up dead in Ireland before he ever got off the ground, and the other one was found dead in New York very shortly thereafter. Now there again we have these suspicious circumstances but with absolutely no proof.

Now where Tyler Kent fits into this thing is in connection with Bullitt and Roosevelt's proclivities for carrying on diplomatic negotiations by verbal means so that he would never be implicated by his "John Henry" on a piece of paper. What could be greater evidence of this fact is when they worked out the Rainbow 5 plan which set the United States up as a virtual ally of the British and with the proviso in that that the effort would all be made in the Atlantic, and the Pacific would be tail-end Charlie as far as military effort was concerned. This whole thing was written up and Rainbow 5 committed the United States to an alliance which committed us to certain military policies and economic policies which of course had never been even hinted at to the Congress, which at that time was still, constitutionally, supposed to have the power to declare war. When this Rainbow 5 was hammered out by the British and American staffs in Washington it was called the ABC 1 plan, to begin with, "American and British conversations"--the British over here secretly in civilian clothes and the whole thing kept deeply secret as to its very existence. The whole set of papers came out, were distributed to the fleet, the Asiatic Fleet, the Pacific Fleet, the Atlantic Fleet, in April or May 1941, but without Roosevelt's signature. He refused to sign it. When they had Admiral Stark on the witness stand in the Joint Congressional Investigation in 1945-46, Stark waffled on the things as to why he didn't sign it and he made some lame excuse that, "Well the President intended to sign it as soon as war broke out but that he had disseminated to the fleets in any case and that it had all the weight of an official order in that Roosevelt had approved it verbally to him." That is a typical example of how he was always covering his rear--whether that is good or bad I don't know, I am merely stating the fact. The same was true as far as getting the Poles to stand up and fight. Neither Roosevelt nor Churchill had any idea what the Poles would do. They were a mercurial lot, unpredictable, and it was just possible, they thought, that they would cave in, in view of the fact that they had the Russians on the other side who were in effect allies of the Germans--they had signed a non-aggression pact or two--what would the Poles do? The thing to do was to buck them up as far as possible. Well the British made an outright guarantee. The British at that stage of the game were pacifically minded. They had no army to speak of. They were not at all warm to the idea of going to war with anybody. The Poles obviously needed some more bucking up so that was done, wholly informally, through Bullitt in Paris. Paris was the headquarters of American diplomacy in those days, moreso than England, because it was the center of the continent, and normally when any embassy in Europe disseminates a dispatch to a direct addressee, a cable, it sends printed copies by letter to other embassies on the continent which might necessarily be interested in the subject. In other words, if Bullitt in Paris sent the American embassy in Warsaw a communication by cable in connection with the possible bucking up of their spirits and so forth, London would get a copy. That too was amongst the booty that Tyler Kent picked up; he had copies of the letters and of course all this stuff that Tyler Kent pinched was sequestered at once.

Q: He had not distributed it?

Adm. T.: I don't know the details of whether he passed any of this stuff on to this daughter of this White Russian admiral or not--that is outside of the purview of my assessment of the whole situation. But I do know that Kent, indirectly through a very dear friend of mine in Norfolk who in turn is a very close confidant of Kent's--Kent had spilled all this stuff to my friend who in turn took notes on it and has given me copies of Tyler Kent's letters telling about these things--the fact that Bullitt was carrying on this very strong propaganda campaign having been told to do so by Roosevelt to bolster up the Poles, telling them we would come to their economic assistance, we would do every conceivable thing we could to support them against the Germans if they would only stiffen their backs and fight. On the strength of the British proposal that they would honor their alliance with the Poles, their agreement to mutual assistance with the Poles, plus apparently what Bullit had told them and which we know existed and which we know happened, through Kent, as truly happened, the Poles fought, they resisted--as precisely what Roosevelt and Churchill had hoped they would do, which sparked the war. Otherwise, you see, Poland would have been divided between the Russians and Germans--as it was subsequently anyway--after the Germans took the place over the Russians moved in from the other side. The secret protocol of the German/Soviet agreement whacked up Poland in that very respect, and also allocated Lithuania to Germany and Estonia and Latvia to the Soviets, it also made some vague promises about the Soviets taking over control of the Straits, the Dardanelles. Those were the secret agreements, which of course were not published when the Ribbentrop-Molotov agreement first came out. Now the Soviet relations with the Germans went sour before any of these things came to fruition because the Soviets occupied all three of those countries, instead of leaving Lithuania to the Germans, as proposed in the secret agreement.

There we have Roosevelt's secret diplomacy at the epitome of it, one of the typical situations.

Now let us take another track and figure out what we shall talk about next.

Q: One of the items would be the Poltava Naval Base.

Adm. T.: Poltava was an air-shuttle base. The original concept was for the bombers to leave England and overfly Germany and continue on to Poltava and rebomb and refuel and fly back again to England.

Q: Where is Poltava?

Adm. T.: Poltava is in the Ukraine. Also there was a possibility of flying to Poltava and to fly over the Ploesti air fields in Rumania and land in Italy.

Q: They did a little of that, didn't they?

Adm. T.: They did both, of course to begin with, the Soviets were extremely reluctant to allow any foreign fighting people in there at all. For example, the British sent a Spitfire squadron to Murmansk because Murmansk was only about 15 minutes away from German air bases in Norway and Northern Finland. The planes were brought over there and landed and the Russians said, "Thanks very much for the airplanes but we don't need the pilots. The pilots can go home", which they were forced to do. The same thing happened during the crisis at Stalingrad. The Americans offered to send in something like 20 or 30 heavy bombers and base them in the Caucasus and fly them. They were pretty complicated bombers. Obviously the Russians had never trained in anything like it before, but they said, "Yes, we will be glad to have the bombers, but no pilots, no American personnel at all."

Q: What is back of that reasoning, as you understand the Russian character?

Adm. T.: A good many writers from the Marquis de Coustine in 1838 right on down to the present day--George Kennan and many others who spent lots of time in Russia, have concluded, aside from all the physical characteristics which are parallel to ours--appearance, height, basic derivation of language, and mode of life in many respects, are so close that they have caused us to make a grand, basic error, in that the

Russians were brought up on one side of the line and the Europeans, such as ourselves, were brought up on the other side. The European side enjoys the heredity of the Age of Chivalry, when there was born in the Western viewpoint our views on womanhood, honor in general, truthfulness, and in a word, the attributes of Sir Galahad, which of course are not carried down to the basic fundamentals in most people now, but that overall viewpoint is derived from the Age of Chivalry in Europe to which the Russians were never a party. They are basically Byzantine Orientals in their religious and psychological makeup. They are extremely suspicious of outsiders, and well they might be, because they have been overridden God knows how many times--by the Mongols, the Turks, the Swedes, the French, the Lithuanians. The Russians have been invaded and subjugated and put upon. So naturally enough, they have a fairly built-in suspicion of foreigners in general and their motives, because the motives have basically never been altruistic. They have been there to squeeze out what they could. That was true from the beginning of the industrial age also, when Russia's industry, such as it was before the Revolution, was built up by foreign capital, chiefly British, French, Belgian, Dutch, and the people were over there (from their point of view) simply to exploit whatever they could from the

Russians. It was perfectly obvious what their views were. So we have these two basic and fundamental bugs that affect the Russian viewpoint:

a - a suspicion of foreigners in general and,

b - the fact that anybody that comes there is there for a material and ulterior motive.

Q: What you say underscores how deep seated those feelings are; their refusal in the face of real disaster to accept American pilots and British pilots.

Adm. T.: Yes, deep seated in the sense that they feel a temporary crisis can be treated at the moment, whereas a long term penetration might prove fatal. Any conceivable foot in the door in the past has spelled 't-r-o-u-b-l-e' all the way through. The other thing is that they have the same degree of reticence to come to a "Yes" or "No", a certain degree of duplicity and mendacity and so forth which is characteristic of the Chinese; it is very difficult to get a mainland Oriental of any description--Chinese, Korean, Malay, or anybody else to come down with the first and last price at the very beginning. There must always be the bargaining with the hand up the sleeve, and, the bargaining having been settled you can never be sure that the quality of the merchandise is what you had hoped it would be in the beginning.

Those qualities are part and parcel of the Russians. Looking a gift horse in the mouth is the basic order of the day as far as they are concerned.

When the Americans wanted the base at Poltava, the insistence was so great and the bait held out was so tempting, in the form of a landing field that they subsequently could make use of themselves, and of course their forces were advancing at that time but they were still hard pressed, the war was by no means won, so anything that could do damage to the Germans was acceptable, up to a point. But to have a very large number of Americans in the USSR--first of all the degree of hospitality which they like to show toward people could not be applied in this case because they simply didn't have the means. They had to start from nothing on the bare field in Poltava. They laid down steel mesh runways (Marsden mats) and made the best attempts they could to house the personnel-- which of course was large. And of course where we went wrong was to go along with their proposal and proviso and requirement that they provide the protection for the base. In other words, there was to be no American anti-aircraft defenses, no fighter planes. It was strictly a squatting place for the bombers to come down and re-bomb and refuel. So, after I think not more than one or two passages on the shuttle deal the

Germans followed them back to Poltava and came in and wreaked utter destruction on the base, cripped, burnt, or otherwise destroyed practically all of the bombers in that flight on the ground and did tremendous personnel damage--wiped out the barracks. The efforts to defend the place with fighters and anti-aircraft guns was so deficient and so piddling that it almost suggested that it was deliberate--that they had no intention of ever carrying the thing through. It was simply a sop; that they tried it on to make the Allies feel good, and having discovered that it was insupportable and impossible to carry through they would abandon it, which they did, of course. The same held true, for example, of bringing planes in by Alaska. It was a thoroughly sensible thing to fly planes up to Alaska, fly them across the Bering Straits through Siberia and through perfectly adequate air fields to the front, particularly for the short range fighter planes. The only other way to get the planes over there, the heavier type patrol planes and whatnot was to fly them--all the way down to Brazil, across to Africa over the Atlantic and then by round-about way up to Teheran. For a patrol type seaplane it was a risky thing. The fighter planes had to be boxed, crated, put aboard ship, delivered, uncrated, assembled and whatnot. It was far simpler to fly the things across. But we never succeeded in doing it; the mere fact that there would be American personnel required on a half dozen Siberian bases scotched the whole idea. The Russians were desperately afraid throughout that early phase of the war, up until about 1944, that the Japanese would attack. They had been able to withdraw their Siberian forces--the best front line troops they had--on the advice of their magnificent spy Richard Sorge in Tokyo. He had told them in October of 1941 through his high connections at the German Embassy in Tokyo and through his association with high individual Japanese, that the Japanese intended to strike at the south and not into Siberia. He was a German newspaper man, purported to be at any rate, but he was one of the best spies, that has ever been fielded by any nation probably--in view of the results he obtained. He established himself in Shanghai as a newsman, for a German news agency--purely a spurious front, he was a good newsman, but that wasn't his real job--then he went to Japan and ingratiated himself with General Eugene Ott who was the Nazi ambassador and likewise with a great many top Japanese. He was able to find out in October of 1941 that the Japanese intended to strike south and not Siberia. At that stage of the game--this is before Stalingrad--the Russians were retreating on every front--

it became apparent to the Japanese that the Russians would collapse; we thought so too, our military attaché over there, Colonel Ivan Yeaton, said, "Give them three months and a minimum of six months at the very outside," and certainly that was the Japanese view, so why go in there and waste their powder on Siberia when it would fall to them anyway. That was obviously the theory on which they were working and that's the word that Sorge was able to send--it was about the last message he sent--the Japanese had been desperate to round the guy up. They found him and hanged him; he has since appeared on the Soviet postage stamp as a hero of the Soviet Union, and well he might be. As a result of his revelations to Moscow the Soviets were able to withdraw large numbers of their best troops and, under the command of Marshall Zhukov (he was then a general) they managed to drive the Germans back a hundred miles from Moscow in the fall of 1941, to save the city, and one man did it--this guy Sorge. Another interesting fact is that as far as we know, the Soviets never told Washington about it, about any of the Sorge's revelations--the fact that the Japanese intended to strike south. Up to the very minute, up until November, Kelly Turner, who was director of War Plans in Washington, was sending messages to the Far East that Siberia was the target. Of course in October, if the Muscovites had told us we'd know perfectly well it wasn't Siberia but it was the south. Obviously the Russians would have been delighted to see the monkey taken off their backs with the Japanese attacking us.

Anyway, in those early days in Moscow, May of 1942, it looked not unlikely that we might have to walk out via Iran, or who knows where. The country was pretty well demoralized. Of course, after Stalingrad things began to look better but by no means clearly seen through to victory. There were all sorts of misgivings amongst the Russians themselves as to the outcome and some were shaky to the point of switching sides. Of course, we all know about General Vlasov, he was a Soviet general who defected with his entire division intact in effect, to the Germans, and fought on their side. He was never given a very important part of the fun because I suppose they didn't entirely trust him. About this time, about 1943, one of the enlisted men in the American embassy, storekeeper, who spoke Russian pretty well and who had some good contacts in town, came back with a leaflet which had been circulated in Moscow, telling about Vlasov. So the degree of defection or the possibility of it was very real. Of course when you see the war maps you see a line stretching from Murmansk down to the Black Sea--there was no such thing as a front, the length of that line was several thousand miles to begin with, so if they put people within five feet of each other there wouldn't be enough of them to go halfway down it. Actually what it amounted to was that the very few east-west roads that connected Germany with the interior of Russia were the only, what you might call, real fronts. The rest of the country had no roads. There are no roads as we know them in the Soviet Union even now, I mean paved roads; it is an adventure to go by motor car from Leningrad to Moscow even now. At that time the few concrete roads that existed petered out eight or ten miles beyond the city environs and you either went by railroad, or in the spring and fall, you were up to your hocks in the transition period between summer and winter--you were up to your axles in mud and the only conceivable time to start a war was either in late spring when the earth was firming up or in the fall when it was frozen. It is an interesting thing that Napoleon and Hitler both started their invasion on exactly the same day 22 June, which was the ideal time to start when the earth would bear you and you wouldn't sink in. Even then they had to go along certain well defined avenues because the areas in between were simply utter jungle and morass and impassable so that was no line--merely clots of resistance and offense, all the way from the White Sea down to the Black Sea. It was possible for anybody who knew the country to penetrate all the way through the lines, way back to the German rear, which was routinely done by partisan bands. In fact, there was one Russian employee of the embassy, one of whose relatives had come back leading a cow from God knows how many hundred miles behind the German lines. It was positively like a huge screen that you could jump through any one of the many holes as long as you stayed off the main routes of ingress and egress--there was no war, you didn't even know there was a war going on. The crops grew, the people worked, of course most of the men were at the front, the women were at home and life went on generally as before. It was only in the big population centers that it was evident; it was a different kind of war, it wasn't like the 1914 European war where there was the solid front--shoulder to shoulder--guns and men from the North Sea to the Adriatic. It wasn't that kind of war, Of course, the distances are so great that it was difficult for the Germans to bring up sufficient, sustaining supplies to maintain any sort of a bombardment so there was very little bombarding of the big cities--air bombardment of Moscow or even Leningrad. The mere physical business of bringing up gasoline, supplies and bombs and so forth--in many cases by horse and wagon. It worked both ways, we don't realize the tremendous numbers of horses that were used on both sides; German artillery supplies, the Russians had whole divisions of nothing but horse cavalry that were able to cover country at two or three times the speed of infantry, and dash back and forth behind the Russian front to bolster up weak points. The classic story of the Russian re-supply system is the horse and the driver and the Russian telyaga--a four-wheel springless wagon loaded with provisions and ammunition. This would work its way to the front and come up to a gun battery. They would distribute the shells, break up the wagon for firewood, take the driver as a replacement in the battery and eat the horse, so there was no problem about traffic going back in the other direction. Of course they were tremendously inventive people, the Russians. We make jokes about their claiming inventions, as being first, at any rate they claim they invented radio first and the airplane first and all sorts of things. In many cases they were either contemporary or they really did do it first. They had the first four-engine bomber--Sikorsky, who was an Imperial Russian, developed it and then came to the United States. They invented the armored cruiser. In 1914 they had the destroyer NOVICK which would make 36 knots, which was 15 knots faster than anybody's destroyer could do at that time. They invented tactical mining, which had never been done before; they invented dropping mines by parachute, they took up mass parachute jumping after they had seen Chennault try it on in the United States in 1928. Of course, during the war they were having the same problems moving their artillery over the wretched roads. Guns are heavy and bridges were insufficient to hold them, so they brought out this mass rocket fire. Now we, of course, developed that during the war, also the rocket launching boats were used to soften up the Japanese positions ashore. But the Russians used these for the artillery. They would mount what amounted to 15 or 16 hunks of 3-inch gas pipe on a truck, a plain ordinary two and a half ton truck, and put some sort of an ignition device in it and send out a salvo of 3-inch rockets which was equivalent to a whole battalion of field artillery and for the purpose of laying a barrage, just as efficient and at one fiftieth of the cost in effort and material. They thought of it first and they carried it out and it was very effective. When they came to a piece of bad road or a bridge which needed to be constructed across a stream, they would immediately tear down the nearest house which was usually stone, and build the road or the bridge; who lived in the house--there was no argument about payment or anything like that. Their rifles for example, had trigger guards which were big enough so that you could get the index finger which was mittened, in it to fire it. The bolt was three inches long with a big knob on the end so you could fire it with mittens on and load it with mittens on. Their automatic rifles were pressed out like tin cans and they rattled. They were called a grease gun, which is just about what they amounted to; they were so effective that the AK-47 in the Vietnam war when an American captured one he preferred it to his own gun because he could drop it in the mud, pick it up and shake it and it would fire. I think at one time they were even making AK-47 ammunition in the United States for our people to use in the captured guns in Vietnam, captured Soviet arms from the Vietnamese. So, their equipment was far more suitable. For example, their boots were big enough they don't use socks, they use foot cloths; it is an endless tape about two inches wide and three or four yards long which they very expertly wrap around their feet and legs such as we would do a bandage and when it gets colder they just wrap on more foot rags.

Q: With all this inventiveness, it does raise the question why did they not provide adequate defense against air attack on Poltava? Other than the theory you explained--maybe they didn't want to.

Adm. T.: The only theory is that apparently they didn't want to save it, that they wanted to see it wiped out.

Q: Did you journey down to that base?

Adm. T.: No, Poltava was established either after I left, I think it actually got into full commission after I left. It was a tremendous job to set it up. General Deane came over there; when Harriman replaced Standley. He had gotten reports on the ridiculous situation then existing, the fact that diplomatic relations didn't exist between Faymonville and the attachés and the whole thing needed a shaking up. When he went over there he went under the proviso that they would fall out and fall in again on the other side of the fence, that there would be no more Naval military attachés. It would all be a military mission and it would be under his trusted friend General Deane, who was secretary to the Joint Staff in Washington at that time, or some comparable position--one of considerable responsibility. They trusted him implicitly in his ability to get on with the Russians, and in his sincerity. When he first went over there, of course the attachés were no longer called as such; we had a party one time shortly after he arrived, with some Russian girls and some of the embassy people, wearing uniform of course and we wore our undress aiguillettes to show the marks of an attaché. The next day, through our then new boss--Duncan had gone home--Admiral Clarence Olsen was then the attaché, the word came down to throw those aiguillettes in the ash can, there will be no more worn. You are no longer attachés; you are military missionaries. Deane had no sooner hit the spot over there than he called all hands together and delivered a resounding speech to the effect that we were there for one purpose and one purpose only and that was to help win the war and do everything we conceivably could to cooperate with the Russians and that there was to be no intelligence activity of any sort whatever.

Q: No gathering of intelligence?

Adm. T.: No gathering of intelligence, no reporting of intelligence, and no attention paid to intelligence, it was solely a help effort. Well, of course the Navy paid no attention to that and went right on as before.

Q: What was the wisdom of that blanket policy?

Adm. T.: He had got his walking papers from Roosevelt. Roosevelt wanted the whole thing done on a purely straightforward basis so there could be absolutely no suspicion of double dealing as far as the Russians were concerned. He even went so far as to say, "I want the situation such that we can invite the Russians into our office at any time and see any piece of paper we have any place in here." Presumably, I don't suppose he mentioned it by name but 'come in the code room and see what is going out over the code machine'. Of course the messages had to be in code so the Germans wouldn't read them and know what was going on. There again, no Russians came into the Navy code room. Whether they went into the Army code room or not, I don't know. I doubt that too. The bloom however was very soon off the rose. Of course the beautiful banquets went on, as soon as they came to Moscow the people in the hotel next door--the National--went on half rations so they could give these huge banquets--caviar, three or four courses, wine--and in very short order Deane tried to make contact with his opposite number and the opposite number was always busy or he was sick. He made it impossible one way or another. If he did get to see him there was equivocation and there was no agreement. In general it took Deane about six to eight months to realize what the face of things actually was. I met him in Washington after he had come back, I guess just after the war, probably 1945. I had heard that he was writing a book. I naturally enough was interested and I went up to him at a cocktail party and wanted to know what the name of the book was. He said, "I haven't figured it out yet but what I would like to call it is, Two Years with the Bastards, but I probably won't be able to get away with that." Actually the book came out as The Strange Alliance. That was the name of the book and it was a very good one too. It well might have been because it was largely the secret report written by his staff. He had a very large Army staff there. I suppose there were 30 people over there and by that time there were about 15 Navy. The Navy part of his book was rather modest because being a military man he gave the preponderance of attention to the Army. I recognize some passages which we had helped to write, in the book, that is actually what he had done; he had put in some personal adventures and unfortunate situations but the lion's share of it was the top-secret report of the military staff.

Q: Did Ambassador Harriman share this same idea of the policy toward the Russians?

Adm. T.: Harriman was so desperately keen to be Ambassador to the Court of St. James that he was making no waves whatever. He was over there simply hoping to God that nothing would happen that would upset the apple cart as far as he, Harriman, was concerned. And he finally wound up getting what he wanted.

Q: Why was this such a burning ambition?

Adm. T.: I suppose it was the certain degree of prestige; he was a young man then and there is a tremendous amount of prestige in being Ambassador to the Court of St. James.

Q: How effective was he as Ambassador to Russia?

Adm. T.: I am not in a position to say. It is possible that he did a lot more than I know about. In the very beginning when we first went over there, the Navy's ciphers were used exclusively for State Department--for business between Roosevelt and Stalin--of course this put us at a grave disadvantage because the message would come from Roosevelt to Stalin via Navy cipher, we would be very careful about how we paraphrased it because slight nuances, slight changes can make a tremendous difference in diplomatic language. It is not quite the straightforward language we are used to in the Navy. Of course then very shortly thereafter would come Stalin's reply in Russian or in English (the Russian would be translated of course) and then send it to FDR back via the Navy cipher, which gave the Russians tremendous leverage in their ability to break our cipher, which I am sure they must have done. Everybody was breaking our cipher--so were the Germans. Then we got cipher machines and the State Department got them too, so then the diplomatic traffic shifted to State and the military traffic stuck with us. But the code was pretty hard to crack with those cipher machines. When Churchill and Harriman came over there in August 1942--you see they had promised the Russians a second front in '42, very recklessly and without due regard for the facts, they simply didn't have the landing craft, they didn't have any of the stuff that they could possibly have made any sort of a successful landing, and, had there been a disaster like there was at Dunkerque or Dieppe, the war would have been prolonged for God knows how long. So, Stalin expected the invasion in 1942, his back was to the wall. He was so upset about it that when he wanted to send a blistering telegram he didn't care who he sent it to nor what he said. The things he sent to Roosevelt at that time and Churchill, made it clear that it just wasn't enough to send him back a mollifying answer, that they had to send people over there. So Churchill and Harriman were sent; poor Ambassador Standley was in the back seat, he was around but he wasn't enough, it had to be Harriman and Churchill. They started off from Teheran in four big Liberator bombers and they had Churchill and crew and his advisers in one, Harriman in another, a third was loaded with staff officers and the fourth was with British General Wavell. Wavell never made it, his airplane had to sit down someplace but the others appeared on the air field. We were all out there as a reception committee, all hands and the ship's cook from the embassy, everybody who could find a place in a car. The guard and band were there, Molotov was there and they all shook hands and the national anthems were played and they played the Star Spangled Banner through twice and then Molotov got in his car and they slammed the door and it sounded like the State Department safe clanging shut--it was an armored limousine--and we all jumped in our cars and back we went to Moscow, the streets all having been cleared and lined with NKVD troops; so the conferences then started with the hope on our side that we would convince Stalin of the futility of trying to make this landing in spite of the fact that it might momentarily take some weight off his back.

Q: Where was the landing to be?

Adm. T.: Where it eventually took place--on the channel, it was supposed to be a cross-channel landing, but as I say, they were absolutely in no position to consider such a thing at that stage. The American troops weren't over there, they simply didn't have the warm bodies or anything to present there. But it was very difficult to convince Stalin of this. He was losing tens of thousands of men on the front every day, and what's the point of not losing a few Americans and British and Frenchmen at the same time--even things up. So they conferred and they got almost nowhere. The day of the farewell banquet--they always wind up with a big hurrah--Stalin and Churchill had been in the last stages of a knock-down and drag-out argument and Stalin made some disparaging remark about the British fighting ability and the army in general that was too much for Churchill. He stood up and threw his cigar down and said, "I didn't come here to have the British Army insulted," and he stalked out without the usual goodbye handshake, which was a pretty serious attitude to take at that stage of the game. After all Stalin, was Russia, he was it--he had insulted Churchill and Churchill insulted him right back. That night, the banquet was supposed to be carried through as scheduled. It was held in the Kremlin in one of the huge old Czarist halls. Present thereat was my boss, Captain Duncan. Of course Standley was there, and five or six generals--Spaulding who was on the supply mission, General Follett Bradley, General Maxwell from Iran, supply mission, and another general whose name escapes me now; quite a delegation. The British had an equivalent number of high rankers. Churchill had arrived thirty minutes late and he was wearing what he called his 'siren suit'. It was a thing like a suit of coveralls and it went from his ankles all the way up and it was a belted sort of thing--a covering like mechanics wear. He normally wore it when he was making a long trip, or when he was about to dive into an air-raid shelter back home. The connotation here was that he was ready to jump on his airplane right then--everybody assumed that that was what he wore it there for; the other thing was to sort of discredit the Russians. Stalin was there in his best dress uniform--great for protocol--with his marshall's star and all that, so it was in effect a further insult. Well Stalin apparently realized he had gone too far that afternoon with Churchill and he was trying to jolly the old boy along, make cracks and so forth, and Churchill came in with a very long, dour face with his cigar hanging down instead of up like it was when he was jubilant. So as the dinner went on with the usual number of toasts in wine and vodka and champagne and whatnot, and toward the end of it apropos of nothing at all old Stalin stood up and launched into a dissertation on the value of intelligence and the fact that it sometimes decided more than battles and, as an example, says he, "Witness the miserable, incredibly bad overall bungling of the Gallipoli campaign in 1917." Well, of course, that was Churchill's baby--that's what he got fired from the cabinet for because it didn't get across. Stalin went on a little farther and of course old Churchill was getting redder in the face all the time and squirming around, so Stalin, very well satisfied with himself, proposed a toast to intelligence officers, that they were the unheralded, unsung heroes of the war in every war. Everybody joined in that and everybody sat down, then old Jack Duncan stood up. He had been lapping up the booze like all the rest of them, and he was way down at the foot of the table. As a captain he was well down below the salt, a long way from where Stalin was at the head of the table, and he said, "Mr. Stalin, I would like to propose a toast too, to the intelligence officers because I am one and I would like to say that since I have been over here I have been unable to function as one because I can't make contact with anybody that would come across with any information." He would never have said this had he not been in the state he was, I expect. Well, Stalin stood up and said, "Mr. Captain, that is the first honest thing I have heard all day," and he was looking at Churchill. He said, "I want to drink to that too," so he picked up his glass, walked all the way down to the end of the table, clicked his glass with Duncan's and they had a drink. So, back Stalin goes (this is almost the end of the dinner) and there were a few more toasts and that was that and everybody got up and Stalin came back to Duncan and put his arm around his shoulder and said, "Come on, let's you and I walk out," and then in a big loud voice, over his shoulder, he said, "Gentlemen, the toilet is on the left," and that was the end of dinner.

That was the state of relations in August 1942 and the reason I know all of these things is because the next morning, of course we all had a post-mortem around the dining table for breakfast. Duncan was there nursing a hangover. The whole crowd stayed around there for about a day after that-- the rank and file. Of course Churchill and Harriman got out quickly. The smaller guys, like Loy Henderson for example-- he was there. Old Follett Bradley said to the army attaché,

"I guess you Army cryptographers had quite a job." They had sent some extra people over. So, Duncan spoke up and said, "Mr. Henderson, about what General Bradley said, --the Army didn't do it. The Navy did it; all the correspondence, all the communications passed through the Navy. Well how did I know that, because I sat up for two nights all night trying to get this stuff off, so that I know whereof I speak."

After that, in general, the seeds of suspicion that had been sown under those circumstances became pretty evident in almost everything we did.

Q: The honeymoon was over?

Adm. T.: The honeymoon never existed, there was never any such, there was a degree of suspicion which was well understood in the very beginning by the Russians, but not for a long time by us. It gradually became apparent that it was a purely one-sided affair. Of course we all recognized that international relations were wholly on a pragmatic basis, none of it was on a friendly basis. All this hurrah about the "allies", the French and whatnot, the French are in it for themselves, and we are in it for ourselves. During the Civil War for example, the Russians sent ships to San Francisco and New York, they were in it purely for the fact that they didn't want them corked up in the Baltic because the British and the French were about to intervene in the case of the Polish-Russian troubles. So all of these things are only pragmatic, and for us to have gone over to Russia saying a new era has dawned, we are all friendly, we love each other, and would like to sit around and swill Vodka together, that's great on the bottom level where people have to get along but as far as any international relations are concerned, we all recognize that is a bunch of hog-wash.

Q: You attribute that to FDR's attitude?

Adm. T.: The friendly business?

Q: Yes.

Adm. T.: He was wholly naive in this. He was a funny combination of--he was a composite guy, he was raised as an only son, he was pampered and petted by an adoring mother and he grew up in an artificial atmosphere in many respects, then of course after his paralysis and his fairly long sojourn of several years, maybe longer, in Warm Springs, Georgia, he then was able to associate with the common folks, where apparently his ideas on liberalism and equality and so forth developed to the point where he had these ideas that everybody could be reached if you treated them in the right way. Not a pragmatic viewpoint, but purely a hand-shaking friendly viewpoint. He could charm the birds out of the trees if he wanted to. He had a tremendous ability to influence people and that is probably what got him in this unfortunate hole with Stalin where he called him, "dear old Uncle Joe," and felt that if he could get next to him he could convert him. He would make a pal out of him. He did so in many instances, very obviously at the expense of Churchill, because by that time the Roosevelt/Churchill romance had cooled somewhat because Roosevelt had made some very straight from the shoulder remarks about what he felt should be the future of the empire--all the empires, British, French and all the rest of them--they were an anachronism, should be done away with and that should be part of the aims when the war was finished up, to give self-determination to all these subject peoples. That brought forth from Churchill the fact that he had not been made His Majesty's First Minister to preside over the liquidation of the British Empire. At Teheran and at Yalta both, Roosevelt did his best to woo Stalin, who hated Churchill with a passion. He just hated the guy's guts. And he always had, as many years before Churchill had said the best boon to humanity would have been to have strangled Bolshevism in its cradle, and he tried desperately to do just that. Stalin had no love for him and Roosevelt realized that he did what he could to make jokes and ingratiate himself with Stalin at the expense of Churchill, which was not at all well received by Churchill, because there are some things you just don't have a sense of humor about when you are being made fun of. Churchill was an imperious and a powerful man in his own right but he had to go along and take it, for after all, he was the beggar at that stage of the game. There was nothing he could do.

Q: He was the weakest one of the three.

Adm. T.: Now let me read you something that I wrote in October of 1943, which I believe reflects what was pretty well the general attitude of all the people over there.

Q: You were still in Moscow?

Adm. T.: Yes, I didn't leve until May 1944 and this was in October 1943:

> "It may on the first glance seem unfriendly to remind ourselves that much American scrap iron and other such materials are now being returned to us with a vengeance by the Japanese--materials which we ourselves could have used to very good advantage had we been more fore-minded.

"The present trend of the official policy in the USSR the tone of their propaganda to their own people, and the growing Soviet independence and lack of trust should give cause for deep consideration of the potentialities of this situation."

That was the last paragraph of an intelligence report I wrote in October 1943. Most of these intelligence reports that I used to write, I know for a fact to have been sent to the White House. Of course, it would be rather presumptuous on my part to suggest or even feel or think that it had any influence at all, but it does make it perfectly clear that Roosevelt was very much interested, or somebody in the White House was, perhaps Admiral Leahy, on what first hand information was available in Russia and what people were thinking there, regardless of what might be the view on this side. Maybe they were trying to protect Roosevelt against himself, but there is no doubt that Roosevelt was, before his death for three or four months, wholly disillusioned as far as the Russians were concerned. He completely recognized the fact I think, and the evidence shows it. He had realized his policy had failed, that 'good old Uncle Joe' was not the kind you could shake hands with and be a good poker player companion. I would like to think that maybe these little words of wisdom that we sent from Moscow might have helped to bring that attitude about.

Q: Because this was a consistent theme in the reports you sent?

Adm. T.: The ones in the beginning, when I first got there, were the best estimates I could make of the Russian character and their behavior as we saw it on trips, on the train, where we got really to meet Soviets, swap drinks, and tell long tales, and of course at the end of the train ride in spite of expressions of deep friendship that we would meet again, call them up, come see them, and they would be delighted to receive us and give us a fish or give us a ride or do that or this, when the time came to try that on, they were gone, they were sick, they had been transferred--in other words they had made the horrifying discovery that association with Americans was poison. It happened every time we made a train trip and there was no way to control it because there were just too many people involved. The controlling force found it very awkward. These reports in the beginning were chiefly on the characteristics of the people, what their reactions were to long conversations with us. We found in most cases that they were extremely dedicated, that they were openly suspicious of anything we told them because they had been indoctrinated since childhood almost; for example, such sentences in their reader as a small child, one kid says to another,

"Oh, Vanya, there goes a foreigner, you watch him while I go get a policeman."

Then as the reports continue, and I became a little more sophisticated--I suppose from the diplomatic viewpoint, was able to read a few more dispatches by people upstairs who knew more about it than I did and who had better contacts, it became apparent that the whole idea of any sort of detente, as they now call it, or any sort of softening of the opinion of the Russians toward ourselves was a fairy tale, a fantasy. It would never happen; the Russian idea was to receive as much as they possibly could, give as little credit as they possibly could and certainly it indicated the fallacy of our thinking that you could bank good will, because everything was based strictly in its own individual merits and it was a quid pro quo all the way through, you gave something and you got something and there was no business of building up good will through unilateral sacrifices or gifts or favors.

Q: No treasury of merit?

Adm. T.: I suppose that is a good way to describe it. Mind, you, throughout all this we certainly didn't in any respect lose our affection toward individual Russians because

there are a great many for example, of liaison officers--
Commander Kostrinski and I were the dearest of friends, I like
to think. We would bare our souls to each other back to the
time we were born and everything that made us tick. He
spoke quite good English and between the two of us--actually
his background is rather interesting and typical in many
cases; during the Revolution his parents had disappeared
someplace and he was left homeless and became one of what
was known then as "byezprzornik" which is 'without backing' in
other words a homeless orphan, a ward of the state. Now,
in the very beginning the state didn't have very much to
offer in the way of being a ward. The kids lived in drain
pipes and scrounged food and lived as best they could, but
as time went on the Soviets managed to improve the situation,
rounding them up, putting them in homes and in his case,
giving him an education. He had been sent to England as an
assistant naval attaché, spent three or four years there
during which time he perfected his English. Then he came
back. And, here, he said, he was a proud commander in the
Soviet Navy and had started off simply as a homeless raga-
muffin. Obviously he owed his whole life and his entire
load of gratitude as to where he was and what he was doing to
his Motherland and his government. Anybody in those

circumstances is pretty hard to wean. Even though he had lived in a democratic environment such as England, he still felt that the solution to the problem for the Russians was not the way the British did it, but the way they were doing it. No amount of argument or reasoning could shake his belief or at least it wasn't evident that he was shaken. Might have been underneath. Who knows where he is now? Maybe in Siberia, because almost anybody who had any relationships with Americans in those days, either civilians working in the embassy or as opposite numbers in a military way, all were rounded up and sent to Siberia after the war. Some have come back, some died, some have been seen on the street, some we have made contact with--I think the most celebrated one the Americans know of is Zoya Fyeodorva, whose daughter, the love-child of Admiral Tate, was rehabilitated after Stalin died after she spent eight years in a prison camp, simply through virtue of having associated with Americans. There is no conceivable way in which she could have harmed the Soviets in passing information; I am sure she had none.

Q: Was that a policy of Stalin's?

Adm. T.: This was the Russian nature. Under Stalin, anybody who had associated with foreigners was ipso facto, likely to be infected by the wrong ideas, were dangerous, and should be put where they could do no harm. That has been the Russian policy for a hundred years or a thousand years, there is nothing new about it. The Imperial Russians, with rare exceptions, the minor number in the aristocracy, couldn't even travel. It was one of the few countries in the world requiring passports before WWI- Turkey and Russia were the only two with passport requirements. Not only did they have to have passports to travel but interior passports as well. All this business about the Soviets overturning the life-style of the Russians is of course a lack of understanding of the facts. It is nothing new, this is simply a reflection of the Russian character for centuries.

Interview No. 5 with Rear Admiral Kemp Tolley, U.S. Navy (Retired)

Place: At his residence in Monkton, Maryland

Date: Friday, 9 April 1976

Subject: Biography

By: John T. Mason, Jr.

Q: On this beautiful pre-spring morning we are going to have Chapter 5 of your fascinating story. Last time you left us still in Moscow. I think you were about ready to come back to Washington and a new assignment.

Adm. T.: I don't recall that on the tape anywhere, mentioning the fact that I had been married over there. The marriage was an extremely simple ceremony. We went around to the agency ZAKS, an acronym for some Russian term indicating service of a household nature to the Soviet people. It was a very unobtrusive office and a rather mousy looking woman with a book, which we signed, paid 15 rubles, and were told by the lady behind the counter that if we needed a divorce later on that would cost 50 rubles. Divorces were very common and very easy to get in those days. Actually, I think you exchanged post cards and that was it. Practically as simple as the Mohammadans where you say three times, "you are divorced" and the deed is done. Of course, concomitant with the simplicity of the ceremony is the ceremony at home which consists of breaking a plate on the ceiling-- you throw the thing up against the ceiling and it is supposed to come down and break. It if doesn't that's bad luck, but the plate broke. This in itself was a tragedy for the old Russian gal who helped keep house for us because I think we had a total of about six plates, six dinner plates and that was one of them.

Q: Was this back at the Embassy?

Adm. T.: It was at the Embassy; things were in very short supply. A lot of these bits and pieces that we had stuck together to housekeep had come from ships in Murmansk. I used to make trip up to Archangel and Murmansk about once every three or four months to bring back, by word of mouth actually, how things were, and I would always come back loaded with loot from the various American merchant ships-- possibly a ham or three or four plates or particularly cooking utensils because when we first set up housekeeping most of the cooking was done in #10 cans. You know, these things that hold a gallon. It was the usual size that they supplied to ships for canned vegetables and things of that nature. As time went on of course the Navy took care of us. It is an interesting thing that when the embassy was first set up in Moscow the State Department, impoverished as it always claimed to be in those days, turned to the Navy for help and all of the crockery and knives and forks and the cooking utensils and things like that in the American Embassy in the early days had the USN mark on them. I particularly recall that when I was there in 1935 for the first time. The same was true in 1941, '42 and all through that area, the Navy was called upon to supply almost everything--antifreeze for the car. When a ship came in to the north we would scrounge as much as we could and one time we had a whole flatcar load come down. Actually it was a flatcar and a boxcar, the flatcar had a Ford automobile on it for the American naval attaché and the boxcar was loaded with about twenty to thirty tons of food, all Navy supplied. Of course, this caused the US Army representatives in Moscow considerable chagrin because they weren't able to supply anything and about the only place they got their foot in the door was when one of the very rare airplanes came in with a visiting mission. We would go out and bleed the plane and get a barrel of gasoline from the aviation gas, bring it back and mix it with a barrel of Soviet alleged motor gasoline, the two mixed together would almost make the car run properly. Soviet motor gasoline was very little more than kerosene. In the wintertime in order to get the fleet under way in the morning, one automobile would have to run constantly, all the time, it would keep warm and it would be used to push the others in turn in order to get them going in the morning.

Q: Too bad you didn't have diesel motors?

Adm. T.: Well they were all just ordinary American cars. There were about four or five cars over there that had been left over from peace time. They were in pretty poor shape to begin with, but the Russian gasoline was so bad that you had to run in second gear most of the time and as I said, in cold weather you had to keep on running all the time or you would never get it started again.

Q: The policy of the State Department to pass it on to the Navy for supplies seems like passing the buck.

Adm. T.: Actually the State Department had no logistic facilities as such. They are geared up basically to work in what might be called civilized countries where all the amenities are available through civilian sources so when they get in a situation like this they have no machinery to back them up.

Q: I take it that the plate you threw up on the ceiling was one of those heavy thick Navy plates?

Adm. T.: It probably was some shipboard crockery that I had gotten from one of the American ships up north.

Q: Tell me, a wedding of that sort registered in the Soviet Bureau, is that recognized as a valid marriage in other parts of the world?

Adm. T.: Absolutely, you get a piece of paper saying that the ceremony has been performed, that you are man and wife. Now, according to the Soviet custom and by law the wife does not have to take the husband's name, which of course, is now, I believe legalized in the United States--fairly recently after a lot of litigation allowing people to keep their single name for business purposes if they like.

Q: Did you have any difficulty as the result of your marriage to a Russian citizen, did you have any difficulty as an American?

Adm. T.: The only difficulty was, if you want to call it that in this case, was that wives weren't permitted to come into the Soviet Union, to accompany their husbands or to be with them there. In this case, of course, there was absolutely no way around it because it was impossible to get my wife Vlada a visa immediately, so they held me over. My cruise was about up, I had been there for about a year and a half, which in wartime is certainly sufficient, you want to get out and get some proper sea duty. They kept me over six months hoping the visa would come through so that Vlada could accompany me out. Vlada would make trips around to the ZAKS agency every week or two and the answer would be "No, not yet." Of course that continued after I left, until 1946. In September of 1946 she finally got out, and we were married in November of 1943.

Q: What did she do in the interim?

Adm.T.: After I left she started to work for the OWI. By the time I had left, one or two women had been allowed to come in to work with the Embassy. One of those was Elizabeth Eagan who was the representative of OWI (Office of War Information) in Moscow and she was involved in this exchange of magazines—*America* was the name of the one in the Soviet Union and I think we called the one that was over here put out for the United States by the Russians and was called USSR in Construction—in any case they had a deal whereby each country would publish 50,000 copies, in effect a propaganda magazine, to be distributed in the other country. Vlada was involved in that operation in the American Embassy and they found her a room in a hotel where she could live until such time as she got out. We never knew what sprung the trap, so to speak. Only one possible connection we could think of: at one of the American Embassy parties, the Fourth of July celebration or some such, there were quite a few Russians of the type who would turn up on such occasions, none of them were what you might call friends. They were all official representatives of the Soviet Union, people from the foreign office, people from the liaison office of the military, and amongst those present was an NKVD general in his full, resplendent uniform. During the course of the evening he danced with Vlada and Vlada explained the situation in which she found herself. So about two weeks later, the next trip around to the visa office, lo and behold there was her visa to depart. Whether that did it or not, who knows.

Q: Had she been subjected to any kind of harassment during this period?

Adm. T.: No, of course almost anyone who had any contact with Americans or foreigners, if they worked in the house as a servant or if, as in Vlada's case, they worked as a translator and general handy gal around the office, they were always subject to questioning by the NKVD. In many cases, of course, they were professionals put on the job. At the theatre for example, there were always some very well dressed, obviously not ordinary type Soviets, because the ordinary type Soviet could not get clothes like that, very nicely dressed young ladies walking around with a flirtatious eye, and always very willing to team up with some foreign individual, usually in uniform, which made them very easily identifiable. And in many cases, a liaison was struck up with these gals and they would eventually wind up back at the quarters and they were always interested in toothpaste or tooth brushes or soap or anything that could be carried out as a little booty and pretty soon they might even move in. Obviously of course everybody understood well that these girls were agents of the NKVD out to find out anything they could, mostly to attempt to get information on personalities, what the vulnerable aspects of an individual would be, presumably to be able to apply a little blackmail --let's say the individual was married and if they got him into a compromising position they might possibly be able to bleed some information out of him on threat of blackmail.

To my knowledge, that was never used. I know it has been in other countries but as far as I have been able to determine nobody was ever blackmailed under those circumstances in the USSR, in my time. Later on after the war, there were cases where there were obvious set-ups where people were taken out on parties and gotten drunk and then it was later claimed that they had done things which the people claimed they didn't do but they could't prove they didn't. That was a pretext to get them out of the Soviet Union. When we were there there was no requirement or no desire, as far as I can imagine to get any of us out of the Soviet Union. As far as the Soviets were concerned we were all there doing a useful job and an exchange of material and information.

Q: You were helping them.

Adm. T.: It was purely to their advantage that we all remained, unless we were obviously of an hostile nature which in the long run would be damaging to the joint interests. But after the war that situation did not pertain. Any Americans or foreigners were there, as far as the Russians were concerned, simply as spies in brass buttons. So, the best thing to do after any one of these individuals was found to be particularly competent in the language or had been there long enough to know his way around the best thing to do was to get rid of him and get a neophyte in, someone new in. So, these various set-ups were arranged and give him the old heave-ho. That happened on a number of occasions, not just to Americans but to other foreigners.

Q: Was there any objection to the fact that Vlada married you in the first place?

Adm. T.: No, because first of all there was absolutely never any machinery in the Soviet government, in their new constitution, or in their laws right down to the lowest levels to make it possible for anybody to emigrate. They would never expect that anybody would either want to nor would they allow them to do so. So there was absolutely no legal normal routine manner in which somebody could leave the Soviet Union. So, suppose someone married a foreigner, they were either stuck in the Soviet Union or they would have to devise a way to get them out and each case was judged wholly on its merits, and each case depending wholly on somebody, somewhere along the line, having guts enough to sign the paper allowing the individual to depart. In wartime USSR, with everybody in a very delicate situation as far as his own job was concerned, their being only one strike for everybody, nobody was about to jeopardize his position by putting an up-check on any such case as Vlada's. So it would get to a certain level undoubtedly and then stay there in the action basket and people would come over to the USSR, such as the Secretary of State even, or the very highest individuals of the government, would speak about these cases. Vlada's wasn't the only one. There were five or six of them, and they would get nowhere. They would get a pleasant "Oh, yes, of course we will take care of it," on the part of Stalin or Molotov--all these things are in the record. The State Department gathers together its correspondence and periodically puts out a large red volume containing all of the exchanges of information and memoranda that has taken place between the two governmments, and there is a considerable volume of such correspondence concerning these marriages, including Vlada's and it indicates that it went to the very highest levels. But it is just the utter and complete inertia of the Soviet government in matters like this where there is no precedent set, where there is nobody who wants to take the chance--I suppose there had been cases when Soviets got out, such as Solzhenitsyn, let's say, but in earlier cases--two or three of these wives got out and immediately started writing scurrilous articles and making unfavorable publicity for the Soviet Union. Well, the poor guy who signed the green light on their exit papers was wholly responsible for whatever she said. Obviously you can see where they might jeopardize their whole life, not just a few points on their job application but the fact that they had any job at all on such a mistake.

Q: So, you had to return home by yourself.

Adm. T.: Yes. I might add in there that as far as the Americans were concerned, Vlada was very well thought of in the embassy and one big boost, which I am sure the Russians themselves observed with considerable interest, was the fact that shortly after we were married, Admiral Clarence Olsen, who was then naval attaché or Chief of the Naval Section of the Military Mission, which it then was--the naval attachés had been done away with in that section when the Military Mission was established, and he gave a very nice reception for us and several Russians were invited to come so the whole thing as far as the Americans were concerned was put on an official basis. The Russians took that at face value and as far as they were concerned treated Vlada as any foreign diplomat's wife would have been treated.

Q: Was she able to continue her relationship with her family?

Adm. T.: Oh yes. As I may have mentioned earlier, she had spent a good bit of her childhood in England where her father was on duty, and that of course, starting in 1937, anybody who had ever been abroad was deeply suspect, all of the ambassadors with the exception of about two and that means something like 14 or 15 major ambassadors, were shot and lesser individuals such as my father-in-law who had been in London as a representative of the Baltic and Black Sea Insurance Corporation, the Soviet organization, was given some sort of a drum-head trial and sent to Siberia presumably for eight years purely for his association with foreigners or having lived abroad where he was likely to become infected with all sorts of wrong ideas. He had been in Sibera from 1937 and this is 1941 and only about then had the family started to receive communications from him and they exchanged letters with him. He was then in Magadan, far Eastern Siberia. After his return from England, before he had been purged, he had been Vice-Commissar of Finance for insurance. He was an insurance specialist. He had got himself an inside job, so to speak at Magadan. He was a wizard in finance, spoke fluent German, French and English of course, and obviously Russian. A self-educated man from a small village in the

Ukraine. Of course, after Stalin died he was rehabilitated and was allowed to come back to Moscow. He had served far more than his eight years, but the fact that you have x-number of years in a Soviet concentration camp doesn't necessarily mean you can look forward to the gates opening at the end of that time. You are frequently forgotten about, and you may stay there forever. At least that was the situation in those days. In any case, he was rehabilitated. I never met him, as he came back to Moscow after I left. He died in 1958, undoubtedly largely resulting from the rough treatment he received while he was in Siberia. My mother-in-law was in Moscow at the time. She was living in a small apartment there and there were no restrictions put on her. She was never harassed or questioned or suffered any opposition.

Q: Was she supported by the State, was she given a pension or anything?

Adm. T.: Everybody works in the Soviet Union. For example, when my father-in-law was in London with the Soviet Insurance firm there, my mother-in-law worked in the office. She wasn't just a housewife who stayed home and drank tea like so many of the English ladies were doing, I suppose under similar circumstances. The same is true in the Soviet Union now, many of the wives are employed one way or another, although with the new aristocracy there are some who spend their days in idle chatter and tea drinking; and some of the youth over there who do nothing productive--the youth of the new aristocracy. But basically all the wives work at something, always have--that is an economic requirement in most cases because the salaries are not sufficient to run a family with only one member of the family working, unless you want to live in a purely marginal manner. In this case, my mother-in-law was working in an office of a small manufacturing outfit in Moscow, getting a small salary. Now, of course, she gets a pension like anyone else who is retired in the USSR. She is also particularly privileged in that she is the wife of what is known as an Old Bolshevik, which is a member of the party before the Revolution. My father-in-law had joined the party as a very young man before 1917. As a result she has a special ID card which allowed her to get on the front end of the street car with the pregnant women and get half-price theatre tickets and have what is known as a "putyeovka" which is a free vacation in the Black Sea area each year, a free ride there and free accommodations at the place.

Q: Then she is, in effect, a member of the new aristocracy?

Adm. T.: By no means. The new aristocracy is the self-perpetuating group that has risen high in the party--have all the best jobs. Their children are eligible for schools which the ordinary citizen would never get into, particularly those for foreign trade and diplomacy where they learn a language, where they have the possibility of going abroad. All these things tie in. When you go abroad for example, you get a large proportion of your salary in the currency of the country to which you are assigned. That foreign currency is extremely valuable beyond just its exchange value in that they have special stores in the Soviet Union where only foreign currency is accepted, and where things are available that are never seen outside these special stores, and they are at very low prices. For example, the apartment that we bought in Moscow about five years ago, was bought for dollars and in that apartment house the rest of the residents are Soviet citizens who have come back from duty abroad and bought their apartment with marks or pounds or dollars or pesos or whatever country they happened to come from. The ability to be educated in the way so that you can be sent abroad is not just advantageous from the glamor standpoint but also from the purely material advantages, the emoluments available there. The thing is self-perpetuating

The army officer's kids go to the Suvoroff Military Schools, which are military high schools and from there they go to the various military academies and from there they have a career in the military forces, a professional career which is wholly apart from a career which would be had by the officers serving a period as a substitute for the time as a conscript--every able bodied individual has to serve military time in the Soviet. But, if you choose to do so as an officer and you have the appropriate education, then let's say you will serve four or five years as a junior officer and then you get back out into civilian life. Obviously it is much preferable to be under those circumstances than to be in there toting a gun. However, the salaries and the prestige of people of that character are far less than the professionals who are in for life. Now those people largely stem from the professional ranks--they are army juniors, navy juniors so to speak, and they are the ones who go up to high rank. They get proportionately much higher paid in the army or the armed forces versus the civilian population than is true in the United States. That is just another example of the hierarchy that is building up a special aristocracy, military aristocracy, political and diplomatic and so forth. It is self-perpetuating.

Q: How does one break into that? Through sheer ability?

Adm. T.: One breaks into it through having had the good luck to start out with it a generation or two generations ago during the Revolution. Of course it is a mushrooming thing, after all every military family has two, three, four offspring, so the thing is simply by human growth. It perpetuates itself.

Q: But I mean somebody who had no background of that sort, would he have any opportunity to break into that hierarchy through sheer ability?

Adm. T.: Absolutely, because sheer ability is what gets you anywhere in the scholastic system in the USSR, up to a certain degree. Everybody goes to a school, some are much better than others depending upon whether you are in a wholly working class district or a rural district or an industrial district or a residential district; the school would vary in quality and the quality of the teachers and the curriculum and the students therein just like they do in the United States. Having done your time in the lower echelons, when it comes time to go to a high school there, your marks and political ability, whether you have been a successful member of the Young Comsomols, which is sort of the junior membership in the Communist party itself, depending upon your composite abilities in that respect is the choice open for you for the high school--it may be a good technical high school, or a good all-around high school in a good district or bad district, who knows. There again your marks determine whether or not you are going to college and what college, what type of college, the thing is laid on not so much by your choice but by what you are able to crank out in the way of marks and to what extent you can impress your superiors, your teachers. Of course, in all of these stages nothing is required in the way of money, and in college you get a stipend which is quite sufficient to live on. So, the financial aspects of education in the Soviet Union are wholly dependent on the ability of the individual in most cases. I have already mentioned that the background of your parents is really the open sesame to the prestigious areas. Now of course they are wholly pragmatic too. If somebody turns up who obviously has superior talents in technology or industry or something like that, obviously his talents will not be wasted, and he will have every opportunity to go on and develop those in some higher institution so they can make better atomic bombs and better mouse traps and better anything else in the way of industry. Unfortunately once he gets into that industry, his efforts will, to a certain degree, be stifled through the stupidity of the bureaucracy which is like any bureaucracy, which is an inefficient thing.

Q: It would seem that they do skim off the intellectual cream and utilize it.

Adm. T.: It sounds utopian almost, that they would capitalize on this, if you can use such a word in such a society, capitalize on the best elements of each coming generation but actually we know that privileged societies and privileged groups sometimes tend to go sour. They certainly do in the United States in many cases, where the offspring of the aristocracy, I can think of a few right now--Miss Hearst for example--where money and prestige and background is if anything, a disadvantage in that it breeds indolence and arrogance in the young individual which is destructive to the family hopes that the kid will take. What better example could there be than young Stalin, Joe Stalin's son. He was made a general in the air force at the tender age of about 24 and was utterly dissolute, he drank himself to death, he was a dope fiend, and he was guilty of every conceivable debauchery. It is almost reminiscent of some of the less savory princes of the old aristocracy. Again, that is of course not a wholly unique case.

Mikoyan, the perennial Commissar and later Minister, when they dignified the position, of Foreign Trade, had something like six or seven sons. Of course the Armenians are great believers in large families--they were all at a very tender age beautifully uniformed, regularly attended the opera in Moscow and obviously were privileged far beyond the average soldier. Whether or not that destroyed them as independent individuals or not, I don't know as I have never been in the position to follow their careers but it certainly gave them every conceivable possibility to follow the route that young Stalin took. On the other hand, some of them may have turned out very successfully, although I have never heard of a second generation Mikoyan--none of them have ever hit the press, never to the point that the old gentleman had.

So it may or may not be an advantage to be an aristocrat. I mean from the point of view of ultimate rise to fame and power. We don't see any of these second generation people sprung from famous names who have gone on, let us say as the Roosevelts have or the Tafts have in the United States. No second or third generation of famous politicians in the USSR, so perhaps the thing is self-eradicating, who knows.

Q: That is very interesting. Now let us go back to your own career when you returned to the United States.

Adm. T.: I left the Soviet Union in May 1944, almost to the day two years after having arrived; flew to Washington deviously. I thought well, I hadn't been out of the USSR in two years--honestly, in those days it was like coming out of a dank cellar that had cellar smells and cellar looks-- you never felt that the daylight really penetrated. There were times when we would go out in the country around Moscow and pick mushrooms in the middle of the beautiful summer when you felt that it was a glorious world, but those were flashes. Basically it is a gloomy place, there is no color, certainly there wasn't then, though it has improved now. The people were drab, the streets were drab, the whole impression that you got was as I say--that you were down in a dank, airless, badly illuminated basement. To get out, even to get to a place like Teheran, which at that stage of the game was not a patch on the tremendous metropolis it is now; it looks like Milwaukee, Wisconsin, now, but in those days it was more or less a dirt street, overgrown country village with slop running in the gutters and people washing downstream from the place where someone was relieving himself two or three blocks high up, but even to get out to a place like that was like a breath of fresh air. I rode down to Teheran and stayed three or four days, I rode down with the son of the Iranian Minister, Ahy--a very famous name by the way. He showed me a very good time in Teheran and there again it was a tremendous comparison between those who had it and those who didn't have it. The Ahys were very wealthy. I managed to get a Jeep from the American Supply Mission Camp down there, to drive around; in fact we had gotten two for one particular party that the Ahys had arranged with three or four or five of their friends. Coming home from the party we were stopped by two drunken Russians with guns who demanded to be taken to the railroad station. It was a very tricky moment because there is nothing more absolutely unpredictable than a drunken Russian soldier. They think absolutely nothing of shooting each other or anybody else or one of their officers or the officers shooting one of them--it is purely a matter of routine and they chalk it all off to the childlike innocence of the drunk; he is not considered to be responsible for his actions per se although the retribution frequently is pretty severe. In fact at that particular era we heard of one case where the Russian officer had been picked up in an altercation in one of the cabarets by an

American military police. They took him back to the Soviet Embassy and dropped him off, turned him over to the guard. And the next day they sent a message over that there were no charges pressed, they simply wanted to deliver the man back to safe keeping. So the Russians returned the note and said "Thanks very much, there would be no question about pressing charges; the man had unfortunately died in his cell that night." Obviously he died in his cell all right but not by natural causes. So, when these two drunken Russians stopped the jeep they fully intended that we take them to the railroad station, and there were no ifs or buts about it. I made a long speech in Russian and the fact that if Comrade Stalin had seen two of his glorious soldiers down there protecting the frontier of Mother Russia that he would be ashamed of them and this certainly wasn't the type of behavior I had seen in Moscow which I had just come from. One of them looked at the other, swaying from side to side, saying, "Do you know what, he called us Comrade. He is not a capitalist after all." I was dressed in my Navy uniform with the gold chin strap on and the gold chin strap is worn in the Soviet only by generals, so as far as he knew I was a general. But the fact that I had called him Tovarich when I made my spiel was what swayed him. I am sure he would have been willing to shoot a foreign general to get a ride to the railroad station. So he saluted and said, "Thanks very much, he would stop the next car that came along." And shoot him or get to the railroad station, that's the way they do business. They are a highly emotional lot in many respects. They tell the story about the Russian soldier who went into a village that had been occupied by the Germans a long time and of course the Russian civilians had stayed-- the Russian men had all been chased out but the women were there and the old men and the children, and here was a young baby about six or eight months old and the poor homesick Russian picked the baby up and fondled it and so forth. It made him homesick to see a baby; then he had second thoughts on it and dashed the kid to the ground and said "Death to the German occupier" knowing full well that the father must have been a German, and he stomped on the baby. They are that way, I have seen that many times--from beautiful smiles to red faced rage, or vice versa, on a word. They are wholly unpredictable people in that respect.

We picked up a major of the Soviet Army one time at the theatre, that was a frequent place to meet people. These Russians would come in from the outside. They had never been briefed on the perils of associating with foreigners although they had been more or less brought up in school to be suspicious of foreigners. But they were curious. They had a child-like and animal-like curiosity almost, about everything, particularly things foreign. So the major agreed to come over to the apartment with us and have a drink. He not only had a drink but he had a lot of drinks, but the time was three or four o'clock in the morning and obviously we had to take him someplace. So, in his inebriated state he described where he wanted to go. So two or three of us put him in the car and off we went. At each place we would stop, which he had previously described, he would say, "No, that is not the place," and he would take out his gun, hold it at the back of Curly Cram's head (my shipmate who was driving the car) and direct him to the next place on pain of having his head blown off. We finally got the guy out of the car after about four or five of these episodes. It was rough treatment but that's the kind you would like to drop off to the police. But there weren't any. We were blacked out. We weren't even supposed to be on the streets. There was a curfew. Conversely, there was another young man we met, a cadet in the Air Force, I still have a picture of him that he pulled out of his wallet and proudly gave me. We brought him over to the house and he was a charming guest. He was probably 21 or 22 years old. His father was a colonel in the Air Force.

He thought we were great, he said, "These are the first foreigners he had ever met, he was delighted to discover we had neither horns nor tails and he hoped to continue the acquaintance." We said we were delighted to do so and he was welcome at any time. About 2 or 3 days later we got a telephone call and he said he was coming over. He had a present for us. Russians are great on presents, they never visit unless they bring a bottle of this or an old heirloom of that that they can spare to pass on; to go to somebody's house without some kind of a present is considered to be rather rude. In any case we waited and waited and the cadet never showed up; of course he had been stopped at the entrance by the secret policeman in uniform who always stood there. That was the last we ever heard of him; which is typical, he had been warned off--that we were out to pump him. I am sure he had a long sermon on the devious ways of foreigners, how we were leading him down the garden path to traitorous conduct.

Q: That actually you did have horns but they weren't apparent.

Adm. T.: We just wanted to talk to a Russian, for God's sake. What secrets could we get out of some poor little cadet? We just weren't that much interested; it was just a diversion, we wanted to talk to the kid, he was nice and just like anybody else that age that you would meet. Those are the frustrations, that sort of thing is what we encountered when we tried to strike up a casual acquaintance with Russians in Moscow. Now the coastal ports, in Archangel and Murmansk; they were quite different. The people had seen foreigners over there for generations that it had been a shipping port. People had come from all over the world. You could make acquaintanceships there, casual friendships, meet people and go have a Vodka with them at the International Club or they would come around to the American Mission. It was never the same freedom you would find in this country in the United States, but it was a far greater laxity in that respect than you would find in Moscow. In Vladivostok, where we had an undercover office, a man in civilian clothes, the whole American Consulte General was surrounded by police flood lights. Anybody who moved in or out was followed. The whole routine was a completely different thing, they were absolutely and completely isolated. Our man was there in civilian clothes, a Lieutenant Commander Taecker to begin with, and Lieutenant George Roullard later. Because if they had been in their Navy uniforms, the Japanese, who were then still at peace with the Soviet Union, would have demanded similar representation in Vladivostok, which of course the

Russians weren't about to allow because it was a military port.

Anyway, we have pretty well covered the nuances of the Soviet Union. We were down in Teheran and then we got side-tracked. Then I decided that never having been to the Middle East before, I was going to take my long-delayed vacation and take a leisurely way home, a month if necessary.

Q: You were under no duress?

Adm. T.: I was under no duress, no dates, they said report to Washington to ONI for debriefing--that was it.

So I flew from Teheran to Baghdad, it was a military plane, bucket seats, no pressurizing or anything like that. We flew pretty high for part of the way, about 12 to 14 thousand feet. So it was a pretty rough trip and one of the passengers on the plane was a British officer. At least he had a British uniform on (he had a pretty good sunburn I thought). I knew nothing about Baghdad so I thought well, I would try to find out from this Jack what is the best hotel and so forth. So he told me what the best hotel was, and I said "Are you staying there?" and he said, "No, I am staying at such and such a place." And I said, "Well now if you don't mind, you seem to know the ropes around here, I'd like to stay in your hotel." and he said, "Oh, no you can't do that." Well, I discovered he was a British

Indian and the British Indians and His Majesty's white officers didn't go to the same hotels and I was presumed to be in the same category as the white masters and I couldn't go to his hotel nor could he go to mine. Anyway I flew on and arrived in Baghdad and phoned up the American Legation. We didn't have an embassy there and the American Minister was Loy Henderson, a Russian expert and veteran diplomat of the first category. You know, of course, being such, he had voiced his opinion as to what the Russians were really up to; he had spent about six months in Moscow while I was still there while Standley had gone back to the United States to confer (for consultation). Henderson had come out there to make an inspection of the various embassy facilities--he was sort of a logistician at that stage of the game for the State Department--and he was there when Harriman and Churchill had come out in September 1942 to explain to Stalin that they could not start a second front that year and Standley had gone back to the US for a short period so they had turned over the embassy to Henderson as chargé--acting ambassador so to speak. While he was there as ambassador, obviously he had said the wrong things in his dispatches to Washington, because very shortly thereafter he was put onto as deep a freeze as you could find, which was the legation in Baghdad.

That was absolutely the backside of humanity from the point of view of the State Department, from amenities, importance, it was nothing, it was absolutely like Addis Ababa or something. That was the form of durance vile to which Henderson was subjected because he knew what the Russian soul was all about and he had told Washington so. That didn't sit very well with people like Harry Hopkins who thought that Stalin was the epitome of the second coming in effect.

Henderson, of course, was delighted to see me because he was absolutely isolated in this place. He didn't know what was going on anywhere. The second front was just about to break, which he undoubtedly was suspecting all along; that it had to happen some time. So he was definitely keen to get the news from Moscow and I was a welcomed guest. He was an acting bachelor. He had long since been separated from his wife, who was a Latvian gal. She had been adopted in effect many years before in Latvia, taken to England and educated and then brought back when he had married and it didn't work. So Loy Henderson treated me royally and I stayed there for about four or five days. I discovered that there was an exotic way to get from there to Israel. I had always heard about the marvelous beaches in Israel, and the gorgeous oranges and I hadn't had an orange in two years. There was a way to get over there which had been written up in the Geographic and was a little slower but certainly far more exotic than the airplane, and that was by a bus line, run by the French from Baghdad to Jerusalem. It was overnight, and the bus followed cairns of stone. There was no road, and even the track of the previous bus might be blown away. But there were these cairns of stones, like the boy scouts used to find their path stretched across, whether it was 150 or 300 miles of desert. The bus had sleeper bunks on it and it had a galley and all that, which in those days was quite a super proposition. You find it now in the United States but not then. So I got myself a ticket on reverse Lend-Lease--very reluctantly on the part of the British. They said "You had better pay now because the bookwork will get things screwed up." I said, "No, No, this is return Lend-Lease, I haven't got the money you will have to give it to to me free," which they did, and the United States probably paid it eventually.

I got to Jerusalem and spent a thoroughly interesting three or four days there. Went over to Beirut and cased that and Lebanon, then flew down to Alexandria and spent about five or six days in the famous Shepheards Hotel, went out to the pyramids. There was a commander there on active duty, reserve, who had been one of the bonediggers (as we used to call archeologists) in those parts, who knew all about Egypt and archeology and whatnot. But they had sworn him in and hung a blue suit with stripes on him and he was used to entertain all the VIPs who came through. There was no VIP at the moment so he was delighted to take me out and show me the pyramids and all of that. From there I went to Algiers and was very interested to find that the American Army was pretty well in control there, including old General Patton. I didn't actually see Patton but the story had just been going around that he had seen someone all the way across this crowded dining room, with no necktie on and in his loud squeaky voice from his side of the room, he screamed across, "Get that man out of here. He has no necktie on!" The man was in uniform.

Then I went on to Casablanca where an old classmate of mine; (he was then lieutenant commander in the Naval Reserve) was the port director. Amongst the other emoluments that came his way was a large chateau, completely furnished with a lovely brunette gal with her hair piled high on her head and she spoke no English and this guy spoke no French but the liaison situation was well under control. From there I flew to Washington. I had had a delightful and highly spicy month (almost a month) enroute, by which time I was almost completely rehabilitated from the Moscow austerity.

D-day occurred very shortly after I left Moscow and this suggests the naivete of some diplomats. The minister-counselor, number two, in the embassy at Moscow was Max Hamilton (familiary known in those parts as Slapsy Macksy) and old Slapsy Macksy asked me when he saw me in the corridor one day and he said "Commander Tolley, what does D-day mean?" Of course that was the clue to me that D-day was just around the corner.

Q: Had he seen it in a dispatch?

Adm. T.: The minister, the number two man in the American Embassy didn't know what the hell D-day meant.

Q: As I recall, it was a new expression.

Adm. T.: Well it might be a new expression to the public at large but D-day and H-hour and all that stuff had been in use since the Civil War as far as I know.

Q: So things were looking up at that point and North Africa was secure when you were travelling there?

Adm. T.: Incidentally, to get back to Loy Henderson again, he didn't let any grass grow under his feet. This was in 1944

May, and he was sending telegrams to the State Department, all of this wrapped up in one of those red volumes I told you about, that the course of the United States at that time was about to start a train of events that would end in disaster for us eventually as far as the allegiance of the oil-producing countries to our interests was concerned.

Q: On what was that based?

Adm. T.: He said that the Soviets are down here, they are very insidious but in a very effective way, they keep a low profile but they are telling the Arabs, the Iraquis particularly (of course Baghdad was the capital of Iraq) that the Americans are not your friends, they are selling you out to the Jews. Now if you will recall the election of 1944, certain pressures were being brought to bear already for the extension of the independence (or whatever you want to call it) of Israel. This whole business built up to a crescendo until the next presidential election when Truman ran against Dewey. Both of these guys were desperately wooing the Jewish vote. Truman in his memoirs has said that it bugged the bejabbers out of him to be importuned and pressured and threatened (in effect) by nternational and American Jews to do something about Israel.

But he did what was necessary to Israel, something like 16 minutes after they proclaimed their independence--it was all set up beforehand. Well, Henderson had outlined this thing in spades with the greatest detail--that this was precisely what would happen; that the Arabs had been anti-Communist and anti-Russian for a thousand years, were inevitably swaying the other way, that they would be animated against the Americans and although they didn't like the Russians, they would fill the vacuum, the empty spot.

Q: Of course that point of view was not popular, in the State Department or anywhere else, because of political pressures.

Adm. T.: Of course not. In addition, it of course did not enhance Henderson's reputation or situation at the time, although he eventually wound up as Ambassador to India and is now residing peacefully in Washington contemplating his belly button and helping out young students who are applying to him as the only man left alive who was a principal in a great many of these earlier world shaking decisions. In fact he is so busy talking to people like me (he didn't say that but undoubtedly I am included) that he doesn't have time to write his own memoirs as he wants to do.

While we are on the subject of Henderson, this is pretty far from the Navy rails on which we started out--but illustrative of the vendetta which for a time was carried on against anybody who had any really solid, well-founded appreciation of the Soviets and what to watch out for and not overwhelmed over what you might call the earlier phases of detente which was espoused by Roosevelt starting around 1932-33-34 and Bullitt--George Hanson had been in effect our unofficial ambassador to the puppet kingdom of Manchukuo, the Japanese puppet empire of what was formerly Chinese Manchuria before they moved in on it. George Hanson had been there for God knows how many years and he had made a liaison with a charming Russian girl whose name escapes me, but he spoke Russian, he could drink a bottle of scotch a day and most frequently did, and thus was very useful as far as vis-a-vis the Japanese was concerned because he could outdrink anybody in town. He had been observing the Soviets in Manchuria for many years because they had owned the Chinese Eastern Railway; (they sold it to the Japanese in 1934) but until the Japanese had moved in in force, they had been very active in Manchuria. He had many Soviet friends and accomplices (probably not the right word but in effect I guess you could say that because they were against the

Japanese and so was George--he was desperately trying to keep open the American pipeline, straight pipelines for American Tobacco, Dodge Motor cars and British-American Chemicals and all those which are gradually being throttled by the Japs). Anyway, George was sent to Moscow as being a knowledgeable guy on Russians when Bullitt went there as American Ambassador. Of course the two services had different pots to boil. The embassy guys go out and do diplomatic things and the Consulate General takes care of the visas and mercantile interests and whatnot. So George stayed in Moscow three to five months and then he went back to New York on home leave. Here he addressed a group of mercantile oriented people, a trade association of some kind interested in trade with Russia and he made what he considered to be a truthful speech. He said that the possibility of the open-door in Russia was out of the window, it had never amounted to anything. The Russians could buy their stuff by their own trade agency, the AMTORG, in New York and ARCOS in London and that it was an utter waste of time to think that we would ever get anywhere as far as individual trading was concerned. When that hit the fan, George had had it. He was no longer American Consul General in Moscow. He didn't even go back. And like Henderson, he was supposed to be sent to "Siberia," someplace that was absolutely the "bunghole" of creation.

So, they chose Addis Ababa to absolutely immolate George where he would be persona non grata with the State Department and certainly unable to communicate his views on the Russians. Very shortly after George got to Addis Ababa, the Italians attacked Abyssinia and lo, they suddenly discovered they had sent George to the hot spot of the world, that he would be absolutely the center of all attention, the fountainhead of all wisdom in American diplomacy, (this was 1935) and they decided that wouldn't do so they had to yank George out of there and they sent him to Salonika in Greece. He had been a Consul General of long standing in these two places and here they send him to a place called Salonika which is a pump town. It had never had anything but a third-class Consulate before. I was coming back from the Far East at that time by flying down from Bulgaria to Athens so I stopped off in Salonika to see him. I had known him out in the Far East, and they said, "Don't come in. Don't bother to come in, because he is in very poor physical shape. He can't see anybody." I didn't know it at the time but found out later that he had taken an overdose of sleeping pills--he had tried to knock himself off. As soon as he was well enough to travel they put him on a ship for home to get him into some sort of an institution. He made the second crack at it and this time he succeeded. He knocked himself off on the way home.

Q: Has this been a long-standing policy of the State Department to demote people whose view they do not appreciate?

Adm. T.: Not the policy of the State Department. In those days, was the policy of Franklin Roosevelt. He didn't care to hear any dissenting opinion.

Q: In the modern State Department does this attitude prevail?

Adm. T.: I have no knowledge as to what goes on in the State Department. I am really citing two specific cases and I perfectly well know all the details of it.

Anyway here I am back in Washington at ONI for debriefing.

Q: What does that entail?

Adm. T.: That entailed largely re-equipping myself uniform-wise and finding out what was what in the United States, taking a little home leave, looking through the papers and discovering that the knowledge on Russia was thoroughly superficial, that anything that we had sent back had not really been digested because the people who saw it back here didn't have the objectivity to appreciate what we were talking about. We found that the country was flooded with Russians. I was dumbfounded to discover that there was something like 5,000 Soviet officers and technicians in the

United States, compared to our roughly 100 in the Soviet Union. You saw them in uniform in the streets in Washington all over the place.

Q: They were in a sense intelligence officers?

Adm. T.: Of course they were intelligence officers. They were sent over here under the guise of being inspectors of material that was being readied for the USSR, or to learn how to operate certain war material, such as seaplanes for example--we had a big seaplane turnover base I believe in Elizabeth City, North Carolina. They had a large order of motor torpedo boats being built in Annapolis. I went over to Annapolis, was invited over--asked, rather, by ONI to go over and represent them, in view of my ability to communicate in the Russian language. There were about 15 to 20 Russian officers over there and it was absolutely the epitome of friendship and good will; the Americans just poured out their souls to make these people feel happy. We had the Russians congregating in one corner of the hotel.

Q: Carvel Hall?

Adm. T.: Probably Carvel Hall, I don't remember now, and they sang Russian songs beautifully--like an orchestra--and everybody thought it was wonderful.

Q: I do know that the men they sent over to bring the PBNs back were without any personal belongings, not even a tooth brush; they came in and had to be supplied with anything they needed other than the clothes on their backs.

Adm. T.: You can't believe the utter paucity of supplies in the Soviet Union. I went up twice to Archangel on what you might call super-missions, in that one was with Harriman when we went to turn over the American cruiser MILWAUKEE to the Soviets and two other times in fact, once with Admiral Duncan and once with Admiral Olsen; in the case with Duncan--

Q: Is that Woo Duncan?

Adm. T.: No, that's Jack Harlan Duncan, he was the last one who was naval attaché. When Admiral Olsen came over they had already changed it to a Naval Mission--that was the big flip-flop which Harriman required as part of the agreement so that he go over there in the first place.

In Archangel they turned over the quarters of the Chief of Staff of the Northern Fleet to us in Polyarnoe which was the naval base that went out from the Kola Inlet which was in effect the Port of Murmansk. This was the quarters of the Number Two guy in the Northern Fleet which

was one of the four major fleets that the Soviets had. I
don't like to downgrade hospitality when it is the best anybody has to offer and when it is given in good faith but
it would have scarcely done credit to a share cropper's house.
It really wouldn't. The fixtures in it; for example each
room had a single wire down from the ceiling with one bare
bulb, if you leaned too heavily on the arm of the settee it
fell off. It could be set back again I suppose. There was
a little square table the size of a card table, no cover,
in the middle of the room. No rug on the floor, an iron bed;
the whole place was utterly and completely bare austerity.
You brought your own towels and soap. They never had any of
that. Perchance they had soap, it was made out of fish oil
and that would attract every cat in town, assuming they had
not eaten all the cats, by the mere smell of it. So I
can easily understand why the Soviets would come to the US
to pick up war planes without their toothbrushes. They just
didn't have them.

Q: So, you were representing ONI with the contingent over
in Annapolis.

Adm. T.: It contrasted very favorably I must say with the
treatment that we had gotten over in the Soviet Union. Here

the Soviets in Washington and Annapolis were treated with such open handed and full hearted hospitality and friendliness and in Russia we, basically, with the exception of two or three individuals with whom we had almost daily contact, we were treated with utmost suspicion, almost like a colony of lepers--we were dangerous to cope with, dangerous to talk to and anybody who had the temerity or ignorance to try it on immediately got turned off and the next meeting just didn't occur. It was a tremendous comparison and a tremendous eye opener. We had lost our objectivity in Moscow, we really thought it was a way of life and then to come back and see the reverse aspect of it, that it wasn't a way of life at all. It was simply a horrible comparison between two ways of doing things.

Q: When you were actually in the ONI offices, examining the materials they had and the interpretations they made on things in Russia, were you asked to contribute anything from your own experiences?

Adm. T.: Actually I found such (I can't say such a state of utter confusion because everybody obviously was engaged in his own bailiwick). That seems to be one of the drawbacks of any organization when they are in a state of high pressure and flux--that they are not too much interested in what the guy next door is doing or what he is seeing or what he has to offer--they are too tied up in their own affairs. So, as I recall there was absolutely no interest in anything I had to say other than the Office of Naval Intelligence and other than checking in with the Chief of Naval Intelligence, I had no conversation with him at all.

Q: Who was he at that time?

Adm. T.: I don't even remember. I can't even recall who the man was, but I think Ernie King wasn't too far off the mark when he established, in effect, his own office of intelligence in the form of the Y-Branch at Naval Operations. ONI had long since been considered pretty much of a dead end as far as a career was concerned and had been more or less designated by people like Kelly Turner, when he was director of War Plans, finally wangled out of supine Stark as far as Turner was concerned--Stark was eating out of Turner's hand-- he would do anything Turner wanted. Turner put through Ingersoll and Stark the unwritten agreement that War Plans would be the one to develop the assessments and judgments for material furnished by ONI, in other words, ONI was merely a collection agency and not one in which to find an explanation of what the various documents meant. So that's what it had become by the time I got back in '44, if it hadn't already been. Operations had already taken over the interpretations of what the intelligence meant that ONI collected. So the only one I saw was the head of the Russian Section of ONI, who was Major Andrew Wiley. He was still a reserve officer. Major Wiley was a charming fellow from a fine old Washington family and lived in a huge, haunted house up on Thomas Circle.

Q: A beautiful Georgian house by the way.

Adm. T.: I lived in that house the whole time I was there. They took paying guests, as the family had fallen on rather slim means at that stage of the game, probably not the same opulence they enjoyed when the house was built. There were two or three of us staying there. I recall coming home one night, had my little key and let myself in. It was about ten or eleven o'clock at night and the voice of the old colored woman down below, who was the general factotum of the house said, "Sir, is dat you or is dat one of them other folks?" I asked her at breakfast the next morning, "Who is them other folks?" and she said, "Oh, they been around here for a couple hundred years, they come around every now and then and knock on de do."

Wiley was sort of a dilettante as far as the Soviets were concerned, he had made a round-the-world trip in the mid-'30s and grown a long beard, and in the proceedings had come by Moscow. The placed intrigued him, so he had applied for a job and they gave him a job as sort of a glorified door man. In other words, he passed on those who attempted to get into the embassy on some business or other, and stayed there for a while and developed an intense interest, if not an affection, for the Russians. He had effected a superficial knowledge of the Russian language and somehow had got himself in as the head of the Russian Section at ONI. He was my mentor there and amongst his prized possessions was a beautiful blonde Wave named Irene Holmes. Irene Holmes was the widow of an American National City Bank man from Manchuria. I had met them out there; she was a Russian, of course spoke perfect Russian and French and a rather highly accented English and in a Wave uniform I would go so far as to say she was about the cutest thing in the Navy Department. Poor old Andrew, with his conspiratorial bent, had attempted to keep her covered up from the Russians. He didn't want them to know that he had anybody that was such a valuable asset over there, who could speak the language. She agreed to go with me to that expedition to Annapolis where they were accepting delivery of the motor torpedo boats, and the Russians were positively enthralled, so bowled over by Irene and insisted that she ride back to Washington with them instead of with me.

Q: She was in uniform?

Adm. T.: She was in uniform and of course as far as they were concerned it was a beautiful penetration presumably, of ONI. Irene was far too smart to play along with anything like that. She rode back with young Tolley, as far as I know she had no further truck with the Russians.

But that was more or less an indication of Major Andrew Wiley's naivete in general of the whole mission of ONI.

Q: So that was the only thing that you could contribute to the fund of knowledge there?

Adm. T.: The only thing that I felt a little set up about was the fact that the distribution on all the intelligence reports that we had sent back from Moscow had an indication that they went to the White House. Now who saw the things over there I don't know but they got there, and knowing Roosevelt's predilection for anything to do with the Soviets it is possible they got read. If they got read by Harry

Hopkins they undoubtedly got thrown in the trash can because mostly they suggested, as least the ones I wrote, and I wrote almost all of the reports, was that the Soviets would bear watching, that after the war they would not be on our side any more, they would be on their own side which is wholly legitimate and logical. This of course was not according to the soothsayers who were advising FDR--such as Loughlin Currie and Harry Dexter White, and Owen Lattimore and Harry Hopkins of course, and Alger Hiss in State--all of whom were, if not actually convicted, pretty well stamped with the Communist label.

Q: Did you also point out in your reports the fact that the Russians were asking for far more than they actually needed and that they were storing supplies for post war use?

Adm. T.: One of the few things that we managed to get through in the days of the Supply Mission--of course General John Deane came over there with starry eyes which said that we have come here solely to assist the Russians that there will be no intelligence efforts made whatsoever by this Mission. Obviously the light dawned on him before too very long because he was a very bright man. He was Chief of the Military Mission and he was a confidant of George Marshall, one of Marshall's chosen boys. Later in the game we did have quite a few Army people who came over there. The Navy section didn't grow; it stayed pretty much as it was in the beginning in 1942, with representatives in Archangel, Murmansk, Vladivostok and in Moscow. The Army wound up with about 100 people over there, some of whom were tank experts and some of whom were specialists in aircraft repair--Aerocobras--which we had supplied to the Soviets--they are very keen on cannons, no cannons, no good! So the Army managed to send some people out, for example, for tank repairs and tank construction; factories had been set up along the Volga. Actually we sent out one or two of our Naval officers too, the places that were building motor torpedo boats, and they all reported that there were vast stores of diesel engines, etc., but particularly diesel engines, small ones that would be ideal for fishing craft and things like that, but that were of absolutely no applicable usefulness in the current war effort; and that was one thing that they kept pounding on--that they are stockpiling this stuff, either through bad staff work and bureaucracy that they don't actually know what they want, or that they know damn well what they want and are asking for these things to stockpile them, knowing that this is the time to get them while the fruit is breaking down the tree.

Of course, when you consider that the grand total of all the Lend-Lease was only eleven billion, now eleven billion sounds like a lot of money but when you consider the cost of tanks from our bookkeeping point of view and airplanes and high value items like that, of which we sent quite a few, and trucks and God knows how many million pairs of shoes and hundreds of thousands of miles of barbed wire and things like that, there is not a whole hell of a lot left over for what you might say stockpiling--not in the sense that it would in the slightest affect their basic military potential, so I wouldn't even consider this of having importance.

Q: I think we are about ready to talk about your next assignment which was,

Adm. T.: --to go to war, huh?

Q: Yes, you were sent to NORTH CAROLINA, wasn't that it?

Adm. T.: I left Washington in September by railway to go across to Seattle where the battleship NORTH CAROLINA had just come out of overhaul at Bremerton Navy Yard. Of course it was quite an experience to ride on a train in those days because they were hanging from the straps. It was pretty much like China at its worst as far as accommodations were concerned. The trip was more or less without incident. Just to show you how a naive young man, unused to American ways and who had spent most of his adult years outside the United States, I had heard, as the fable says, a pig can go through Chicago without changing trains but people couldn't in those days. So, I had to get off one train and wait half a day and get on another train. In the interim I went to a restaurant and had a meal and a drink or two and three or four tables away a couple of ladies were sitting and the waiter came over and said, "One of the ladies would like to offer you a drink." So I thought that's fine, I'll take the drink and then I'll offer them one; which I did and we waved thanks and that was it. When I went outside to pick up a taxi, here was one of the ladies and she said, "Do you mind if I share your taxi? They are very hard to get now." So I said, "Of course, where do you want to go?" She said, "It's right on your way to the station or wherever you are going."

Q: Were you always the focus of designing females?

Adm. T.: I'll be damned if I know Jack, but this I am sure was meant for any innocent passerby. So, on the way she got to talking about how lonesome she was in wartime Chicago and the fact that she had a nice flat up there and how about coming up and having another one of those drinks? In fact she got rather insistent about it. I explained very carefully that I had a train to catch and had just about enough time to do so--thanks very much but no thanks. After I had let her out, rather disgruntled, the taxi driver said, "I didn't say anything to you, mister, but you sure were smart not to take that women up on that--that was a trap." So I went and hopped on the train feeling much better about the whole thing.

Q: What was the trap?

Adm. T.: I learned later that the process was that you were up there and they would get you in an embarrassing situation or desperately try to and some man rushes in and claims to be the husband and demands ransom or retribution or whatever you want to call it, at the peril of being beaten up by a couple of his friends waiting outside. In other words a shake-down proposition.

Anyway, I rode on out to Seattle--one incident on the way: A Chief Petty Officer came back, he went through the train, and he said, "Sir, you are the senior officer on this train as far as I can determine and I have a carload of sailors who are giving me a bad time. Every time the train stops they get out on the platform and take off their jumpers and raise hell and swear and embarrass the civilians and get drunk and I don't know what in the world to do with them. They won't pay any attention to me. Will you please come up and read out the law to them?" So, I went up there and here was a whole carload of sailors, a draft going someplace, they looked like ordinary sailors to me--civilians in uniforms--and most of them non-petty officers. I gave them a little speech and that was the end of that and there was no more trouble. They were just trying this guy out I suppose, just baiting him.

We arrived at Seattle and I chugged out to the USS NORTH CAROLINA that was lying at anchor. I climbed up the gangway with my two suitcases which was all you needed in those days--formerly a young officer with all his dress uniforms and sword, and evening clothes and tennis togs and riding pants and whatnot, this would occupy three or four trunks. But, I had all my necessary belongings to go to war in these two suitcases. When I got on deck the OD assigned a messenger to me to take me to see the exec, and I said, "What's the exec's name?" And he said, "I don't know, sir." And I thought, my God what kind of a ship is this when a crewman doesn't even know the name of the executive officer? That's a poor way to start. Well maybe the guy had just come aboard. I don't know, but I determined henceforth that I would emblazon my own name on my shirtfront where everybody at least would know my name was Tolley, so if I had to be found in a hurry they would know who to look for. That was, as far as I can determine, the start on board that ship of everybody being required to wear his name in a conspicuous place. The NORTH CAROLINA, as far as I was concerned, was just absolutely monstrous, I had served on the battleships FLORIDA and UTAH and you could have hoisted them aboard the NORTH CAROLINA almost as if they were liberty boats. You just walked and walked and walked to get someplace, with men literally by the hundreds all over the place.

I took over as navigator. As a midshipman I hated navigation. I can't add up a column of figures with any promise of accuracy and I am slightly near-sighted so I couldn't see the stars without specs and as far as I was concerned it was a very unpopular choice. But, it had a certain prestige to be Number Three on a battleship and it made my wife very happy because I had told her before that my new ship had about 18 inches of armor plate on it all over the place and was practically unsinkable. We went down to San Diego. We managed to find our way down there all by ourselves with me navigating, then we went out singly to Marcus Island, way down south, to get back up to join the fleet in the Ulithi area. This was my first introduction to radar. I had heard about it, but imagine--this was in 1944 and I had never seen an operating radar--that's how divorced I was from the facts of life in the new wartime Navy, and I was dumbfounded to see what it could do.

We had a very uneventful trip; the long loop around was to be able to operate independently, without escort. The fear of Japanese submarines had largely evaporated because they had been used chiefly for re-supply of island bases and very little in a combat role. We joined the fleet and from then on, the next one year, we operated almost continuously as part of either the Fifth Fleet or the Third Fleet. Actually, they were the same groups of ships but it was the Third when Halsey had it and the Fifth when Spruance had it. Whether this was supposed to fool the Japanese I don't know. Still it was a very transparent stratagem.

Q: You refueled and re-supplied at sea?

Adm. T.: For week after week, a month at a time, we would go on such expeditions as down off the Philippines to support

MacArthur at Leyte--that was later in the game--in one case with Halsey who was the complete reverse of 'Careful' Spruance. Halsey was, as someone said one time, too stupid to know when he was in trouble. On the other hand, he was precisely the man they needed because he was a wonderful morale backer. He would think up the most stirring epigrams to put out over the radio, which meant nothing at all but they made everybody feel good when they were broadcast. Such as one of his later ones, "If you see any Japanese come out, shoot them down in a friendly way," this was after the surrender. It was that sort of stuff. For example, he took the whole fleet over there through the Formosa Straits over to the coast off Indo-China, in a fog, at the very end of his logistics life line, with just barely enough stuff to get back to fuel on the safe side of the Formosa Straits. That was Halsey. They went over and bombed the be-jabbers out of Indo-China, sank a French cruiser over there that had gone to the wrong side, and I am sure this didn't do a lot to further the war effort, but it was a tremendous morale assay when we could penetrate right across the Japanese life line with impunity. Then we operated off Japan and every morning, an hour before sunrise, General Quarters--clang, clang, clang-- up we would get, man the batteries for the possibility of a dawn attack. Then about possibly eight o'clock our planes would take off from our task group. There would be four carriers in the center (or three), then the next outer ring would be one, two, or three battleships and an equal number of cruisers, the total would be about seven heavies. Then on the outer ring would be as many as twenty-five destroyers.

Q: The mission was to bombard the coast or what?

Adm. T.: This was a circular formation and there were three of those in the fleet, sometimes four. They were large concentrations and that would mean a total of 12 or 16 carriers at one time. They would not necessarily correlate their strikes--one would always be replenishing and two or three would be on the line bombing, but one might be a hundred miles south or north of the other, or east or west of it, but basically in the same campaign area, either off Leyte, or off the islands of Japan or off Okinawa. Then of course, about eleven or twelve o'clock the strike would be due back and everybody would be on deck to count the airplanes to see what we lost. It was always a tremendously scary thing to see these planes come back. We would turn into the wind and as navigator I was always on call. It was an exhausting year. I lost weight. I was really debilitated at the end of this year because I was up an hour before sunrise normally with the crew, the same in the evening at sunset, you had General Quarters until an hour after sunset. I would have to take star sights, morning, evening and at noon--sun sight at noon--but the worst part of it was that the skipper, all of them of course were a little reluctant to leave the bridge except for calls of nature and to take cat naps--because the ships, particularly at night, they were all operating without lights and within 500 yards of each other, not much more than 2 or 3 ship's lengths and a wrong turn would be disastrous. It would mean losing two major ships. Once or twice it happened, a battleship ran into another battleship, the TENNESSEE rammed somebody in just such a case, and it could mean the loss of thousands of men; so the skipper was out there on deck practically all night and he got lonesome. They would nab me out there and I was a conversation piece for them. I had been around and they wanted also to unburden themselves. Many a night I staggered out there half dead on my feet.

Q: You were telling me about Ozzie Colclough.

Adm. T.: Actually Ozzie was one of the more erudite of the skippers we had and one of the most articulate. He was a very bright man. Basically the NORTH CAROLINA and perhaps some of the other battleships were merely finishing schools for captains selected for admiral, when they had to put in sea time. So in the year I was aboard, I was more or less an instructor for skippers in the ways of battleships, they probably had served on battleships before; that is probably pushing it a point to say that I was instructing the skipper. But when I went aboard, for example, the skipper was Captain Frank P. Thomas and he was relieved before we left the United States by Captain Frank G. Fahrion and he is the one who took us across to join the fleet. Next came Ozzie Colclough (Oswald S.) and following him came Byron H. Hanlon and he was the one who was aboard when I left. So you barely got one broken in and it was pretty tough on a navigator because the skipper had nobody else to depend on whatever. The exec was always in a purely administrative role down below decks someplace; the officer of the deck was one of four and they had four lieutenants j.g. who were officers of the deck and that is all they ever did, and my assistant navigator at general quarters took the deck. None of them were Naval Academy. They were all reserves who had specialized in this one activity and they were absolutely superb and they would get the directive to change course which had come over scrambled, it would be unscrambled in the communications office, right next door, passed out on deck number of degrees change of course or the axis of the new formation; they would translate it into what the new course should be, bring the ship on the new course with speed and precision. But they were only j.g.s. They had no real Naval background, so the only guy the skipper had for continuity so to speak, was the navigator, and this was old man Tolley who was out there day and night either wet-nursing a new skipper or trying to morning, noon or evening position or changing the axis. Every time the wind changed 15 degrees the axis of the fleet had to be changed and that entailed a mathematical calculation and in some cases a considerable change in relative position as far as the center of the unit was concerned (the mythical center, there was no ship at the center, it was always a theoretical center). So, it was a constant grind, out there with the maneuvering board or exchanging banter with the skipper.

Q: What was the purpose of the battleships with the fast carriers, were they engaged in bombarding coastlines?

Adm. T.: The battleships were basically the anti-aircraft gun platforms. Sometimes it was rough, which makes gunnery difficult on a destroyer. They were all like buckets and the mere business of tending the guns became difficult and of course their accuracy is lessened. And they are on the outside fringes where they get the first crack at the intruder but many of these guys came over at such high altitudes. We were frequently (at night for example) pestered by 'bed-check Charlies'. One Japanese plane would groan out there.

Q: Reconnaissance?

Adm. T.: Reconnaissance presumably, or purely for morale purposes. You would have some one guy overhead all the time. It means the expenditure of one or two Japanese aviators but it means the requirement for all hands in the entire task group to man the guns and it would interrupt their sleep which can be a nerve-wracking thing over a long period of time. When you are out there a month at a time, this thing goes on day after day and you operate for six or seven days and then you replenish for two days. You withdraw let's say 200 miles to seaward out of range of Japanese planes. You are still in Japanese submarine danger and there is the constant minor peril of being alongside a tanker that something will go wrong and that you will have a collision. One or two of the destroyers we have seen that came alongside the NORTH CAROLINA that had minor collision with the ship, so you are never divorced from some sort of peril. Of course in the latter days when the count of casualties became the order of the day there was never an encounter that somebody didn't get hit. You would be up on deck, I never missed the show, I got up there and watched, my General Quarters station was any place I wanted to make it because my assistant took the OOD. The skipper was on the bridge and I could go where I wanted and for my place I always took out on the wing of the bridge so I could see something-- I was supposed to write up the war diary which was an enlargement in effect, to the log. That is one thing that rather surprised me in some of the skippers; very few in fact had any appreciation of descriptive prose and I recall one time offering Ozzie Colclough my war diary for approval and he took one look at it and he said "Ouch!" I had described a scene of the Japanese planes coming in, something like 'the wings falling off like autumn leaves' or something like that. Just a little touch of descriptive phraseology, but as far as Ozzie was concerned and as far as all those skippers were concerned that was a waste of artistic talent. All they wanted to know was how many planes got shot down. Well, you can find that out in the log book. I considered and I have since discovered, the fellow that runs this NORTH CAROLINA Memorial Ship organization, Captain Ben Blee, USN Retired, has applied to me for anything I have in the way of memorabilia from the NORTH CAROLINA, and he said, "By the way, I would like to mention the fact of your war diaries. They have been extremely useful to find out what some of the battles looked like, because there is no other way to find out. The logs don't tell you anything. That is merely a time sequence and what specifically happened, where you were and so forth."

Q: Dry as dust!

Adm. T.: Hopeless, I have tried to find something useful in it. The only other source of information of course, is personal letters. Now of course they were closely censored. I was one of the censors and in port I would spend a day running through thousands of letters. There was a whole group of us; about 15 censors and I was the chief censor. The sailors' letters were almost like they had been mimeographed: "Dear Mom, The chow is lousy. We have been out for the last three or four weeks having a big time. How is Henry the rooster. I will certainly be glad to get home and get some of your cooking. Love, Willie" and that was it. There was absolutely nothing on anything that would give you a clue on what the ship had done. Of course we were supposed to cut that stuff out though I am sure it wouldn't have harmed us in the eyes of the enemy if they had known a little more.

An interesting fact about Frank Fahrion, by the way, as far as I know he was the first man who ever commanded a ship as a flag officer. Now I believe another one is John McCrea. When he was Aide to the President, he was ordered to command the battleship that took Roosevelt to Casablanca. I think he commanded that as a flag officer one time, I am not sure. Fahrion was allowed to break his flag and was congratulated by the division commander. When he was skipper of the NORTH CAROLINA he wore stars for two weeks until he got to port and was relieved.

Q: He was selected then while he was at sea?

Adm. T.: All these guys were selected long before they ever got command. They would never had gotten the command in the first place. It was too prestigious a job. But they had to wait their turn and they had to have a certain amount of sea duty and this was it. They got their three months sea duty, got their stars and were relieved, except for poor old Thomas. He didn't make it. He is one of the few. I don't know what happened to him.

Q: In the final days of the war we used battleships for the bombardment of the Japanese coast and of industry that was situated there.

Adm. T.: In that final year that I was there the homeland was in extremis. We would go in and bombard let us say, at Okinawa, in a useful manner. We would bombard shore positions and soften up the beach for landing forces. For a specific example, at Okinawa we made a feint bombardment on the southeast coast and sent in some landing craft empty as a feint to draw off the Japanese forces from the actual landing beach which was around on the west coast about the waist of the island. Then we went around and actually bombarded the real landing beaches. Basically those beaches were taken care of by the old battleships that were too slow to keep up with the carrier task forces. Then we would make two other bombardments which I participated in as navigator and can therefore give pretty good testimony as to their usefulness. One was the steel works at Muroran on the Island of Hokkaido. The other one was the plains area just slightly northeast of Tokyo and in both cases it was an utter waste of hardware. It was murky both times and we had only radar to guide us in the area off Tokyo. The coastline was so low and so without prominent land marks that the radar was pretty mushy. I was plotting the ship's position all along as we were supposed to be picking out our targets and it later developed that all the shells went into a rice paddy. Nothing hit anything of any consequence. The amusing part of the whole thing was that it was done in absolutely dense fog and overcast. You couldn't see a thing and it was raining from time to time. We could hardly see the ship ahead. So, it was all done by radar and of course they had the internal broadcasting system which rebroadcast news that emanated from the United States and we were all very much amused shortly after this bombardment to hear the press announcement how the glorious American battleships had gone in within spitting distance of the Japanese coast. "We could see the roaring salvos arching across the open spaces of the empty Pacific and landing with huge red splashes on the Japanese targets, flames leaping up. The whole thing so spectactular it was almost impossible to believe it as we watched it from the fighting top of the USS NORTH CAROLINA." Utter horsecrap—they made it up as they went along. Such things as this might be just dandy for the public, very exhilarating. But for the poor crew who had seen all this stuff with their very own eyeballs, they would wonder how much of these lies can we believe about everything else.

Q: Is this typical of the flip-flop of the silent Navy?

Adm. T.: I don't think even the Navy with its hell-bent outside position on public affairs and relations ever stoops to utter prevarication. This was just completely made up out of whole cloth, nobody was even there watching to my knowledge, certainly there was nobody on the NORTH CAROLINA. They even made up the locale out of the whole cloth. Utterly unnecessary. It was a revelation. We used to laugh at Tokyo Rose and we could have an equally good laugh at our own people. It was wholly unnecessary because we were on top already, it wasn't required that we should make such balderdash.

Then we continued the close-in aerial bombardment, flying off air groups, watching them come back and hearing some of the agonized reports from the planes' TBS. I particularly remember one where apparently the radioman had been badly wounded and he was screaming and praying and importuning the people on the carrier to get the plane down. He was bleeding to death and "for God's sake the pain is absolutely insupportable." It was one of these awful gruesome things that you some times see in the movies or on TV now and don't believe it is possible, but to hear it with your own ears it is something else. Another equally stirring situation was the tremendous typhoon that Bill Halsey's weather man erroneously got us right into the middle of off the Philippine Sea. We had been operating off Leyte Gulf and the storm was prognosticated. So we pulled up and got well out to sea and ran right into the middle, the eye of this typhoon. Of course the old NORTH CAROLINA bulled along, rolling about 30 degrees, which was a lot for her, white water over the bow. There were two chairs on the bridge, one on the port and one on the starboard side, inside. The Skipper always sat in one and I sat in the other. The only time I ever got out of mine was to go to the head or to eat or to take a cat nap. On the rare occasion when the exec would come up to view the scenery he would oust me from my port chair and sit in it himself. I sat in that chair during most of that storm. The skipper and I were up there all the time. The PITTSBURGH, one of the cruisers, had her entire bow break off in this storm. Well, we thought the NORTH CAROLINA was pretty tough. But anything could happen, and some of the dispatches that we could hear, the chit-chat on the TBS from destroyers; we had been under way for some time and normally the destroyers like to top off at least every three days and fuel up because at the speeds we went to operate aircraft-25 to 28 knots--they couldn't last long. So they were almost down to their lower minimum level when this storm started to get worse and there was always the hope that they might be able to come alongside a battleship or a carrier (that's where they got their fuel from in this task group) and get a pipeline over, rolling though we were. In order to be ready, they had unballasted. Normally when a destroyer uses up oil it replaces the used up oil in the tanks with sea water to keep stability. But in this case, they didn't want to do that because they wanted to be ready to take fuel. Some of those destroyers were down to 5%, which is almost to the point where you're on the Brooklyn Bridge at rush hour with no gas in the tank. So their stability was absolutely marginal and these reports would come in--there were three that actually rolled over. One would say, "50% roll, very slow recovery, hung there for five seconds"; another would come in saying, "water down the engine room skylight, water in the engine room ventilators, recovery very, very slow, doubtful we will recover from next roll." Then you wouldn't hear him anymore. Just the laconic reports. Then you would get one from one of the cruisers converted to a light aircraft carrier, "fire on the hangar deck," another one, "planes broken loose crashing uncontrolled on the hangar deck;" another one--"bombs loose, bombs uncontrolled, fires," and then later there would be, "fire under control." Actually they made out all right on the carriers, but they were rolling some horrendous amount: 45 degrees on some of those converted carriers. The big carriers did all right because they are far more stable. The next morning, absolutely incredibly clear sky and the ocean was so flat it looked just like a large sheet of glass. A little debris floated around, no people.

Q: Was this the typhoon for which Halsey was almost yanked in? Almost relieved of his command?

Adm. T.: Halsey was highly censured and shortly thereafter Admiral Nimitz sent out a letter on behavior when approaching bad weather, which is a classic. And it of course, was spawned by that. Halsey didn't get fired; after all it was his weather man; bad judgment on the weather man's part.

Another stirring close-range tragedy was when the FRANKLIN was hit. Each one of the battleships, of course, was normally in a brother-sister relationship with a carrier, purely due to distance from her in the formation and you felt a particular responsibility toward that carrier. If you saw a dive-bomber, a Jap kamikaze, headed that way you forgot about any other planes in that area--maybe on the distant horizon--and concentrated everything you had to protect your chosen carrier. The FRANKLIN was about 700 yards on our port bow, maybe not quite broad on the port bow, and it was overcast, scattered clouds but we were shooting off planes and retrieving planes. It was still flying weather. We had a combat air patrol up--we had those up in almost any weather because they were all-weather planes. They could see in the fog, as they were radar equipped. It was General Quarters and I was up in my usual spot on the wing of the bridge and Tom Morton was the gunnery officer and he was down there on the port wing of the deck next below me with his head-phones on. He was up there in his control position. That was his control spot, on an open deck on the port side. I saw this single plane coming in in an attitude that couldn't possibly be an American plane. It was coming in from the FRANKLIN's starboard bow at about 4 or 5 thousand feet at just about lower cloud level, going like hell. It was a fast airplane. It came in almost to the FRANKLIN, went into a steep dive, almost a vertical dive and I yelled over the bridge, "Tom Tom, for God's sake, here comes a Jap." He didn't hear me. He had his head-phones on, and as far as I know I was the only one who spotted this Jap because nobody opened fire on him. He came down in almost a vertical dive, flattened out just before he got to the FRANKLIN and let go just on top of the flight deck, which was loaded with airplanes. Of course she burst into flames. Bombs started to explode. Huge clouds of smoke went up. The formation changed axis at about that time, or course, and this put the FRANKLIN slightly on our starboard bow. She was still ahead of us; she started to slow and dropped astern of us, just like passing in review, not more than 4 to 5 hundred yards on our starboard beam. As we passed (we were making about 25 knots, and she by that time was probably making about 15, slowing down, I guess, to try and better control the fires. Maybe she lost power. I don't know. Anyway over her stern was a constant stream of people, mostly in life jackets, and as far as the eye could see, astern of her was this string of sailors swimming in the water, that had jumped over the stern, the fire had driven them overboard. They had no place to go. Now how many of those guys we picked up, I don't know. Of course the destroyers were in the fringe of the formation, four or five miles outside of the central body. So it is doubtful if many or even if any of those poor guys who jumped over were picked up. We couldn't stop. Of course it would have been absurd for us to have picked any of them up. She was an immense pillar of smoke and flame but she still survived. We continued, there was no point in stopping the formation. There was always the submarine menace, and we had to fly off and take on planes at the same time. The FRANKLIN more or less disappeared over the horizon as we drew on, and as I later learned, they were assigned a cruiser and she was towed in and rescued.

The only real close-in casualty. We didn't have any kamikazes land on us but there were some very near misses.

Q: Were you a target?

Adm. T.: They weren't after the battleships, they were after the carriers.

Q: But they would take anything?

Adm. T.: They would take anything I suppose, in extremis but they were all shooting for the carriers, normally. Now down at Lingayen and places like that they hit the command ship, the EL DORADO I guess it was, and three or four other non-aircraft carriers in the landing force. But normally they were just after one target and that was the aircraft carrier and they hit quite a few. Of course when 15 or 20 ships are all shooting, especially when these kamikaze would come in low, mostly they came in at a high altitude and came down in a steep dive, I presume the idea being that if they got hit and lost power they could always glide into a target, whereas if they came in low and got hit they would go straightaway into the drink. In any case, we were off Okinawa and the NORTH CAROLINA got a five-inch shell hit in her five-inch directer tower, which is about amid-ship on the port side. It was from one of our own ships, in a low trajectory, probably one of the destroyers on the scouting ring. The thing blew the directer tower pretty well to pieces and killed, I think, three men in it and there was a cloud of little splinters and about fifteen men on the signal bridge just below the navigating bridge, were badly wounded. I went down below for a quick check and there was blood all over the place. It is just hard to believe how profusely people bleed when they get hit. One guy had been hit in the crotch. The kid had just been selected for the Naval Academy. He had an appointment, and he had gotten one testicle blown off, among other things, so that fixed that career for him. I guess admirals have to have two of them, I don't know; anyway he had a puddle of blood under him that would have filled a basin I guess, sitting there holding himself waiting for the medics to come up. There were people lying around all over the place. I was hit too. Like a stupid ass I was up there without my tin hat. You get careless after a while. You figure that you have never been hit before so you won't be hit this time. So this thing went off with a loud bang. I didn't feel anything, but people started getting solicitous all the way around, starting to look like they wanted to hold me up. And then the blood started to trickle down. I had been hit on the front of the forehead just at the hair line and in the back at about the same hair line spot. Both bled like scalp wounds do, very copiously.

Q: But it hadn't penetrated?

Adm. T.: They had just gone under the skin. They were little scraps about the size of a pencil eraser but my comrades out there all thought that the thing, whatever it was, had gone straight through the skull and were wondering what was inside that I should be still on my feet and they were rushing up to hold me up. I wore my tin hat after that.

Q: It was a part of regulations, was it not?

Adm. T.: Well, you know there are a lot of regulations that people sort of let go slightly by the board. They are cumbersome things, tin hats.

I guess the most glorious part of that cruise though was when VJ Day came. Of course we had an interesting interlude when the atomic bomb was dropped. Obviously none of us had the slightest inkling that such a thing was in the cards. We received a message on the following dates: "All ships would remain (some very respectable distances, I remember some 150 miles) from the southern islands of Japan."-- Kyushu Island. So there was speculation that perhaps we had brought over large quantities of buzz bombs, things the Germans were using on England and that they would be launched from Okinawa and that they were so unsure of their accuracy that they wanted us well out of the way. We were thinking up all sorts of reasons. Why the hell should we stay 150 miles away from land on this particular two or three days? Well, we soon found out. It was the atomic bomb. Shortly thereafter of course, came VJ Day and the NORTH CAROLINA was one of those pulled off to put a landing force ashore, an occupation force in Yokosuka. I was the only guy on board who had any inkling of the Japanese language. I remember this unusual scene of this large group of sailors on the fantail of the NORTH CAROLINA. It was beautiful calm weather, no Kamikazes overhead, no General Quarters at sunrise or any of that;

lazing off Tokyo awaiting the word to go in. About 4 to 5 hundred bluejackets there with Tolley up on a rostrum with a microphone attempting to teach them elementary Japanese. Whether any of them used it or not I don't know. Before she ever went in I was transferred to an airplane carrier for transportation back to Honolulu and back to the United States.

Q: Was there any feeling of apprehension of possible treachery or anything of that sort at that moment?

Adm. T.: What we knew about Japan of course was what the popular notion was--that they intended to fight to the death. About a week before the surrender actually came, we were copying Japanese newscasts that came out in English and I still have copies of a number of those, making it clear that the Japanese authorities were preparing the Japanese people for surrender. In the very ambiguous terms the Japanese always seemed to use, they were explaining that the glorious empire was experiencing an era of unprecedented hard luck and reversal of fortune and in order to preserve the Imperial and August Majesty--all this ambiguous horsemanure you know about. Well in other words, we have had it, boys, stand by. We are about to throw in the sponge. We knew perfectly well at least a week before that the game was up, even before the atomic bomb. Those things were all on record. They would have surrendered without the bomb, and of course, the speculation has always been since (as showed up in this movie we saw last night) that Truman's idea was to impress the Russians with the fact that we had the bomb and would use it on people if necessary, including Russians. Truman had no illusions about the Russians by that time. As a matter of fact, the delusions about the Russians had been growing for a long time in quarters that probably Roosevelt wasn't aware of, such as, for example, the fact that 2-4-D, this defoliant that now has been more or less common property on everybody's agricultural shelf, was basically concocted to stand by to sprinkle it on Russian wheat fields. In 1943 that experimentation started 2-4-D that they thought the time might come when we would be facing the Russians and the best way to combat that would be to starve them to death by dropping 2-4-D on their wheat fields. I am sure FDR didn't know about that, but somebody saw the shape of things to come well in advance. Of course, was it Molotov or Vishinsky, one of those boys, was asked by one of the allies, "We assume you intend to stop at Cologne," and he said (pretending to fail to understand) "Boulogne?"

Life on the NORTH CAROLINA in wartime was a most unusual procedure for the navigator. I had an emergency cabin on the bridge level and this is where I lived, week after week. The only time I ever descended from that place was when the ship was in Ulithi for replenishment.

Q: And there was a certain amount of relaxation, wasn't there? When you went ashore?

Adm. T.: You could relax to a point, but I recall a case there where we were all sitting around on the top deck enjoying the sunshine and there was one hell of an explosion down the harbor and a Japanese submarine had torpedoed a tanker and there were flames as high as you could see. It was right in the inner lagoon at Ulithi.

Q: That was the HOOD?

Adm. T.: No, you are thinking of the MT. HOOD that blew up down in Marcus Island. That was an ammunition ship. This was a tanker. So you never really relaxed, and of course, as far as recreation was concerned, it didn't exist in Ulithi. There were one or two islands; they had moved all of the natives to one of the remote islands where they would be out of the way and what few remaining islands there were were so distant.

It is a huge place. I remember going ashore one time with Ozzie Colclough, and it took us an hour and a half at least in a motor whale boat; we were soaking wet when we got there. They had a little club set up on the beach and you bought a book of tickets for about ten bucks and tore off these pieces of paper for a slug of what was known then as 'black death' because it was Three Feathers whiskey and had a black label on it. It was pretty awful stuff. Ozzie very kindly took me into the wigwam that was normally reserved for flag officers. He knew he was about to become one, and he had a lot of flag officer friends, so I was ushered into the august presence of people like Chink Lee and Admiral Halsey and three or four others like that and amongst other subjects discussed was MacArthur, which was inevitable in any such gathering. And of course they all hated MacArthur's guts, all except Halsey. He thought he was great and he was fighting a single-handed battle for Mac while all the rest were trying to put him down. I remember that very distinctly. About the only other thing we ever did was an occasional picnic on a slightly near island. No booze, but just a sandy beach and ground under your feet, or skin dive. The water was crystal clear. Coral was rocky and sharp. It was in no sense relaxation.

On my little bridge, the skipper and I lived up there. As I

say, we never went down, and Joe Stryker the exec, made the observation, he said, "This shower on the bridge deck was the only one in the Navy that he knew where you could urinate and take a bath, legally, at the same time without feeling guilty." It was such a cramped place they had to combine the two. My mess attendant was one of the blackest blacks you ever saw and his name was appropriate--Starling. He was a minister's son and was a very devout young man and of course, like all the mess attendants his General Quarters assignment was somewhere in the powder train. He was down in the magazines, way down in the bottom of the ship and it scared the hell out of him every time we had General Quarters. He figured that if the ship sank nobody would let Starling out and of course they wouldn't have. He was locked down below God knows how many watertight doors. Furthermore, they would take the lids off the powder cans and the place was heavy with the scent of ether. Old Starling would come up dancing on his toes like he had had a couple of shots of bourbon after every long General Quarters. He liked that aspect of it as he got a cheap drunk. Of course he was always hungry. He was a thin, bony kind of a guy and he would bring me up this tray of chow--far more than I could eat, but I found out later that he had double that amount to start with.

He would say, "Suh I don't think you would like the soup tonight so I didn't bring no soup up," and of course he had eaten it on the way. He would bring me this huge amount of ice cream and I would leave about half of it and he would finish it off. I came back unexpectedly one time, and here he was in the cabin cleaning up the mess. He had a mouthful of stuff and he was so embarrassed because he couldn't talk with his mouth full of the remains of my dinner.

Q: What are your recollections of Admiral Lee?

Adm. T.: I never saw him except at that little convocation ashore and of course that was a very fleeting recollection.

One other excuse Starling used to give for all the chow he brought and I sould say, "Starling, I can't eat all that food, you are just wasting it," and he said, "Suh, fat mens float better."

I got a letter from his father one time, the minister in Texas some place, thanking me kindly for the words of encouragement that I had given his son.

All of the major aspects of the use of American air power out in those parts were more or less lost on us in the operating area and level, because we didn't see the big picture. One thing, of course, we did understand and immediately generally questioned was the fact that Admiral Halsey was not present when the Japanese battleships attacked the landing force at Leyte Gulf and chopped up the jeep carriers, when he was off on a wild goose chase taking the bait that the Japanese had so gratuitously offered with their carrier fleet with no planes aboard. The reason we knew that and were in a position to question the whole deal was the air was filled with messages. Things had gotten so desperate that they didn't bother with code any more. Of course, there was another aspect of communications that certainly against a more astute enemy would have been a very dangerous one-- that was the business of everybody deciphering every code they had the key to work on. That stemmed from two reasons. First of all the address frequently was buried in the text of the message so you didn't know to whom the message was addressed until you broke it down part way. Of course, the logical thing was to stop right there. It was not for you, so you throw the rest out. They didn't do that. The coding boards were made up of the supply department and any spare pump handles that they could jar loose from the communications outfit--five or six people and of course they were deeply curious to know what was going on. Here we were completely isolated, immolated from the world in general. We didn't even know whether Europe had sunk beneath the waves, or what. So the only way you could find out was to crack all the messages you could lay your hands on and inevitably it would be leaked to the wardroom and inevitably everybody on the ship would know about it because in a small community like that you think, well, good heavens we are completely isolated, the place isn't bugged, nobody's going to the bar and spill it to some bimbo, so what's the point in keeping it a secret and the enemy probably knows anyway. All the messages were being broken whether they were addressed or not. In this case in this particular haul didn't think it was so urgent and so critical and it went out bingo in plain language.

Q: What was the fleet policy on prisoners of war?

Adm. T.: You mean in case our people fell into enemy hands?

Q: No, I mean in case you had an opportunity to take some Japanese?

Adm. T.: The question never arose because we were miles at sea. How would we ever get a prisoner of war?

Q: If a Japanese plane was shot down?

Adm. T.: It was well understood from the very beginning

that they always refused capture. They shot themselves or allowed themselves to drown. As far as we knew they never had any parachutes, you never saw a parachute blossom out of a Japanese plane, never, anywhere. They went down with the ship. They didn't expect to be captured and we didn't expect to pick up one.

Q: There was always the possibility of gleaning some intelligence from somebody whom you do lay hands on.

Adm. T.: We were in the wrong league for that. We were just members of the warship community, that was somebody else's business, working prisoners over.

Q: What was the flagship in your task force?

Adm. T.: I don't recall offhand. The NORTH CAROLINA rarely was the flagship of anything. As far as I know from the time she was built she didn't have a flag officer aboard more than a few months, which was for a period of four or five years. At one time, I can't imagine for example, a more useless thing than four or five tails on a cat, than a battleship division commander in a task group. Here were three battleships, a division, and presumably the tactical and administrative commander of this group was a rear admiral (commander battleship division X or whatever) and he had a flagship. In our case we had Ross Cooley aboard for about four or five months. His function was zilch. Absolutely nothing. There was nothing administrative for him to do, nothing tactical. We were completely under the control of the air admiral who was commanding the task group. He rode one of the carriers. Even in the case of Chink Lee, he was never in our group as I recall. He was always in one of the other two or three groups. His sole function was no more than Cooley's--simply in case Japanese heavy ships emerged in the task group let us say, as Halsey had broken off a heavy task group to go up and meet the Japanese outfit, then Chink Lee would take over tactically, then Ross Cooley would be his subordinate as the group commander or the battleship division commander.

Q: Commander of fast battleships?

Adm. T.: That's right, but the fast battleship task group never formed except on rare occasions--as in Halsey's case when he went up on this wild goose chase. Normally the ships were scattered around as part of an entirely different task organization. These guys were simply riding in the back seat as a spare pump handle in case the original motive for the task group changed into something else. They rarely had either the opportunity or the excuse to exercise any command of any description. They were merely spare parts waiting to be called into action.

One thing I would like to add here on the personnel aspect of this war is this: When we got hit at Okinawa we had to go back to Pearl Harbor for repairs. We went back independently as best we could and, as is usual for any ship which was detached from the fleet, to go back to "civilization" we took a load of people being returned for one reason or another; either they had broken down physically or they had desperate requirements for them elsewhere or officers who had come to the end of their tour of duty or some such and were being sent back and replacements would come back in a like fashion on a ship coming back from repairs or overhaul. In this trip we made back, after Okinawa, we had a load of about 250 officers who came aboard as supposedly being shell shocked, being disturbed by having been blown up or sunk or something.

Q: They call it battle fatigue.

Adm. T.: Battle fatigue was the overall term to cover it. But they looked like anybody else, they moved around the ship, sunned themselves, ate in the wardroom and joked and watched the movies--they seemed in every respect, normal. Then we had a kamikaze alarm before we got clear of the area, and these guys went absolutely berserk, they screamed, they hid under tables, they fainted, they did all sorts of weird things and it became apparent why they were with us on their way home. This obviously was not a fake and they just did it.

Q: Hysteria.

Adm. T.: Yes, and I suppose it was a mass affair, one of them did it and the rest fell into line. But it was a revelation to the rest of us relatively normal human beings to see all these birds absolutely climbing the walls. The mere shriek of the siren was all it took.

Well that's it, I was on my way back to Washington. I was so intent on getting back to the United States I really don't remember much about that trip. I do remember this. We went out and fueled in a task group and I was put aboard a tanker and the tanker (I don't remember where) transferred me to an aircraft carrier and that's the way I got back to the States.

Q: You didn't come back all the way on the NORTH CAROLINA?

Adm. T.: No, the NORTH CAROLINA stayed out there and went into Tokyo Bay with a landing force which I had trained so magnificently in the Japanese language. Very shortly after that I suppose she came back to the United States herself.

Q: So you got back to the States.

Adm. T.: Well, I got back to San Francisco and a good many of my classmates some months previous to that had already been upped to captain. Being an executive of a battleship, of course, I was not eligible for promotion. You had to be in a job that merited four stripes before you could be promoted, even though you had been selected and certified for same. So, my first official move on arrival in San Francisco was to check in with the appropriate authority and have a physical exam and get my four stripes pinned on. I don't recall whether I got the back pay for the hiatus or not, it was about three or four months that I had lost by being out fighting the war while these other gentlemen, my contemporaries, were sitting on their fat backsides in an office somewhere wearing four stripes; but that's the way things sometimes were done.

Q: And because of the nature of your previous career you hadn't had any sea duty for a long time.

Adm. T.: Probably a lot of these guys hadn't either. There were some very astute avoidees of hazardous duty. I felt, as far as I was concerned, that my fortuitous escape from the Philippines made up for a lot of deficiencies elsewhere. I shouldn't even have been alive.

Q: You were coming back to Washington to a very interesting assignment.

Adm. T.: Actually I had the strange idea that, when I got back there--I had already written a letter from the NORTH CAROLINA, knowing that the war was about over and my one-year tour was about over (a one-year tour was about normal for a tour aboard ship in the war zone)--and I had requested duty as naval attaché to China. When I got called back to Washington to report to ONI I thought maybe that was the next step and, it wasn't until I actually got back to Washington when I discovered that they didn't have any assignment for me at all. I was completely at loose ends. They were looking around in fact, where to send this guy next. Everything was in utter confusion after the war. When the war was over everybody wanted to go home and who knows what unit could even move for lack of personnel to go down and build the fires under the boilers--it was as bad as that--some of the ships were lying immobile for lack of people to make them go. The confusion was almost equal to that in Washington. I hadn't had any leave of course, had been out there for a year, so I had a 30-day leave coming to me which I took here at home. And then I got called by Smedberg and he said, "What are you doing? What is your assignment?" and I said, "I don't have the foggiest idea, I don't have any assignment." He said "Get over here right away, I have a place for you." Smedberg was in Washington and he was, at that time, Chief of the Y-branch of Naval Operations and the Y-branch of Naval Operations was, in effect, Ernie King's ONI, his private Office of Intelligence and of course it was chiefly involved in either clandestine intelligence or Communications Intelligence, both of which were closely allied with the actual mechanics of communications rather than with gathering documents, which was a part of it-- the routine sort of stuff that ONI normally goes in for and which in many cases is considered public knowledge, gotten out of public documents, newspapers, magazines and technical journals--but Y had nothing to do with that sort of thing. When I got there I found out I was to relieve William Sebald,

Commander USNR, who was in the class of 1922 or 1923.

Q: You had known him, had you not?

Adm. T.: Bill Sebald, of course, had been a language student in Japan. He had married a Japanese Eurasian of excellent background. Her father was a British lawyer in Japan, one of the very few foreign lawyers. He was given permission to practice in Japan and of course, the state of tolerance of brown skins in the Navy was not what it is now, so Bill thought that his naval career would be jeopardized under those circumstances so he finished his Japanese course and resigned. She was a beautiful gal too, Mrs. Sebald was one of the prettiest people you could imagine.

Q: And from a wealthy family, was she not?

Adm. T.: Wealthy in the sense that her father had done well in law in Japan; I don't know what the Japanese side of the family was like, whether they had money or what the background was. In any case they were high in diplomatic and political circles in Japan. They were really well thought of. Bill finished his stint as a Japanese language student, three years, resigned and came back and studied law. Then he went back and took over the old man's practice in Japan. In about

1938 his many Japanese friends all concluded that it was time to disappear from those parts, gates were closing and he had better liquidate what he had there and get out; which he did. He came back to the States and then the war broke out and Bill came back in the Navy and his wife went to work for OSS. Of course she spoke fluent Japanese. They were both in Washington. Bill was on the Washington end of an interesting net which included Pearl Harbor and the CinC Pacific Fleet, when afloat or any other major command afloat in the Pacific. Of course, there was a comparable net in the Atlantic, which I think was responsible for our ascendancy over the U-boats more than any other thing, which was manned by K. A. Knowles. I think he also was a commander, he had been retired for physical reasons and called back; a brilliant man.

Q: This was the Tenth Fleet?

Adm. T.: Tenth Fleet. So, Bill, of course, was the Washington anchor of a private communications circuit, which gave him direct access to his opposite numbers in the fleet in Pearl in delicate questions. Sometimes he would get messages in the ambiguous Japanese language which was difficult to make sense of, not the code cracking aspect of it but this simple

Japanese meaning. The nuances of the Japanese language are likely to escape anybody but somebody very well schooled in the Japanese mentality. This was Bill's chief function and when VJ day came, of course, the whole picture altered completely then. New targets appeared and the old target was gone, the German and the Japanese targets no longer existed. So Bill decided he wanted to get out; they foolishly had failed to promote him to captain in the short-sighted manner that the Bureau of Naval Personnel often did. So in combination with disgust at his treatment and a basic lack of requirement of his specialized ability, caused him to turn in his suit and he went out on MacArthur's staff in Japan as an advisor, legal advisor. To wind his career up in that area, he stepped into George Atcheson's shoes. Not the George Acheson who served in the State Department, the spelling is slightly different. He was killed in a plane crash so Sebald stepped up with the rank of Ambassador under MacArthur although at that time there was no such thing as Ambassador to Japan. Then he subsequently went down to Ambassador to Thailand and later as Ambassador to Australia. He is very wealthy.

Q: A whole new career.

Adm. T.: He wrote an excellent book on MacArthur, called <u>MacArthur in Japan</u>. It is one of the best I have read on MacArthur. He wrote another one on his experiences in Thailand and couldn't find a publisher so it is still in ms. form.

I relieved Bill and was given carte blanche by that very intelligent and excellent administrative guy, Smedberg. Smedberg had been familiar enough with the seats of the mighty long enough to know that the best way to get something done is to find somebody who knows how to do it and give him complete authority to do so. There were two people in the Y branch at the top, one was Smedberg, who had overall authority and the second one was D. F. Frost, he was known as Jack Frost and his office was on Nebraska Avenue, in the former girl's school which was then used at the Naval Communications Center where foreign language codes and whatnot were broken and worked on. Smedberg (of course there was a whole new picture with the disappearance of the German and Japanese targets, the whole situation had changed) told me to establish liaison with anybody I deemed appropriate and of course, chief amongst those was the Army opposite organization which was headed by Carter Clarke who was then, as I recall, a colonel. He had been a brigadier general and he had gotten in trouble with Marshall. From the very beginning, of course, Carter Clarke, like anybody who had been involved in the intercepted enemy messages, was well aware of the fact that they had been ill used or mis-used in the beginning warning Kimmel and Short of the probability of a Japanese surprise attack. In his rather blustery and undiplomatic way he had made his feelings toward the administration fairly apparent--that he felt there had been a lot of misplaced allocation of blame certainly for the Pearl disaster, and possibly the lack of use of the Japanese intelligence later. For example, in the spurious appeal to Dewey not to reveal any of this material in the election. To put it shortly and not contravene security, Carter Clarke was in a wholly different camp, because he had worked with and fully understood the ramifications of the intelligence gathering by intercepted messages. He felt that they had been misused, so of course when in a confrontation of a more or less enduring nature with George Marshall, who was wholly in Roosevelt's pocket and later in the same respect in Truman's his position was insecure to the point that he was not allowed to retain his rank of brigadier general which he had held during the war and which he felt (and certainly by dint of service and aptitude) he was entitled to. So, when I met Carter Clarke in about September or

October of 1945, he was a very bitter individual. He had been demoted and he felt that he had been side-tracked and was unappreciated. He was rather an irascible type in any case. He was not an easy man to shave. So the degree of cooperation I got from Carter Clarke was near to zero. He obviously was not interested in any continuation of the exchange. I don't know what his relationship with Sebald had been but as far as I was concerned he wasn't interested. I was a fairly junior guy and was new to the game as far as he was concerned, so that was the end of that line. As far as the State Department was concerned, as you probably recall they were so riddled by Communists at that time, alleged and convicted and obvious, that it was considered far too leaky a vehicle to confide in them in any respect. There were only one or two over there that I personally knew and the advantages of any exchange of information with those particular individuals wouldn't justify the possibility in this case; in fact the vital possibility of not only leakage of vital information but also considerable embarrassment in more ways than one--personal and professional.

Q: So there was no possibility of any thought of a unification of effort after the way, in these areas; the Navy was going one way...?

Adm. T.: None whatever, only on the working level and that was purely in the spirit of comradeship, rather than in any official or scheduled arrangement between superiors who were actually managing the project on either end.

Q: Was OSS in this area at all?

Adm. T.: We had no contact with OSS. Our only other contacts were with the British liaison which was established in Washington solely for this effort. Lieutenant Commander Shepherd and after him, Lieutenant Toplas; both of the Royal Navy. Toplas was Royal Navy Reserve. Shepherd had married a very rich Chicago girl many years before and he more or less was an ex-patriate, probably a very good one for Washington duty because British naval officers are notoriously underpaid and I suppose the extra money available through his marriage was very useful to him in Washington. Toplas was so-called Wavy-Navy, he was a British Royal Navy volunteer reserve.

We had occasional contacts with the FBI. Beyond the ones I have just mentioned we were strictly on our own but the network still maintained itself, the one I spoke of before, where we were able to communicate directly and without interference or being looked over the shoulder by any other communication facilities.

Q: Directly to other locations?

Adm. T.: Yes, to other places. It was a very convenient thing in the exchange of not so much the type of intelligence for which I was set up but for, such purposes as for example-- after the war was over shortly, Anna Louise Strong was on her way back to the Far East. Of course, as you know, she was a well publicized Communist witch of long standing; she had been in the United States during the war and obviously she was on her way back to join with the Chinese Communists to see what they could do toward overthrowing the Nationalists. I got a report from my man in Okinawa that Anna Louise Strong had arrived on an Army Air Forces aircraft and from then on, of course, the service was Navy. She had a VIP passport from the State Department, and what should they do with her. So I said, "Hold her as long as possible till I find out what is behind this." Of course, the complexion of things as far as the Soviets were concerned, had flip-flopped in Washington but not in the State Department, so I got in touch with the appropriate State Department authority and in effect I was told it was none of my God-damned business. She has a VIP passport and the passport says Shanghai. She goes to

Shanghai if she wants to go. So that was it. Then, of course, we did a little more investigating and discovered that the agency that issued this was a relatively minor outfit down in the basement, more or less, of the State Department and it was in no position to issue such passports. This more or less confirmed my previous decision to steer clear of State as far as any exchange of information was concerned.

Q: Of what use did Admiral King make of this office?

Adm. T.: Admiral King was interested in what was going on in the Pacific area during the time of hostilities. The main use of this intelligence was tactical. Such, for example, the ability to outguess the Japanese and be on the spot when they were there at Midway. Even though we had an inferior force, the mere fact that we knew what their operations would be in advance enabled us to concentrate what small forces we had, and with a little luck and a little expertise we managed to knock out the Midway deal and change the course of the war. After that there were many instances where we were able to pinpoint the location of Japanese forces and the composition of the forces, and sometimes, their mission. So it was purely of a tactical nature and obviously King was interested in what was going on in all the oceans even though he wasn't basically involved in tactical decisions except possibly one of a major nature like the Midway thing where actually he wasn't sure it was Midway. I think it was Nimitz who was convinced it was and King who had rather (I may be wrong on this but this is my recollection) a considerable doubt whether they could trust the information that led to Midway. Later on, our ability to come to these conclusions was much enhanced because the people had increased ability-- people like Commander Joe Rochefort in Hawaii and three or four others of like professional caliber who concentrated on these things. So he got to know the Japanese more or less rat-like proclivity for repeating themselves in various tactical situations, even though they didn't have full information, they could more or less prognosticate what would likely be the course of events. Now, of course, the usage of this information after the war is quite different, and I won't go into that.

Q: How long did you stay with that outfit?

Adm. T.: I left in April 1947--about two and a half years. During that period I was also in charge of the Map Room. The Map Room was Admiral Sherman's pet project. In it were wall displays of the world situation and the various troop dispositions, force dispositions of everybody in the world of any consequence, and it was frequently used by Admiral Sherman to discuss military and naval matters with members of Congress. That was my first encounter with the Legislative Branch in that four or five Senators at a time would come over to justify their opposition or backing of something that the Navy asked for. I was a sort of combination of depressed, disgusted, and impressed with the behavior of some of these people. They didn't act like either gentlemen or people of high mentality. They were abusive of Admiral Sherman, which I thought was absolutely uncalled for. It simply tore me to pieces to see these uncouth louts come over and abuse Admiral Sherman, dressed in a blue uniform with an admiral's stripes on, in a way that you would hardly use an office boy. Now they weren't all like that but there were enough of them that were like that to absolutely disgust me about the way in which a senior naval officer could be treated by, as far as I was concerned (I won't use a four-letter word), the elected representatives of our country. Of course, this also was a very good opportunity to apply what information we had, plus information that came from diplomatic sources and others to show what possible trends were. And during this period there were very delicate situations evolving from Soviet occupation of Iranian Azerbaijan and also the projected demands on Turkey to return Kars and Ardahan, the abrogation of the Montreaux Convention and the intrusion of Soviet influence to Iraq and the Soviet military activity on the newly occupied Japanese Kurile Islands; many things that were bits of information from all areas filtered in and all showed up on the Map Room walls.

Q: Some of this was classified was it not? And yet it was revealed to members of Congress?

Adm. T.: That's correct, and I am sure that the appreciation of the classification of some of this was not uppermost in the minds of these Congressmen and they either used it or bandied it about. Of course there is a vast difference between seeing the information displayed on a map and what the sources were from which that information was derived. The sources of course were obviously not revealed nor even the fact that the sources existed.

At the same time, of course Vlada wasn't over here yet, and I was interested in the Soviets and maintaining the Russian language and for one purpose or another it seemed a useful thing to cultivate the Soviets in Washington.

This was one of the reasons why this tied in, and when I first got there, I don't recall the mechanics exactly, but I got to know and to be accepted in the Soviet Embassy and was usually invited there for important receptions and after Vlada came over that continued. I got to know the assistant naval attaché quite well and later on I learned that a rear admiral had come over who had been superintendent at the Naval Academy at Baku when we had visited there in 1943 along with Admiral Duncan. He was a very charming Georgian-- Georgians as you probably know are people who have no use for the Russians, they are a wholly independent breed and they are continually giving the Russians trouble by their efforts at economic independence and their lack of Communist motivation and all that.

Q: You remember, of course, that Stalin himself was a Georgian.

Adm. T.: Right, but the manifestations of the Georgians as a whole have nothing to do with Stalin's basic performance as a dictator and a rough customer. It's an entirely different breed. In any case he is a charming man and I made contact with him and had him over to the house. Every now and then I would give a party for American associates and perhaps Toplas or Shepherd and perhaps one or two of the Soviets from their embassy. Years ago I had had a supply of Russian type shirts, the ones you wore with the tail out, high neck and a belt around the middle and embroidery on some, because we found out in Shanghai and China in general, that in many of these international parties where you had individuals from diverse backgrounds and countries that they were a little ill at ease. But you get their jackets, neckties and shirts off and get them into a masquerade party, they forget their inhibitions and everybody feels a common denominator and there is more fun. We used to do that at these parties in Washington very frequently and everybody would have a marvelous time. The vodka would flow freely and I had long since been a fairly good cook and everybody enjoyed the informality of these things. The only difficulty that ever developed from this, which one of my good friends immediately relayed to me, was that a WAVE or WAC who had come along with one of the bachelor officers, a lieutenant or some such, she had gone back and reported to her boss all agog and breathless that here was a subversive individual in Washington who was entertaining at wild Russian parties, Soviets all over the place, and in a sensitive spot furthermore and possibly a grave leak to national security. What had set this gal off, I hadn't realized at the time, was that I had been at another party of contemporaries and colleagues and she had been present there too, and I had passed myself off as a Soviet that wanted to defect, speaking in broken English and giving this story that the whole thing was a terrible myth, the Soviet Union, and that I wanted to get the hell out of their control and so forth. She had reported that to her boss. Of course the fact that it was just a huge practical joke and had made an utter fool out of the poor girl and she was out to gig me in return. It never got her anywhere because the boss laughed at the whole thing because the whole deal was fixed up and I'll tell you about it later. It didn't faze anybody except eventually Sherman said (long after this episode), "You have a Soviet wife and there are a lot of people around that feel it's not the best situation to have you in this sensitive spot so maybe you better go to sea. I'm giving you a good command." So I said, "That's great, I've been here two and a half years, I'd love to go to sea." So that was the end of my Washington career.

Q: Did the Russians know about your occupation?

Adm. T.: I told them that I was in the control of shipping and that I kept track of foreign merchant ships. They were very curious, because I am sure they had a copy of the Navy Department telephone directory, which is more or less a public document and I wasn't in it. My office had no name on it and I was not in the telephone directory. In other words I didn't exist as far as the Navy Department hierarchy was concerned.

Q: That's why you said what you did, that you had a Bigelow on the floor but no name on the door.

Adm. T.: I had rather an embarrassing situation one time. The Chief of the Political and Military Affairs Division came down; he was a Navy rear admiral. He had heard about my whereabouts; I had a secretary outside--you pushed a button and that opened the door, otherwise you couldn't open it. The secretary said to the rear admiral, "I am sorry, I'll ask Captain Tolley to come out." He said, "Oh no, I'll just go in there," so he pushed the door and it wouldn't open and she said, "I'm sorry sir, you can't go in there," and he said, "Why not?" Of course I came out, but he never did get in.

Q: How was the place secured when you weren't there?

Adm. T.: It was secured.

Q: Did Admiral King ever come to see you then?

Adm. T.: Oh no.

Q: That was not a part of his immediate interest or use?

Adm. T.: He may have seen Smedberg, but I doubt even that.

Q: You were leaving Washington and this highly interesting and important job, and you were going to sea again. This was in the Spring of 1947.

Adm. T.: As far as I was concerned it came at a very opportune time, aside from the fact that every sailor likes to keep on the move after two or three years. They feel the grass has all been clipped.

Q: In spite of the importance of the job they are performing?

Adm. T.: Everybody thinks his job is supremely important, but when you try to shift it against the comparable aspects of history elsewhere you really reduce it to its honest common denominator; very few things are really important unless they are able to trigger great events, which I don't think my experience ever did. It was merely keeping the wheels turning until somebody else moved in and made it turn some more.

Q: I suspect that what you were doing was capable of triggering great events.

Adm. T.: That is true. That's what the fire department exists for. You may lie in the fire house for a long time ready to go and only when the fire breaks out you appreciate its presence and capabilities.

But to get back to leaving Washington. Our landlady came back and we had to move and finding a house in Washington in those days was close to impossible, so that eased us on our way with more joy than probably we otherwise would have found in leaving. Our landlady, an interesting concomitant to all this, was Estelle Frankfurter, the sister of the esteemed Justice Felix, and she had a marvelous collection of Queen Anne furniture and oriental rugs and so forth in this very old apartment which was close to Connecticut Avenue and the center of things. I could walk to the Navy Department. She interviewed me when I first came there from my bachelor digs in the Army-Navy Club and she said "Will you have a drink," and I said, "Perhaps a sherry." "Cigarette?" And I said, "No I don't smoke," so that put me right where she needed. She didn't want anybody dusting whiskey or cigarette ashes on her Queen Anne furniture or her oriental rugs, so I was in.

Q: That was a testing process.

Adm. T.: That was a checking out process. She went over to Germany, of course, to heckle the Nazis. She was a blistering anti-Nazi, as one might expect. And having given them a proper drubbing she came back and wanted her apartment. So that is when we had to leave.

Q: Before you leave, tell me something about Admiral Sherman, you had some close contact with him.

Adm. T.: Admiral Sherman I would say, was a humanitarian of the first category. He seemed to take a personal interest in everybody who worked for him. Furthermore, he would never pull the roses from somebody else's vase, so to speak. If somebody came in there and wanted something explained, they would ask Admiral Sherman--Admiral Forrest Sherman. Of course he knew the answer, he knew more aspects of it by far, than I did, but he would say, "You tell them, Tolley, and go over and point out on the map what the situation is." He would always hand the baton to somebody else that he thought would be encouraged by being allowed to speak his own piece.

Q: He has been pictured to me as a very cold individual.

Adm. T.: I don't think so at all. I'll tell you about him later, over in the Mediterranean when I met him again.

Q: All right; now we go to Norfolk.

Adm. T.: Well, we went down to Norfolk and finally found a place to live and I discovered, after having gone through about two weeks of refresher training on what to do when you go to sea, at the Naval Amphibious Base, that my new command the USS VERMILION - AKA, an attack cargo ship, had been skippered by Monty Eggers of the Class of '25 and it was in magnificient condition. He must have been an excellent skipper in all respects because her crew was in fine shape. The ship was in good shape and it was a pleasure to take over a ship like that. Mind you, I am a pretty honest guy and I don't say things like this unless it is really the way it was. We had barely got the commission pennant up and down when we discovered that the ship was about to deploy to the Mediterranean. They sent units of the amphibious force over to the Med on a six-months rotational basis and this was in the very early days of what is now the Sixth Fleet. It was called something else then, six or seven destroyers, a couple of cruisers and that was it. In my case, the AKA, had aboard the tank platoon and 250 Marines.

Q: How big was this AKA?

Adm. T.: The AKA is rated at about 15 thousand tons, it is a big ship about 500 feet long and they were built in numbers during WW2. Their purpose was to form part of an amphibious unit, usually consisting of two APAs, which were Attack Personnel Transports that would carry a battalion each, and the AKA would carry, as mine did, a tank platoon, or, could be loaded with various replacement cargo or back-up cargo for the attack combat assault. But the principal specialty or peculiarity of an AKA versus an ordinary cargo ship was that it carried a large retinue of boats--four LCMs which each would carry a heavy tank, and about twelve LCVPs each to carry about 25 combat equipped infantrymen or a jeep or a small truck; so they were able to land their own cargo over the beaches. That is why they were called Attack Transports or Attack Cargo Ships, they had their own facilities to land their own, whatever they carried. We made this trip across, and before I left I got a message from Admiral Red Yeager in Washington that I was having a very special passenger aboard that I was supposed to take good care of and give him all the best hospitality and he turned out to be a Captain, USNR in the Chaplain Corps, Msgr. Fulton J. Sheen. In any case he was an extremely welcome addition to my solitude up in the cabin. As you know, the skipper always eats alone in a ship like that. He took off his eagles and spent most of his time below deck chatting with the 500 people we had aboard, my own crew of 230 and we had about 230 or 240 Marines. He must have done a lot of good, because during our entire tour over in the Mediterranean we had absolutely no delinquency problems or any morale or any other sorts of problems at all. I certainly attribute a good bit of it to his interest in each individual's problems and so forth which he in his expert way straightened out.

Q: Why was he termed a VIP, so to speak?

Adm. T.: Why Father Sheen was a VIP I discovered later. He was on a special mission to His Holiness the Pope. His mission was secret, and as such they didn't want him going over there in any manner in which he could be publicly noted and publicized. Apparently this whole thing was strictly a cover operation. What the mission was I have no idea; obviously he wouldn't tell me.

Q: It was Pius XII in those days, I guess.

Adm. T.: I don't remember. In any case we had a very uneventful trip across and we got almost to Gibraltar when we met up with the Cruiser Flagship of what was to become the Sixth Fleet, and several destroyers and they said "Form on me, we are proceeding to Gibraltar." So off we go at about 17 knots. We were supposed to keep up, and the best we ever did was about 15 knots. So, I sent down to the Chief Engineer and said, "You keep up with that cruiser or don't come up at all," and he said, "Captain, we have never made that much speed before," and I said, "Oh yes, you are going to do it this time." So we followed the cruiser in and I called the chief up later and I said, "Chief that was a marvelous job. How in the world did you get 17 knots out of this?" He said, "God damn it, skipper we held down the blowers, we held down the blower trips so the blowers wouldn't trip out. I expected them to burn up any minute but they didn't." That, as far as I am concerned was the spirit that that ship showed the whole time over there. It is a long story about how we made it through the Med but we were largely independent. The place was a cauldron of disorders at that time. The first Palestine disorders were about to break out in 1947; you will remember that is when the first of the so-called wars started. The French political situation was so bad that none of our ships were allowed to go to France. The flagship itself had given up Villefranche as the headquarters port, so to speak, and Italy the same.

We didn't get to Italy for the same reason--political disorders. But the fleet commander, who had known me as his subordinate in Washington, said, "Go where you please, make up your own mind, make up your own schedule, just let me know where you go and don't get too far out of line on your situation position."

So we started the "Tour de Grand Duke" as the Russians used to say, and in the Mediterranean we started off.

Q: With the Tour de Grand Duke?

Adm. T.: We started off in Gibraltar of course, then to Algiers, then to Sfax in Tunisia, and while we were in Sfax, Admiral Sherman's flagship came in. Meanwhile I had made very good friends with the colonel commanding the fourth regiment of Tunisian Spahis, based in Sfax. My French was good enough to communicate easily with these fellows, so by the time Admiral Sherman's flagship got in I was on extremely good terms with them.

Q: He was in command of the units to what became the Sixth Fleet, and you were a unit of that fleet.

Adm. T.: This was in the days when American warships were fairly new in the Mediterranean, in other than the wartime basis which of course ended with VE day. So every place we went the Americans were very well received. Over the red wine and snails in the French officers club Sfax, the colonel of the regiment and I decided we would welcome Admiral Sherman in a very special way. So they planned to outfit me in a Spahi Lieutenant's uniform and put me in the review, which was supposed to be put on for Admiral Sherman, and see if he would recognize me. So they got me all gussied up and lined me up with a bunch of Tunisian sergeants and I said, "I have ridden a horse before but I haven't the foggiest idea what I'm supposed to do when I ride past the review," and they said "All you do is sit on the horse and hold on to the reins. The horse knows what to do. Nothing that you will do will make the slightest difference, he's done it a thousand times." So I said, "Okay," climbed into all this gear and we prepared to pass in review when the said word came that Admiral Sherman had a hangover, or words to that effect, that he couldn't make it. The festivities of the night before had laid him low, so we had to settle for a picture of the "Lieutenant de Spahis Tunisien Tolley" and let it go at that. I have always wondered whether Admiral Sherman would have noticed me galloping by with sword held up.

Q: And how he would have reacted.

Adm. T.: And how he would have reacted had he known it, but he would have felt I was in character. In any case, the old gentleman was very glad to see me and said, "I wish to God I had you as intelligence officer, I don't think much of the one I have, and any time you've got any ideas please let me know." Of course what he was worried about at that time was the explosive situation in Yugoslavia. The Yugoslavs and the Italians were feuding over the Trieste area, to whom should it belong and we had two or three destroyers up there. The British had two or three and not too long before that, maybe six months, they had shot down an American military plane that had strayed over Yugoslavia by mistake. The situation was pretty tense and he appreciated the fact that I had some Russian background and, of course, he felt that Russia was all tied in with this thing anyway. I used to go over and see him whenever we were together and we would talk matters over and we carried on the same friendly rapport that we had enjoyed in Washington.

Q: He had yielded to the pressures applied to him in Washington to leave your job there but he didn't believe any of it.

Adm. T.: He never brought the subject up. It was purely a new deal as far as he was concerned, my having come over to the Med. He was obviously delighted to have me, because he was most friendly on all occasions and in fact sought me out. Another little aspect of Admiral Sherman: We were over in Argostoli, which is one of the islands off the northwest coast of Greece, and at this particular time Greece was still in a highly divided state; there were bandits in the hills and in fact there were bandits ten miles from Argostoli and we were told not to wander outside the immediate limits of the city and we had armed patrol boats every night, all night circulating around through the anchored ships. We had the PHILIPPINE SEA in there, the aircraft carrier, the ROCHESTER which was the flagship and the CALOOSAHATCHIE - AO the oiler, and probably half a dozen destroyers, quite a little fleet. In the way of hospitality and reception, the city fathers had set up a 'vin d'honneur', which literally means 'wine honor' or honor of wine, something like that. In effect it is a cocktail party with wine only. They had this thing in the city hall, which looked like something out of Greek Mythology. Everything stone, everything heavy pillars, stone floors, And you might also say stone faces, because most of these Greeks were seamed by exposure to the elements. They were common, ordinary fisherman, the townspeople in a purely rural aspect community. It was particularly touching in that this was back in the days when food was extremely scarce and it really sort of hurt us to go over there with full bellies more or less, and see all this smoked goat and lamb and hen and all sorts of delicacies spread out on the table and we knew they were depriving themselves of this food. The whole atmosphere of the place was unlike anything I had ever seen before. They had a Greek Bazouki band, which sounded like something out of the Arabian Nights, absolutely unfamiliar music to which we were supposed to dance on these stone floors. And rather weird looking people I might say. Their clothes were almost like a costume party. Some of the old gentlemen were in Greek shirts like the Evzones wear in the palace guard in Athens. In general the entire thing looked like a theatre set. One of the things that I was particularly struck by was that Admiral Sherman never missed a dance. The old boy was, I am sure, dead on his feet. He couldn't communicate in any common language with these people, but he would go over and invite some old dowager to go out and while around with him. He never missed a dance, and he certainly represented the United States marvelously. And we made a great many friends in that place. I still communicate with one family that I met in Athens when I went around the world in 1973. They had a terrible earthquake there in 1952 that practically shook the town to the ground and they almost abandoned the place.

Q: Tell me about Sherman, since he was reputed to have been an extremely brilliant man, an outstanding man. Did you discover him as such?

Adm. T.: He was, I would say, certainly a wholly down-to-earth individual. In my conversations with him, many times and in many places, it was such utter matter of fact conversation, after all he was a vice admiral and I was a fairly junior captain and our age differential was certainly half a generation, but he was utterly at ease as far as I was concerned. There was no stilted aspect to our conversation or the subject of it or anything else. He was just like a contemporary as far as that goes. However, I was over on the PHILIPPINE SEA one time to check in with George VanDeurs, the skipper, and two or three officers were over there from some of the other ships looking for gold braid and they were joking about it in George's wardroom and the fact that anybody who came out there had better have good shiny braid or Sherman would see that they got some when they went home. He must have been, if not a stern disciplinarian, at least a stickler for the nicer things. As far as any manifestation of stuffiness or rough treatment of any of his subordinates, I have no recollection nor have I ever heard anything; except, possibly one clue; when I left, I left Suda Bay on the way home and passed the flagship somewhere off the bay's entrance and sent a message to Com-whatever the name of the fleet was, ComSixthFlt, thanking him for the hospitality of the Mediterranean and wishing him the best of luck, goodbye, and Admiral Sherman came back--From Sherman, To Tolley "Congratulations on an excellent cruise (or words to that effect). You have been a great asset to the fleet, we are sorry to see you go." And when I got back, of course obviously enough, I sent a copy to my boss, Commander of Amphibious Force Atlantic, and when we got back Admiral Wright (Jerauld Wright), when I went in to check in with him, said, "Say, that was a nice message you got from Admiral Sherman. He has never done that before with any amphibious ships." So whether I really did the old man a good turn or whether the other amphibious ships were pretty lousy I don't know, I don't know what the answer is.

Q: Tell me a little about the Trieste situation and what the US Navy could do under the circumstances.

Adm. T.: As far as I can determine neither the US nor the British Naval presence up there had any particular bearing on the situation. The only thing I remember was the cute little tale about the American captain. All of us were temporary ranks in those days, in fact a good many captains in my category, the Class of '30 for example, were pushed back to three stripes. They had their fourth stripe unzipped and they had to make it the second time. I just escaped that, but we were still all temporary ranks.

Q: Did this make any difference in your pay?

Adm. T.: No, no difference in the pay, merely a difference in your vulnerability if you did anything wrong. Your permanent commission might be withheld or revoked.

Q: You were probationary?

Adm. T.: In fact you were probationary. So the American ships went up there under the command of, obviously enough, temporary captains or commodores, and the British on the other side of the fence, would, naturally enough, want to know what the date of the rank was because that determined who was the senior officer present regardless of what nationality you were. That is the reason we did away with commodores in the US Navy because we were always out-ranked by foreign rear admirals. The British sent back, when the captain sent over his date of rank, "Yes, but what is your real date of rank, not your temporary date." They refused to recognize the temporary date as the real date of rank of the people so that they could take command. It was very much like--to hark back to earlier days to the joint expedition intervention in north Russian in 1918 to 1920-- we had a brigade up there, really a reinforced regiment of about 3800 people and they were thrown into the front lines and although their position was supposed to be solely to protect war material against the possibility of its falling into the hands of the Germans, they served largely under British officers in small units, platoon units mostly, under British company commanders let us say. This I think, is a true and actual story, that these British officers always carried in their pockets the pips for one superior rank in case any of the Americans should get promoted and they would thereby be qualified to take over command of the local unit.

Q: I supposed you can't make any other sort of arrangement to meet a contingency of that sort?

Adm. T.: It is purely a matter of looking up the figures in the book.

In general the flag showing cruise and the usefulness of the cruises in the Mediterranean was again, like our fire department which might be called on to do something. The ship that relieved me was rushed over to Israel to deliver some communications equipment and things that they felt the Israelis were desperately in want of, but by that time our tour was up, our six months were up and back we went to Norfolk.

Q: During that time you didn't touch base at all, on land?

Adm. T.: After Sfax, as I say, Admiral Sherman said make up your own schedule. Go wherever you want to. So I chose Rhodes in the Eastern Mediterranean, and then we went to Athens, to Argostoli, then back to Algiers. Actually we went over to Algiers and Tunis again to take part in digging up the American unknown soldier from the North African campaign. Then we marched in several parades and as was usually the case they put cavalry up ahead and we were always sort of having to toe dance during the parade to take care of what the nervous horses had left ahead of us.

Q: As a footnote to the remark about the American unknown soldier in North Africa, where were his remains interred?

Adm. T.: The whole thing, as far as I was concerned, was another one of these cases where history is a lie that the living play on the dead. There was a major in command who was a member of the American Graves Registration and he was in charge of this thing. They took aboard not only the unknown soldier, but there were 50 or 60 coffins they had dug up. It was the tail end of gathering up the remains of the American dead over there and they were brought back on a merchant ship called the BENNY KIRSCHBAUM. I asked this major about the unknown soldier and he said, "Hell, he's not unknown. We know the names of all of them. We just put the sticker on any particular one and that's it."

Q: Where was he to be interred?

Adm. T.: Somewhere back in the States. I don't know. But the whole thing was such a charade; big parades, lots of Frenchmen, bands played, speeches, piled all these coffins on the BENNY KIRSCHBAUM and the supposed unknown soldier and they knew who he was all along.

One of my more interesting hosts over there, a vice admiral who had been in command of the JEAN BART, a French battleship at Casablanca, where she fired a few shots at the Americans. He was a genial type, and of course I went over and called on him as soon as I was in Algiers and asked him if I could expect the honor of a return call, so I could get out the brass band (we had a little band on board) and Marine guard and all that. He pleaded to be excused. He said his feet hurt, and so he never did return the call but he said, "In exchange for my not having made a call on you, you come up to lunch at my place." So I went up to this opulent castle that the old boy inhabited, including three or four lovely blondes I might add, and had a gorgeous chow which caused me about four or five days in the bunk with dysentery shortly thereafter. I guess Frenchmen can eat and digest anything, but I couldn't, even washed down with a copious amount of his wine. He said it was a very friendly battle that he had. He said "Yes, we've got to fire a few shots in honor, but we didn't particularly try to hit anybody. The battle ended very shortly and I met the American commander of the opposing ships and we became great friends." So, as far as he was concerned the thing was purely a matter of Gaelic honor. He wasn't mad at anybody.

Q: As I recall, that wasn't the impression of the commander of the MASSACHUSETTS, which was the principal adversary, and I don't think he had that impression at all.

Adm. T.: Maybe when you are on the losing side you are more generous in your assessment of things.

Q: You might tell me about the status of the Royal Navy in the Mediterranean at that point. Did they still maintain superiority over our units?

Adm. T.: Not to my knowledge. I don't recall their actual horsepower there, but we were never in company with a single British ship anywhere. I never was. No, I take that back, we were in Gibraltar. Now, we were very well treated there; entertained by the commanding officer, Vice Admiral Archer, who had also been in Murmansk. So I had known him from up there.

Q: You didn't put in at Malta?

Adm. T.: No. The only even near approach to Malta--we had somebody who had appendicitis and needed instant care, a medical case like that so we came close by, sent in a boat, delivered the man and came out again. We didn't go in at all.

If the British Navy was around they certainly made themselves scarce because they certainly were not operating in areas where we were.

Q: You have a note about the British truculence in claiming SOPA.

Adm. T.: That's it, that was the Trieste incident.

Q: And you also have a note on independent duty, this was the carte blanche given you?

Adm. T.: That was the carte blanche that Admiral Sherman gave me; turned me completely loose. My opposite number you might say, was Captain George O'Keefe of the Class of '25, who was the skipper of the destroyer tender SHENANDOAH. George was an absolutely superlative one. Of course, he would always be SOPA; he was four years senior to me. But he was the most considerate guy imaginable, a wonderful host. He did everything he could to promote international relations wherever he went. It was just a pleasure to be associated with him. Of course he always went to ports where the main body (if you want to call such a modest force) congregated, because the destroyers, obviously enough, and the cruisers and the carriers operated as a task group. But I was left wholly on my own.

Q: This involved you in what you term "Captured on Crete".

Adm. T.: We went into Suda Bay, Crete, like everybody else did, for logistics. It was simpler to go in there and fuel from a tanker than it was to go out and attempt to fuel under way. The tanker had enough problems that way with the carriers and the cruisers and so forth.

Q: Crete by this time had reverted to Greek rule?

Adm. T.: Heavens yes, this was 1947, but Greece was still torn by dissidents and the communist underground and so forth, even though, in effect, the Truman Doctrine of assistance to Turkey and to Greece had fairly well stabilized things, there were still lots of disorders around fomented by the Communists. In Athens for example, all over the place, again in '47, you would see the initials KKK which was the acronym of the Communist Party. They were too numerous to even bother to go around and try to eradicate.

In this particular case in Crete we had a carryall on board. So it was very easy to put one of these carryalls in an LCVP and land it on the beach and run around in it, use it for transportation. Some of us in the wardroom and myself decided we would go out in the country and have a picnic. It was a Sunday, so we stopped by the nearest big town. Everything was closed up tight and we beat on the door of a winery and the man opened up and said for nobody else than Americans would he allow any sales on Sunday but you may have anything you want. So we got ourselves a couple of big bottles of wine and tootled out in the country and settled ourselves under a tree alongside a stream and a few cows around to lend a bucolic aspect to the whole thing. We started to munch our sandwiches and swill our wine and pretty soon, out of the bushes, jumped about five or six of the wickedest looking bastards that you have ever laid eyes on, dressed in a peculiar mixture of what looked like had once been army uniforms and all of them with big long rifles. The rifles were pointed in our direction, clearly indicating that we'd better get up on our hind legs and explain what we were doing there. Nobody could communicate in any common language. They came over, looked us over fore and aft, no guns, we offered them all an apple and a sandwich which they gingerly started to move in on, then they took some wine and pretty soon it was clear that we were not on the wrong side. Then by motions we were directed to an upper road and pretty soon we came to an inn. I guess there must have been ten or fifteen people in there, on long benches and at rough wooden tables and in one corner was a barrel of wine, about 50 gallons worth, and over top of that a beat up china closet with a lot of cracked and broken crockery in it, a very poor place. On one side of the wall was a great huge cut out newspaper picture of Churchill. So we suspected that at least we were on the right side. We waited around, sat on the benches and pretty soon they produced a gentleman in a coat all spotted with egg. He was all out of breath, they had gone off and dragged him in from someplace. He was originally from Utah, about 40 years hence and about five by four and he was supposed to be able to speak English. He could make a few noises in English--he was the pivot on which the whole proceedings turned. It was the Greek Easter, that's why everything was closed up so tight. We spent about three hours there and about ten gallons worth of wine and then finally started off, more dead than alive, down to our carryall and then got back to the ship. But they had thought that we could be Communist guerrillas. We were funny looking guys as far as they were concerned. They had never seen anything quite like us before. They figured maybe we had been parachuted in to cause trouble. We all parted good friends.

Q: Not so far distant in the past they had experienced this kind of thing, Germans coming in by parachute.

Adm. T.: Sure, these fellows were local partisans, white partisans, and they were out keeping a sharp eye for anybody who might be on the wrong side and couldn't explain himself. Of course we had the camera along so we got pictures to prove all of this stuff.

That was the general spirit in which we were met all the way around. We got over to Rhodes, for example, and of course it had been in Italian hands. I had been in Rhodes in 1936 and on the way around in independent duty, when it was Italian and it was a burgeoning place with lieutenants all over the shop and I was very well handled by a lieutenant in the Italian Navy whose family had come from California. It was kind of fun to go back, that is why I told Admiral Sherman I would like to go over there. Well, you can't imagine the change, the Italians had all been run out, of course. The monasteries and churches that were Catholic had all been closed up, and the place just looked like a huge Roman ruin with about one tenth of the number of people rattling around in there that it was supposed to accommodate; all Greeks. The Italians were all gone. They had been chased out, and the head man was a grand old Greek vice admiral by the name of Ionnades. He had been tutor to the then King George II of Greece, when the king was a kid. They had a big dinner party one night to which I was invited, and I suppose there were twenty notables on hand, most of them, the educated Greeks, pretended to be able to speak French, and some of them spoke it pretty well. Some of the other Greeks, part of that very large Greek colony on the north shore of the Black Sea, spoke Russian. There was a very large colony of Greeks both there and in Turkey until WW1 was over. So I had two languages in which to communicate and was chatting back and forth in French and Russian and one of the Greek guests said, "Are you really an American? You are speaking French and English and Russian?" "Yes, I'm an American." "No" she said, "you can't be an American, you are too intelligent." Which I suppose is a reverse boost to my ego.

There again, we found the most incredible hospitality. There was a member of what was comparable to the American Coast Guard, the Greek Coast Guard, named Kootsekopolous and he spoke perfectly unaccented British English, had a charming young wife who spoke nothing but Greek--their pay was very low--and it was really embarrassing to be invited over to the hotel by these people, to see him blow a week's pay on about a dozen bottles of beer to entertain me and some of my shipmates. There wasn't much we could do in return except to invite them out to the ship, which we did. We had to lie out about a mile from the beach and take them out in an LCVP, the ship's gig. It was a covered boat and very comfortable, but when they came alongside it was quite rough (in the open seas) so it was impossible to bring the boat alongside the gangway. So we hoisted the whole boat on board by the boom. Of course, Mrs. Kootsekopolous wet her pants at that. That was too much for her, the excitement. But to them it was almost like something from outer space. They had never done or seen anything like that, and they were so gracious on board. While we were there, one of the sailors--this was a rare occasion to have problems ashore--for an utterly unknown reason, unprovoked, he had zapped one of the local Greeks over in the market place and then run away and they couldn't catch him. The Greek came out and protested. This was in the harbor at Rhodes where the Colossus was supposed to have spanned it, and the thing was like it was in the days of the Knights of Rhodes during the days of the Crusades. It hadn't changed. In any case, the Greeks came out and said one of their citizens had been bopped and could we please find the culprit who had done it and admonish him not to do that any more. We didn't know who to look for, so we brought the boppee out, along with three or four of his friends and a very cute little girl who brought me a single rose as a peace offering, and I said, "We have four or five suspects and we can't nail anybody on this but we think it should be in this handful of people and we will parade them on the deck alongside my cabin. You stand here and look out through the screen door and point out the one you think did it." So, we got these guys up there and they very willingly paraded and the girl with the rose fainted. She was up there with the four of them. She had been in the party ashore when this incident took place. She turned white, sank down, and we had to lay her on the couch. It mystified me. The four guys with her, one of whom had gotten bopped, were from Athens and were over in Rhodes on holiday, and they spoke perfectly good English, I mean understandably, so we had no problem with communication. When the smoke cleared away we discovered that she had gone through this routine when the Germans were there and that the whole thing had brought back this horror of the German occupation when they were forced to identify people through a screen like that. Of course I was the innocent perpetrator of this thing. We found the guy later. He confessed and he said, "I couldn't be more sorry and anything I could possibly do to make up for this I will be glad to do." He was a radioman second class or some such thing, a very responsible guy. He must have had too much ouzo or something. All was forgiven and the four Greeks and the girlfriend invited me over for a tour of the city. I willingly went and they showed me all over Rhodes and we had a good time. That's another one of the incidents that we had, one of the small things that happen, and the friends you make as a result.

Then we went over to Athens and I guess one of the most colorful guys who ever went through the Naval Academy was on duty over there; he was a gentleman of Greek descent of the Class of '31 by the name of DeMetropolis. He looked like a Greek, acted like a Greek, talked like one and had all the good attributes most people feel about Greeks. For example, during the war he was skipper of a destroyer and he came alongside the NORTH CAROLINA one time to get refueled and here was a great, big banner on this thing with some screwy name that DeMetropolis had figured out as the name of his ship. He had a band up there; on a destroyer mind you, and he said, "We have come alongside to render any assistance we may be able to give you," says DeMetropolis on this big sign, coming over to get fuel from the NORTH CAROLINA. He was that kind of a guy. He and about three others were over there on some species of supply mission, and they were living in Athens. They had rented a place on the top floor in one of the brand new big buildings in Athens. Sixth floor with a picture window about ten feet square and you could see the entire city. They paid about 500 bucks a month rent for this place, which was a fantastic sum in those days. It was literally a palace, with rooms 30 to 40 feet long, it seemed to me, with two or three pictures of sea battles up there about 8 x 10, and they were holding court in the most magnificent fashion. Through that party I met quite a number of Greeks. They were still having semi-blackout. The lights on the car were just slits; didn't show the full headlight. Well, driving back to Pireaus one night from Athens, we got stopped by a gun aimed at the radiator and it was a soldier who wanted to know what the dickens we were doing out at that time of night. (I presume that's what he wanted to know, in Greek) and we had a bad time to get through him. Things were that rough, that marginal in Greece even in 1947, in Athens yet.

Q: This was the Communist threat of takeover, was it not?

Adm. T.: The Communists presumably, had been subdued, Mark Clark had been over there and the whole Truman Doctrine had been applied. The Yugoslavs had decided they weren't going to back the Greek rebels any more, the Greek Reds, so the whole thing, presumably, was pushed underground, but they were still very spooky.

I went to the Hotel Grand Bretagne in Athens, to a big party that the Greeks were giving for all the commanding officers and diplomats and I had a letter to mail and all I needed was a stamp. So I asked one of the Greek bellhops in the hotel where I could buy a stamp; "Follow me," said he. So I followed him for a while and I thought, this is damned odd, we were going down a lot of corridors to buy a stamp. Why couldn't we go over to the lobby? But I couldn't communicate with this guy. Pretty soon, we go around three or four more sharp turns, up a few more steps and what not, and he knocked on a door, opened it and here is a lovely young Greek inside and he motioned for me to go in. I said "All I want is a stamp, pal." Obviously he had misunderstood my request, maybe that's the way you ask for it in Greek. I don't know. I didn't go in, and I don't recall whether I ever got the stamp, the episode left me so shook. All I was going to do was go to the party and have a martini.

Interview No. 6 with Rear Admiral Kemp Tolley, U.S. Navy (Retired)

Place: At his residence in Monkton, Maryland

Date: Tuesday 10 August, 1976

Subject: Biography

By: John T. Mason, Jr.

Q: Today we are coming back to the United States from the Mediterranean that very colorful period when you were there in the VERMILION. Now you are back in the United States and will you take up your story at that point?

Adm. T.: Obviously the messages Admiral Sherman had sent back or sent to me, which I had, of course, forwarded to ComPhibLant, struck pay dirt, because even before I had arrived in the States, I had received a dispatch that my next job would be commander LST Ron 2. This I thought was not only thoroughly pleasant but most unusual because I had already had a year and a half of sea duty and command on the VERMILION and back in those days that's about all a captain got in any command capacity. It was nice to be called commodore of course, and doubly nice to be more or less on my own. Commander of LST Squadron 2 operated out of Annex 3 Naval Amphibious Base in Norfolk and he was completely separated from any other authority. That little annex in effect belonged to him, he was the senior guy there.

Q: Were you under the Second Fleet? What was the chain of command?

Adm. T.: The Second Fleet was sort of a skeleton command
which is ready to be implemented in time of war for special
exercises and it doesn't actually exist as an operating
fleet. It is merely a paper organization which is constituted
under special circumstances and it has no command capacity
in other respects. The real command structure was the
Commander in Chief of the Atlantic Fleet which was concurrently
the NATO Commander in the Atlantic, four or five hats really.
Then under him were the Destroyers Atlantic, Submarines Atlantic,
and Air Force Atlantic and the Amphibious Force Atlantic.
The Amphibious Force was at that time commanded by a
rear admiral which has since been upped to vice admiral, I
believe, on both coasts and under him was Amphibious Group 2
and another paper organization called Amphibious Group 4,
which had a commander and a flagship but no ships regularly
assigned to it. It was a standby organization that would be
set up in time of war or a time of special exercises when
it would be assigned ships from other units. Amphibious
Group 2 was an operating unit and, as I recall, it had three
or four transport divisions and those divisions usually
consisted of 2 AKA (attack cargo ship) and 4 APA (personnel
attack cargo), and two converted destroyer fast transports.
An independent organization, not under Amphibious Group 2,
but directly under the Commander Amphibious Force was LST
Squadron 2, which then consisted of 12 LST (landing ship
tanks), ships of about 4500 tons commanded by a lieutenant,

who usually had 3 or 4 officers aboard with about 50 men at that time. And additionally attached were 2 ARL (they are LST hulls but they have a complete workshop on board equipped to do repair work on small craft and also more or less active repair ships for the LSTs themselves). Basically they were to be available at the time of landing operations to haul damaged landing craft, small boats, the type of small wooden or steel boats that the landing craft and tanks and the troops are taken ashore in. They get pretty rough treatment in the surf, on the beach, so these ARLs are specifically designed to take care of such repairs. Anyway, it was a 14-ship group and practically an independent command and the only time that I was ever encumbered by somebody upstairs, so to speak, was when we had exercises and I would be included in the task force and one or more up to 10 or 12 LSTs would be incorporated. Occasionally I would go on what would be called semi-independent operations. For example, there was an alleged winter operation to be held at Argentia. So they sent, independently of me, several of the bigger ships, an APA, and AKA and one or two others, but with Marine troops loaded aboard and they were under a senior captain a division commander, I think, and I went up independently. I had 2 LST and I used the ARL as a flagship because it had a nice carpenter shop and I would play in the carpenter shop on the way, and we had a couple of destroyer mine layers and a couple of rocket boats, in other words a small task group of about 10 ships. On this particular exercise we started around October; the theory of the thing was that we wanted to have cold weather operations where it was not too cold but where it would tax the capabilitites of the troops to jump ashore in marginal conditions.

Q: Was that the sole objective?

Adm. T.: Yes, that was the sole objective. Of course, all of our landing operations had been done down in Vieques or down in Virginia some place, where it was almost you might say, tropical. Sadly enough, for the purposes of the drill, when we got up there, it was practically tropical in Argentia. But we held the exercise anyway. On the way up, the seas were absolutely glassy. I have never seen such gorgeous cruising weather. For three or four days out of Norfolk almost all the way up there. But one of the most interesting aspects of it was, at about two days out of Norfolk, and that is not very far, because these craft are slow, they make only 6 knots, and their top speed is about 8 knots and they cruise at 6, the LST I mean, the destroyer and mine layers could do much faster but they had to stick with us. They were acting as screen. Now of course their submarine detection apparatus was obsolete and they had no depth charges and in fact their main part of the screen, they were in fact dummies because they would, in no respect, have been effective anti-submarine ships but they could, at least, listen. On one of these very glassy days somebody spotted a periscope and the word was immediately passed. We were in what you might call battle cruising formation because we were after all on exercise and supposed to simulate war conditions as much as possible. The destroyer/mine layers were out on the scouting line ahead to pick up any subs that we might encounter and they picked this gentleman up and obviously it was a Russian. We checked in later, there were no American subs in the area and, as far as I can determine this was one of the very earliest spotting, sightings (actual sightings, we saw the periscope and the feather of it) of a Russian submarine off the American coast and this was in 1948. The destroyer/mine layers had recording devices attached to their sound gear and of course, they were able to take a sound recording of what they heard and it was sent back to Norfolk and it was assessed as a probable submarine. Long since before that I had learned what we called the Morse code, but the Russian version thereof. They have several additional letters to make up their comparable code. So I composed a friendly message to the Soviet submarine and had one of the destroyer/mine layers send it out on the underwater transmitter in Russian, inviting them to come up and shake hands or words to that effect, which he didn't do and we sailed on.

Q: He didn't respond at all, did he?

Adm. T.: No response at all, and we would dog him for about five or six hours. We were on top of him, but, we, after all had a schedule to keep and our speed was so slow that we couldn't afford to play games. So that was the end of that story.

Q: What would have been his objective?

Adm. T.: Of course, they are carrying out surveillance on our coast now with regularity and it is well known where they are. They are spotted at normal scouting intervals and so forth; in those days I presume it was strictly exploratory to see whether their submarines were capable of it and what they could find out, if anything, worthwhile. Of course, we know that during the Cuban blockade there were quite a few Soviet submarines active, that was before the days of large numbers of nuclear subs so we were able to sit on top of some of those and force them up. We actually saw those. Undoubtedly they were interested in our electronic emissions-- radio, radar, and so forth, to type our radar search pattern along the coast. This is a common practice on all sides now.

Well, the Argentia exercise was more or less perfunctory. It was a bleak place. We felt extremely sorry for anybody that had to be stationed there permanently. As had frequently been my situation in the Mediterranean, I asked the boss if I might pick my own liberty port and he said, "Sure, give us a reasonable one." So we picked Halifax and Lunenburg. At

Halifax we were taken in hand by the local Canadian military. There wasn't any Canadian Navy there but the Army was on hand and it was striking for anyone, who like myself had associated with British in Hong Kong and places like that and in England too, to find here almost a replica of a very modern British regiment but in fact speaking American, with all the gorgeous red jackets and the numerology and the naming of the units and the pomp and ceremony and stomping of the feet, everything except the accent. Even the games that they played, for example, they played a game called "Artillery", where you turn up in full dress uniforms, everything very decorous and you have a few drinks and then you have dinner and then the game starts. The dinners are very elaborate. The port is passed in the right direction and the Queen is toasted and they go through the whole rigamarole just as though you are in jolly old England. Then when the game starts the whole complexion of things changes. In this "Artillery" thing for example, they have a bunk in each of two adjoining rooms, a steel cot, and they put a victim on each one of these cots, which is called a gun caisson. The object of the drill is to get your cot with the guy on it through the door connecting the two rooms before the people in the other room can get theirs through. Obviously enough you meet in the middle of the doorway and you must get your caisson through without dumping the guy that's on the cot. Of course, he generally suffers at least some superficial damage in the process and it's pretty rough on the uniform, as I can attest. Well it was quite an entertainment and quite an experience. From there, we went to Lunenburg and found an absolutely different situation. The only Navy there was a Canadian commodore, a captain like I was but we called each other commodore. But when he got drunk enough he had an odd sense of humor and he would always ease it around a little bit to 'commode', it was Commode Tolley and Commode whatever his name was. But the Lunenburg people really turned themselves inside out, gave me this key to the City of Lunenburg, brass and one foot long; they had a state dinner and all the townspeople in tuxedo and we were just absolutely given the run of the place. That, incidentally, is the home port and the building site of the famous schooner BLUE NOSE which, I think, was for some decades the champion racing schooner in those parts. It is largely a fishing town. Everything is based on fish in those parts. On the way over from Halifax to Lunenburg we ran into some really foul weather and anybody who has gone to sea in an LST can appreciate what you are up against; the ARL in which I was is exactly the same. They have a five-second snap roll. In other words, it takes them five seconds to go through a full cycle from one side to the other and back again. If you are rolling $15°$ to $20°$, that takes you through a pretty fast arc and you have to hold on constantly. You can't sleep and you can't eat properly in all that. I remember my midshipman days sleeping in a hammock where the ship rolled around you and you stayed stable, just like a gyroscope.

So I had an ever-faithful and absolutely indispensable staff lieutenant, an old signalman, and I told him to go get me a hammock. It took some doing, but he came back with a hammock and slung it in the cabin and that's where I slept the two days enroute and got some proper rest. It was some time after that at a cocktail party, when my staff lieutenant had had a couple of slugs, said, "Commodore, I never told you this before and maybe I shouldn't tell you now, but that hammock you slept in aboard the ARL belonged to the previous commodore and he used to put his dog in it when he went to sea. The dog got seasick."

Aside from that we had various independent jobs down in Vieques and in my little kingdom out there an occasional contretemps turned up there. In those days the American ships in port were pestered by what you might call travelling salesmen, peddling insurance, peddling correspondence courses, and every conceivable thing that they might unload on some unsuspecting sailor. I hadn't realized the extent of this until I followed my predecessor's custom and had lunch on board one of the LSTs, a different one every day. My predecessor, Al Boyd, of the Class of '30, had set up a system of signals, and at about ten minutes before twelve each day each LST in our private harbor over there would hoist the signal and what the piece de resistance was for lunch. He would have the signalman go out there and look over all of Annex 3 and pick out whether it was pork chops or roast beef or rice and curry or what and that is the ship he'd pick out to go to for lunch and I used to do the same, except I didn't bother about the signal flags. I found out that these ships were being pestered by all manner of people who pretended to have some influence (and it was a sorry thing too, that some of these people were retired Naval officers, selling insurance, correspondence courses, etc.) and they would come down and announce themselves, "I am Commander such and such, and I would like to see the captain", and what does the poor guy on deck, watch officer, a chief petty officer or first class signalman or whatever-- there were no officers on quarterdeck watch on these small ships--what does this poor guy know and obviously he leads the entrepreneur on to the skipper, who of course, is one or two ranks junior to him even though this other character is retired. So he wastes half an hour over a cup of coffee while this guy ingratiates himself into the good graces of the skipper and then the first thing you know, he wants half an hour of the ship's time for an educational speech, an "eductional address" he would like to make on the benefits of this particular life insurance. First of all he wants to explain the vast benefits to be gained by sticking with your government insurance. That's the come-on. Then having delivered himself of that, he adds that he would also like to say a few words about some alternate possibilities. The same thing went with the correspondence courses. In many cases they were aimed far above the capabilities of the people they were being sold to and they are sold on the installment plan. The kids would get these things thinking that all they had to do was open the package and somehow or other by osmosis what was in the books would seep into their brains and pretty soon they would be highly educated if not a doctor of something or other, increased in rank and pay and all the rest of the stuff that was faithfully promised by the guy who peddled this thing. After about two or three installments it would be obvious that that is not the case, that they were not mentally equipped to take advantage of what they had paid up to a hundred dollars for. So they would quit paying. Meanwhile the fellow had made some money and the people continued to get dunned and it made a lot of correspondence for the ship to try to turn this stuff off. Norfolk jewelers were the same. In those days the jewelers would send letters to the commanding officer to try to collect the money. It meant a lot of book work. I thought this was a vast imposition not only on the individual sailor and the skipper, but in effect it was just plain highway robbery. I instructed the man at the gate to let no further civilians in, except with a letter of introduction from someone who was inside the gate. You can't imagine the storm that broke. My telephone was absolutely crowded with calls from irate salesmen outside. I started getting communications from Washington from officers fairly high up in the Navy Department that this was not legal to bar civilians from this Navy base and I began to be disturbed about this thing, whether I was on the right side or not. I stuck it out and went over and explained it to Admiral Jerauld Wright and Jerry said "It's your base. You do what you damn well please with it. Kick them off if you don't like them." He was a great man, that fellow, very forthright. It worked. Everybody was thankful for it, but it was just one of these facets that goes on that I am sure that lots of people who are supposed to be in command don't know about. It has been controlled since then, but up to that time it was a gross misuse of government time and an intrusion on what little privacy the average sailor has.

Having finished that delightful cruise, which lasted for about a year, I was transferred to the Armed Forces Staff College in Norfolk.

Q: Was this something you asked for?

Adm. T.: This again, just like Com LST Ron 2 was something completely out of the blue and I have since discovered that it was on the advice of an old China friend of mine, Brigadier General Bankson T. Holcomb, (Banks) who is one of these rare birds, in fact the only one that I know of, who has taken both the Chinese course and the Japanese course. He is now retired and living in France. I was called over to the Armed Forces Staff College for this three-year tour to fleet up to be Director of the Intelligence Division. When I went there the current director was a colonel in the Air Force and the Staff College is a tri-service institution with, as far as possible, an equal number from each of the services.

The command of it and the assistant command is rotated among the three services, usually a lieutenant general or a vice admiral or a rear admiral in command; at this time Vice Admiral Hall was commandant (Jimmy Hall, one of nature's noblemen), he is one of the finest gentlemen I have ever met. I worked as one of the peons, so to speak, in the Intelligence Division.

Q: What was this division and why did they need an Intelligence Division?

Adm. T.: The Armed Forces Staff College teaches staff work in general and on any staff you have operations and logistics and communications and intelligence, just like you do in the general staff of the Army or the various staff branches in the Navy Department, or any subsidiary staff, any admiral's staff at sea or at a base ashore. So the Armed Forces Staff College is just what the name suggests. It provides staff officers for the various aspects of staff duty, intelligence is obviously one of those. Now one possible reason why I was chosen for this is that I had been in Intelligence for some time but the basic target at that time was obviously commencing to be the Soviet Union. I took advantage of my background knowledge in that to combine the technique of intelligence gathering and the recognition of what constituted intelligence and the uses of it and how it fitted into operations, by, instead of delivering lectures, putting on skits. We used Russian uniforms and we transferred the whole thing to the Russian scene, and in due course the whole operation was known as "Tolley's Follies". I have been greeted all over the world by graduates of the Armed Forces Staff College by, "You remember Tolley's Follies, one thing I'll never forget about the Armed Forces Staff College is those shows you used to put on." We had two very pretty secretaries and from time to time we would dress them up as Russian WACs or WAVEs or put them in there in a cloak and dagger act when they would be wearing slinky clothing and their opposite number was wearing a boat cloak, with appropriate music and appropriate decorations; it really got to be a professional performance.

Q: How did you succeed in keeping the proper balance to convey the lesson you were trying to succeed with and yet not make it a farce?

Adm. T.: Well, first of all the Intelligence Division was basically trying to do two things. One was to show the process of intelligence, how it is obtained, how it is used, how it is recorded and how it is evaluated, and to what extent Intelligence ties in with Operations and who actually is the adjudicating authority between those two. Of course, for years there has been this basic argument--where does Intelligence stop and where does Operations begin? Ernie King, during WW2 distrusted ONI and considered it was merely a Post Office, that they were not supposed to actually be in a position to give opinions, they were simply supposed to furnish material. In other words, Intelligence in the field is supposed to be able to give basic intentions and basic capabilities of the enemy but it is up to Operations to adjudicate what our side in turn will do to counter those intentions and capabilities, and therefore Intelligence is static and a data collecting agency rather than an adjudicating agency; it is up to Operations to say that on the basis of the intelligence capabilities and intentions that intelligence has given us, we will than make the decision on what the enemy will do. You have given us only the basic facts. We will decide what the enemy can do with those facts, as opposed to our capabilities against him. There is always this argument back and forth, whether just plain intelligence is sufficient or whether intelligence should be able to say what the enemy will basically do. Operations said no. Intelligence can't say what the enemy will do. We will have to say that, because what the enemy will do is dependent not on what they have available to work with but what we will do against them. At that stage of the game, and I am not even sure yet that this question has been solved to the satisfaction of both sides. That one we worked on.

The other thing obviously enough, that they were all interested in to the extent that we could give it without revealing things that were too sensitive, what the Russian armed forces consisted of and what their personnel were like, educationally; what their views were, how they lived, what they ate, what they got paid, and what we could expect of them in the field. All that aspect of it was much more easily put on by this Tolley's Follies type of thing; they could see the actual characters in action. The thing was so successful that at the end of the course the students were asked to fill out a questionnaire; what they liked and what they didn't like; which guest speakers they thought were adequate and which ones were boring and hopelessly useless, and it was in effect a fitness report written by the students on the faculty. Admiral Hall meanwhile had been relieved by a Lieutenant General in the Army whose name presently escapes me. He was a combat general, had served in the invasion of the Philippines and had done very nobly and felt highly of the Navy. He passed the word along to me, saying, "Well, Captain Tolley, we think very highly of your performance, and as a matter of fact the questionnaires of the students have shown it to be so far superior to all the rest of them that when you leave, the end of your tour tour will be in a few months, you might as well set your successor up to doing away with that completely, because it so far outshines the other departments, it destroys the balance of the course." In other words, drag Intelligence down to the level of the others, don't drag them up to your level. That would have been anathema to somebody like Admiral Hall.

Q: What was life like at the Armed Forces Staff College when you were there?

Adm. T.: It was unique in that you had a very deep sampling of not only all the three basic US military services but we had three French representatives, three Canadian, three British and usually one from the Coast Guard, one from the State Department, and these individuals from the other countries were asked to participate in not just a student capacity but also to give lectures. And believe me, the people who were sent there in that category must have been the pick of the crop. They were superior people and they were perfectly fitted. The average rank group was commander, there were some captains, some lieutenant commanders, mostly commanders--senior commanders. So they were all, foreigners and Americans alike, in their mid-thirties, mature people. These foreigners were extremely well equipped to enlighten the student body, through lectures that they were invited to give, on various aspects of their own military service and their views on the world situation and all that. Of course we would have symposiums where we would work out staff problems, and the whole student body would be divided up into groups of about 14 people, each one with three faculty, each of the three services in attendance to thrash out some sort of a problem, either in logistics or intelligence or in operations from start to finish--write up an operation plan, precisely as though they were staff officers in that particular category on someone's staff in the field, which meant that you would have some, if the symposium were on intelligence you would have two or three in there who knew a good bit about it and the rest of them probably would have only a fringe knowledge of it but they might be well versed in other aspects of staff work. As a result, they came off considerably enlightened on the aspects of Intelligence. One of the interesting aspects of that whole thing was the attitudes of the three services. The Army people almost 100%, had been to some species of school before; School of the Line, or some school slightly down the slope from the Staff College and they were used to this type of procedure. They were professional scholars, you might say.

Q: That's typical of the Army.

Adm. T.: The Army is very keen on all sorts of subsidiary schooling. The Navy, of course, far less so. Most of us have been to some specialized school somewhere; the submarine school, and of course, there is the usual percentage of aviators who had been through Pensacola and all that, they were in a sense scholars or had been to something comparable to the Staff College. Both the Army and the Navy students were almost all in effect, college graduates, because they had gone to one of the two Academies or some college ROTC course. The educational level from the Air Force was far, in a way, inferior. There were some who were not college graduates. Only about 50%, I think at the time were, as we discovered at the Staff College. And as far as any process of give and take or dialectic materialism or whatever you would like to call it, there was none on their part. They simply stated their positions and that was it. There was no budging whatsoever from the original position that the Air Force took in their one-third of the group. It was impossible to reason with them or to advance or retard the spark as far as they were concerned. It was a very revealing thing on the mentality of the Air Force as a whole and rather startling and rather frightening. I have heard since that things have improved. As one example, we had six officers in the Intelligence group, 2 Navy, 2 Air Force and 2 Army; I was a captain about midway senior, midway between top and bottom serially. I had entered as an ensign in 1929. This Air Force officer was a colonel, senior to me, who had entered the California National Guard in 1941 and as far as I knew he had no formal education. He wasn't much on the faculty, as far as I could see. He needed a lot of direction and it would have to be very delicately done because, as I say, like most of his contemporaries at that time, he took a firm position and that is where he stuck. For some peculiar reason he was chosen by the US Air Force to be air attaché in Moscow. We met them after they came back and we asked the wife, who I would say was more or less contemporary brain-wise with her husband, what she thought about Moscow, their museums, the theatre, the ballet and the various sights to be seen around there. We knew she couldn't meet too many Russians, because that is the way things were over there, and we didn't even bother to ask that. She said she was sorry to say she didn't see much of those things. She was so busy with cocktail parties all the time, diplomatic cocktail parties.

Q: Was Vlada with you down at the Staff College?

Adm. T.: Yes, she was there and thoroughly interested. The classes were for six months. The classes having been for six months and our having been there three years we went through six classes, each with about 250 people of widely diverse backgrounds and experiences and there was a good bit of partying that went on. We had to work hard, but over the weekends they let their hair down and there was a lot of beer drinking and harmless partying and vast mixing because the students all lived in apartment houses, all furnished so they didn't bring any stuff with them. They weren't supposed to. So everybody lived in everybody else's pockets so to speak, and a lot of friendships were formed between the various services. By and large it was a most enlightening and pleasant experience.

Q: That was one of the objectives, was it not?

Adm. T.: It was. It was a cross-pollination thing and it was educational and it served its purpose. Well do I remember before WW2, the average American Naval officer never exchanged a single word, either socially or officially with an Army officer. And the results showed all over the place when the war came and it was a year or two before there was any real meeting of the minds in the two services. The relationships between the Army and the Navy in the Philippines and in the

Far East at the beginning of WW2, and of the Air Force, which at that time was part of the Army, but it thought it was independent even then. The diversity of action running off in all directions without collusion, we were almost as much our own enemy as the Japanese were. When you consider that there were 200,000 armed men (if you want to call some of them armed men--they were Philippine reserves) but basically we out numbered the Japanese at least two to one. They had slightly over 50,000, and they were obviously at a gross disadvantage, because they had to get a foothold ashore and there were very few places suitable for that in the Philippines. So we knew precisely where they would come. But this utter lack of collusion between the Army and the Air Force and the Navy in the Philippines was obvious in the inevitable disaster. So that is the sort of thing the Staff College was basically, I think, set up to do, to break down those prejudices, let the people get to know each other on a working level.

Q: You made a trip while you were still on the staff at the college?

Adm. T.: Not only did I make a trip, I made a number of trips, because in connection with my lectures I probably was in Washington at least once a month to check in with ONI or various operational activities in Washington for background material and also to recruit guest speakers. We had a guest speaker in Intelligence about six times during the course.

Q: You had your own program of speakers?

Adm. T.: Yes, we had such people as Anthony C. McAuliffe (Nuts McAuliffe) the Battle of Bastogne, and Joe Wenger who was a communications expert, basically people who were almost unique in the Intelligence field. I would go up there to brief these people and to scout out possibilities; of course all the other divisions in the Armed Forces Staff College also had guest speakers. As a result we had about one a week. Admiral Hall would give a luncheon for the guest speaker after the twelve o'clock presentation and very frequently I was invited. Admiral Hall seemed to take a fancy to me somehow, because he felt that perhaps I had a broader view on a great many subjects, although I didn't know a hell of a lot about anything specifically, and I admired him so deeply he must have felt it.

Q: Was Mrs. Hall incapacitated in those days?

Adm. T.: Mrs. Hall was practically crippled with arthritis and I recall one time when the pair were over at our house for cocktails. I was cutting a Virginia ham, one of these Smithfield hams, and Mrs. Hall was watching from the sidelines and she couldn't stand it. She struggled to her feet and came over there and said, "Give me that knife, I just cannot stand to see you hack up that beautiful ham."

Aside from these frequent trips to Washington, I also had a marvelous opportunity to go up to summer school at

McGill University. Actually, it was a small college taken over by McGill in a place called Stanstead, which is on the Canadian-Vermont border. They hired this school for the summer and sent in special professors for a course in Arctic Climatology and Russian Winter Capabilities, and all things to do with cold weather operations and particularly as far as I was concerned, how it tied in with the Russians. They had people like the arctic explorer (whose name escapes me now), in any case they had top of the pile people, ones like Professor Hare for example, who knows more about Arctic Climatology than anybody else I can think of, and another Canadian who is the father of the musk-ox propagation scheme-- the ones who rescued the musk-ox from near oblivion and has now gotten them established in colonies all over the Arctic. The unusual part of this program was that we lived in Vermont, across the border from this little town that the border straddles. I would go to Canada in the morning for school, come back to the United States for lunch, go back to Canada for school in the afternoon, come back for dinner and then frequently go back to Canada in the evening to either go to the movies or pick up some groceries or vegetables or milk which was cheaper on that side. One of the vagaries of officialdom, Canadian versus American, was most apparent here. The Canadians gave us a little maple leaf to stick on the windshield and they said "Come by the back road and forget about the customs inspection, because we know you are back and forth all the time. You don't bother us and we won't bother you." Coming back into the United States however, we had to go through the entire routine. If there were 75 automobiles lined up, we got in line. Fortunately they weren't there most of the times I had to go through. They would sometimes search the car, even though I was living in the house of the widow of the chief customs official. It was simply a matter of harassment, as far as I could see. It served no useful purpose and they knew perfectly well who I was. It was a highly successful course. There were about ten US Naval officers there and the rest were all Canadians, with a sprinkling of British. One of the things I learned early in the game, that I had never even suspected before, was that the negro problem in the United States is microscopic as compared to the Quebecois versus the English-Canadian thing; I learned that at one of these sit-down beer drinking things we used to have on Friday evenings where all the students gathered around to exchange reminiscences and ideas, and invariably the basic subject would surface about the embroglio between the Canadians and the Quebecois, and how they hated each other. You never knew quite who was who because many of these Quebecois spoke perfectly unaccented English. The blood would rise and their faces would get red and then you would know who was who.

This, of course, was a whole summer proposition. Another trip I made was to Frankfurt to the Attaché Conference. All the attachés from all over Europe gathered in Frankfurt to get together and exchange notes and for a little champagne drinking I suppose. So we flew over on a special government airplane and I was in civilian clothes. It was a long, tiresome ride and I was wandering around looking for somebody to talk to and I sat down in a vacant seat next to a likely looking gentleman, very nicely dressed, and I stuck out my hand and said "Tolley". He didn't do anything. He just looked around and said, "What is your rank?" So I said, "I'm a captain in the Navy." So then he stuck out his hand and shook hands with me. It developed that he was the Chief of Intelligence to the State Department, a retired colonel in the Army. I don't suppose he was about to soil his hands with some second class civilian. This was obvious by his actions.

The Attaché Conference, as far as I could determine, was a large boondoggle.

Q: Do you have the rank of an attaché?

Adm. T.: I had no rank at all, I was merely a captain of the USN in civilian clothes, getting a free ride over to flap ears on the shape of things to come, or was, or is in Europe at that time. As I just mentioned, like a great many attachés, either they didn't know, or if they knew they didn't tell. So I didn't learn very much except that Paris was expensive. We stopped there on the way back. In general, it was a very pleasant trip but, as I say, something of a boondoggle.

Well, having been exposed all that time to the various

presumably good influence of the Armed Forces Staff College, my next job was assistant chief of staff for Plans and Operations of Amphibious Group 2. Here I was, back in the Amphibs again, which in those days was a very large hunk of the operating Navy. Still is, for that matter--and immediately launched into the operation.

Q: This being in the Atlantic still?

Adm. T.: In the Atlantic, based in Norfolk. By the time that was finished I would have been seven years in and out of Norfolk, which I learned rather to admire, if not love. It has a great many good points.

I spent two years aboard that staff and it was a big one. There were forty officers attached to it. It was a very large staff because an amphibious staff has a tremendous number of ramifications--gunfire support, landing plans, communication plans, logistic arrangements, contact with the Army and liaison with the Air Force. You need a special guy for each one of these things, so you have a broad mix. Aside from the educational aspects of putting into practice some of the things I had learned, it was also a marvelous opportunity to assess junior admirals, some of whom became important later, and to try to figure out why certain people's careers had gone the way they had. For example, the first admiral I had was Rufus Rose. He was an extremely bright man. You sometimes hear about the gal who is often a bridesmaid but never a bride. Rufus was often a brilliant staff officer but never a commander and this was his first crack at it; and last I might add. A sea-going command he had never had. He had been chief of staff to Admiral Wright, who was commander of the Amphibious Force Atlantic, and had done a marvelous job. He was a fantastic staff officer; had just absolutely a rat-trap brain. He caught something and it never got away from him. Unfortunately, he was brighter and quicker than most of his staff officers and he made it evident that that was the case, so you always had the feeling of never quite catching up. It was one that I would say was not conducive to a happy staff. He desperately tried. He was a grand gentleman and he tried his best to be socially impeccable, which he was. He was wonderful in entertaining foreign officers when we were on operations at sea or abroad. Then, he was followed by what I suppose was the most complete opposite that you would find in the US Navy, Gus Wellings. Wellings was strictly a logistician, he used to tell us about the time he was a small boy and had to stand on a box in order to steer one of his father's tugboats. The old man had a towing business and I believe it was in Boston. He was a nut on gardens. He loved to go out and dig in one that he had previously had when he was commander of the amphibious training command. He would take his flag lieutenant out there hand him a shovel and get busy and dig out the turnips and so forth. In every respect he was a different type of man. For example, we were in a storm one night and Gus was very fond of ice cream. So he told the boy to go down to the ship's service and let us all have ice cream. We ate in a flag mess-the admiral, chief of staff, flag lieutenant and myself. Just the four of us. "Go get some ice cream from the ship's service." Down goes the Filipino boy and came back empty handed, no ice cream in the ship's service. "What, no ice cream on my flagship? Don't they know I like ice cream? You go tell the captain to go alongside the nearest ship in this formation and get some ice cream." Well there was one hell of a storm; I suppose we could have done it but it would have been a dangerous maneuver. Well, in no less than fifteen minutes up comes the captain, personally, carrying a consignment of ice cream. Where he found it I don't know, but he had it. That's the way he did business. He was a chain coffee drinker. He would put a thermos bottle of coffee on his desk and drink a quart of it. Then he would send down to get another quart. He constantly smoked cigars, and he wore a vest like one the railroad conductors wore in the old days and it was always completely gray from cigar ashes. Some of his attributes were really unique. For example, in Amphibious Group 2, there were approximately 20 big ships and they were basically on a cargo-type hull and they had lots of booms to hoist out cargo and ship's boats and of course, all the boats had wires and the wires wore out. They got frayed on the ends and had to be renewed. Gus figured out that there was roughly two hundred fifty thousand dollars worth of wire in the group and he said, "You know what those fools do, when they get frayed on one end they throw the wire away. What they should do is end for end the wire, put the worn end back on the drum where it never comes off anyway and put the unused end which has been on the drum all the time on the business side in the open. Ipso facto, we have saved a quarter million bucks." Nobody had ever thought of it before.

Q: He was an ideal man for that time was he not? Weren't we going through conservation and cutting down in the Department of Defense?

Adm. T.: He would be an ideal man to have any time when it comes to that sort of thing. He was simply a practical logistician. As a kid he had grown up in a seagoing atmosphere. There was a dog eat dog commercial competition and every dime on a can of paint and every nickel on a piece of wire saved, meant that they stayed in business. As far as he was concerned that's how he was running the Navy. He liked me very much because he liked to talk about gardening. I was very lucky with some of these people. Gus thought I was a prince because I knew when to plant peas and what to do for the asparagus and a few things like that. Also that I went along with him on some of his mechanical ideas, because I am basically a mechanic myself. His chief of staff he had absolutely no use for. The only thing as far as Gus was concerned that that guy could do was play tennis. I won't quote his name, he was a friend of mine and is dead now and I'll call him Joe; Gus would say, "Joe how can you be so God damned stupid?

Go home!"

Q: Did the amphibious forces suffer at that time from lack of equipment?

Adm. T.: The amphibious force in general at that time was the same type of stepchild that the entire Navy was. There was no new construction. We were still pooping along on what was left over from the war and of course the amphibious force was built during the war. It was dreamed up during the war. It hadn't existed before the war. The only really new ships were the LSTs and the LSDs, the ones that carried smaller landing craft in them. And in those landing craft were tanks. Those were the only, what you might call new, ships that were built during the war. The cargo ships in many cases, had been commandeered merchant ships that had been built many years before. There were some new Victory type cargo ships, such as my VERMILION. That was a wartime ship, but it was built in a hurry to minimum standards. Just cranked out like sausages and certainly not of the best materials and it was constantly a logistic job to try and make these things go. As I say, the VERMILION was fairly new. But on one of these older ships that relieved us in the Med, she was in such rattletrap condition that my crewmen, half jokingly and half seriously, suggested that we put rat guards on the lines which were tying the two ships together. I went over and made a tour on the thing, went down in the engine room, and there were cans hanging under the steam pipes to catch the drips and everything was rusty and in general it was in very poor shape. The whole amphibious force was in that marginal condition because the ships were old to begin with. They had very little money for maintenance, but they went. The crews at that time were pretty much professional. There was not much come and go. It was almost like the pre-war Navy. I recall in the VERMILION, for example, it would seem that every week a sailor would come up in his dress blues with the ship's cameraman to get a photograph shaking hands with the skipper, shipping over, it really was a professional outfit.

To get on with the various admirals--when Gus Wellings left, the next one was H. Page Smith, and there you have a real prince of a man and a brain and I think all the things that an admiral should be. It was certainly a pleasure to be not only with him in the messroom, but to see him in action. When I would write up an operation order and bring it up to him the only thing he would say was, "Give me a brief rundown on it. What's the basic principle involved? What's the disposition of the forces?" All of this would take me about 20 minutes, I guess. He would have laid out initially what had to be done and he would say, "Tolley, you go and fill it in," then I would give him a rundown on the finished article, all typed up ready to go and he'd say, "Where do I sign?" There were others in the amphibious force at that time, one whose name I won't mention. He was in one of the other groups, one of the paper groups I have mentioned in the amphib group before. He delighted in giving his staff an operation order to write up, let them make it complete, never interfere as they went along, and then on its completion would absolutely gut it and say this is where its wrong, that's where I don't like it, such and such has to be revised, go do it all over again. And if he could do this on Christmas Eve or New Year's Eve that would even delight him more. I recall another instance when the ships were in the Virgin Islands, St. Thomas, and booze was cheap over there, so lots of people smuggled booze back aboard. This guy got wind of it, or suspected it, and passed the word around, the first night under way and he said, "I'll be around about ten or eleven o'clock to inspect, I understand there are some unmentionable things aboard ship, I just want to be sure we don't get in trouble with the customs when we get to Norfolk." Very shortly therafter there were sounds of splashes on the port side and splashes on the starboard side and bottles went out port holes but the guy never came around. He never intended to in the first place. That was the irony of it. If he had come around and inspected, everybody would have said, "Well, that's the way things are; we have to put up with it." In that form you see, he left them all absolutely speechless with rage.

H. Page Smith gave the impression he knew what was going on, that he was completely in control of things. If something went wrong, he would immediately know what to do to correct it, and the only time I ever heard him use a dirty word was when the same admiral I have been telling you about who had the booze thrown overboard, was umpire in an operation off the beaches below Norfolk. Out came these messages as we were sending our ships in, LST and the smaller craft to storm the beaches. Over would come a word from the umpire "LST 746 hit by a bomb, out of action," which meant she had to anchor. She was out of the operation. Then another one would come, "casualty to LSD #, unable to proceed, out of action" (of course they weren't, they were perfectly okay). I would take these messages over and show them to Admiral Smith and finally he said, "Piss on him, pay no attention to him. We're down here to train troops, not the umpire."

Q: There wouldn't have been any ships left?

Adm. T.: He was such a practical man. Of course I thought at the time, "there's a man who will go places", and he did. He was debonair in appearance and absolutely superb as a Naval officer. So there you have those three. I'll name more as we go along. By and large I would say the vast majority of them deserved wearing a flag but every now and then one sneaked through that was a mistake, and there were some down below who should have been up there but never were.

That two years with the amphibious group also involved two trips to the Mediterranean to engage in exercises with the foreign Navies, NATO exercises. One was in the North Sea and involved exercises in company with Belgian, Dutch, Norwegian and British ships of all categories. There were submarines, destroyers, mine sweepers and stuff from the smaller navies and most from our side were amphibious ships with Marine troops on board. Small operation, nothing bigger than a battalion, but the forces involved were so mixed that it was amazing that things got done as well as they did. We had a critique in Oslo aboard a British aircraft carrier, and present was King Haakon VII of Norway, a very tall, angular, gray old man with a big, long, turkey neck in Naval uniform. He seemed very jocular. He was having a nice time and he must have been over 80 at that time. I don't remember very much of the conference that went on but the British had refreshments set up on the hangar deck and the sugar looked like rock salt. This was about 1951 and austerity was apparently still with them. The side effects of all this, the visit to Oslo for example, was a tremendous treat. The complete difference between the city itself and the population, the things we had been used to like Norfolk for example. Everybody was blond, everybody was cheerful, the girls and the boys going around hand in hand. In general, it gave you the impression of a thoroughly well satisfied and down to earth populace. Everybody was helpful. From there, we stopped at Iceland on the way back to the States. Iceland is a very unusual place in many respects. It was a marginal operation to get in and stay. We were all ashore--the admiral, Rufus Rose, and myself and five or six staff officers. Meanwhile the ship was more or less lying to in what passed as a harbor and one of the unexpected blows came up and she had to go to sea leaving us stranded overnight. The Minister to Iceland put us up during all this time we were ashore, about three days, before the ship could come back in to pick us up. We borrowed razors and wore our dirty shirts. We learned a lot of things about Iceland which none of us knew before. Chiefly that the boys didn't like the Navy because the Navy, which was established at the air base mostly, along with the air force, always snatched the Icelandic girls, some of whom were absolutely raving beauties. The sailors had more money and were more interesting and more outgoing and so forth (the Icelandic types were rather on the stolid side). Then we went out to the Keflavik Air Base commanded by a brigadier general in the Air Force and we were very much amused to find one of the colonels out there who had been a great football player at West Point in his day. At the cocktail party while we were out there the colonel and an Icelandic girl were sitting on a sofa together and somebody said, "My it must be very difficult in the winter around here, the weather is so bad. Colonel how about that? What do you do in the wintertime?" So he looked around at Dua, the Icelandic girl and said, "I don't know, I never go outside in the winter." The Navy wasn't allowed to take wives over there. Red Rusenberg of the Class of '21 or '22 was the Navy head man there, and he had a very nice apartment but there was very little to do except what became necessary in the way of administration. So to while away the time, he had gotten about the only tree in Iceland, and it had grown so successfully that he had to cut a hole in the ceiling so that it was then growing up into the bedroom on the floor above. Such were the indoor and outdoor sports that one found in Iceland.

Q: On the whole, did the populace welcome the Americans?

Adm. T.: They did not. Even then, possibly even more than now, they had a large contingent of Communists in the Althing, the parliamentary body. The townspeople, basically a stolid lot, they are undemonstrative and I suppose bad for the business, but as I say, the young men didn't care much for the situation because they were at sea a good bit of the time and weren't able to keep their eye on how things were going with their girl friends.

We went from there down to the Med and put on another NATO operation with the Greeks, the Italians, the Turks and the British. Of course, the Greeks and the Turks were at loggerheads even then. They were certainly not on what you would call friendly terms. The French were then still operating with NATO and there we had command relationship troubles and the French admiral that was riding their aircraft carrier was senior to Rufe, Rufus Rose, who was commander of the expedition. So there were times when out of courtesy and to keep the French from possibly pulling out, we would pass command surreptitiously to the Frenchman to make him feel good for a while. Of course, the other grave difficulty we had was communications. On the Turkish ships and the Greek ships there usually would be one officer who could communicate in English and at the end of three or four days operations that poor guy would be dead on his feet unable to talk in any language, at which point the thing fell apart because you simply had to have somebody who could talk fast and recognize things. I suppose that is probably a weakness of any international force even now, the mere simple ability to communicate.

Q: Which exercise seemed to work the best?

Adm. T.: The one in the North Sea was incomparably better because those people are inherently attuned to the sea, all of those people that we worked with up there. They are at home on the water as they are on the land. As far as the Italians are concerned, obviously they simply are not sea going. Their Navy didn't give us that impression at all and that corroborates their performance during the war. For example, their destroyers which were supposed to screen us, were so short range, range in such things as water that they would have to come alongside for boiler water about once every two days, which is unheard of in any normal warship. You make your own water in an American ship. You have to go alongside for fuel but not water. I recall one case where this Italian destroyer made an attempt to come alongside to get water, failed, made another attempt, failed, and couldn't make it and finally backed alongside. Of course, our impression at that time was that they were just along for the ride. It was most interesting in this wise, we had a senior Turkish officer, a senior Greek officer, a senior Italian officer as observers. They were in the rank equivalent to captain, though in some cases a flag or general officer. I sat next to the Turk in the mess. There were about fifteen of us at that time. We had really expanded. The Greek was across the table and one time the Turk leaned over to me and he said, "Those Greeks, we ran them out of this country once before, let them try it again, we'll run them out again." The whole thing was on a slightly lower level than what one would call an allied cooperative enterprise.

Q: You spoke about the difficulty in communications because of the different nationalities, did you have any difficulty in the North Sea in this respect?

Adm. T.: None whatsoever.

Q: What about the effect of the aurora borealis on communications?

Adm. T.: None at all, it was all relatively short range stuff, mostly TBS, Radio between ships and that type of communication is rarely disturbed.

Q: This was during the time of the Korean War. Were you affected in any way by that?

Adm. T.: This was pretty much at the tail end. This was in 1952, near the tail end of the Korean War. The only way that Amphibious Group 2 was involved in the Korean War was that one division under the command of Captain McWhinnie was sent out with three ships as I recall, with supplies and troops from Norfolk all the way to Korea. There again, Gus Wellings was the group commander at that time and again he manifested his remarkable technical knowledge. He said "Tex", meaning McWhinnie, "I want you to make an experiment on the way out with that APA. It is loaded down, it is in wartime configuration, as far as load is concerned and I want you to test it in various trims. It is my belief that if you trim that ship down one foot by the bow that you will make better speed with the same fuel consumption than if you trim it flat up or down by the stern." They tried it and of course what happened was normally a ship squats when it is under way, so with the ship one foot down by the bow the ship squatted all right, it squatted the foot and in other words it was levelled out; its keel was horizontal with the surface of the water so it made the best efficiency in fuel consumption that it had ever made in its career. Nobody had ever thought of it before Gus did. And that has probably disappeared into limbo. I have never seen it written up in doctrine anywhere, nor have I heard of anyone using it since. Of course some ships couldn't do that. My VERMILION drew 15 feet forward and 23 feet aft, because she carried tanks aboard. A platoon of Marine tanks, and that simply wasn't enough cargo to put her down on an even keel which she was designed normally to float at. So that couldn't be applied to her. But any ships that has a roughly equivalent draft fore and aft could make use of it.

Q: You are going to shift your activities to the Pacific and you are still going to be with the Amphibious Forces. You are in command of Trans Ron 5. What was the date of that?

Adm. T.: That was about September 1954, and I must say that somebody upstairs must have been watching out for me because I don't have any influential friends anywhere. I never tried to make any. I just felt that I would never wind up CNO so why not have fun in the process. Whenever I got any of these what I considered plush assignments, I never ceased to wonder how it happened. In this particular case, here I had already had two amphibious commands, the amphibious attack cargo ship and the LST squadron, two years with Amphibious Group 2-- which was a total of five years straight sea duty, and here I was back to sea again, which was something and which the average naval officer never dreams of. He is lucky to get three years at sea, particularly in this command I am speaking of. The amphibious force, during the war was brand new and it was manned largely by spare parts, people who had been either thrown off or fallen off or otherwise had become detached from what you might call the fighting Navy, the battleships, the cruisers, the destroyers and so forth. Its reputation had to be built. By the time I was busy in it, I think it pretty well had been in spite of the fact that most of the ships were old crocks. This squadron I went to had had its terminology changed. Before that, it had been TransDiv 13, and under that numerology it had the usual 2 AKA and 4 APA and 2 LSD. Then they got together with the east coast here and changed the set up and changed it to a transport squadron from a division, cut it into two divisions of transports and attack cargo ships and LSD, one AKA, 2 APA and 1 LSD in each of two divisions, plus two fast destroyer transports, plus the LST squadron. In other words, when I took over, Trans Ron 5 had 25 ships.

Q: With a total complement of how many men?

Adm. T.: Total complement of 4,250 men. So far as I was concerned, you couldn't have found even a closely comparable command in the US Navy. An aircraft carrier or a cruiser or any single ship command wasn't a patch on it. First of all, those squadrons rotated to the west coast, there was 1, 3 and 5, three squadrons. So one was constantly in the Far East.

Q: One was operational and the other two were what?

Adm. T.: All three were operational, fully operational. Of course individual ships were constantly being overhauled. Now the squadron that was scheduled to go out to the Far East was always at full complement. The repair schedule and upkeep schedule had been such so that all hands and the ship's cook were present for that particular deployment because they needed, in effect, full battle efficiency from the thing. Just before I took over the unit, it had been TransDiv 13 before. It had undertaken this tremendous transfer of Vietnamese from the north to the south, something like a quarter of a million had been transferred by this outfit and very effectively, a beautiful job. So that's the sort of thing they were prepared to do and eminently suitable to do. Very shortly after I took over, about two months, I was on my way to the Far East and when you got out there the designator changed from PhibRon 5 to Commander Amphibious Group Western Pacific, which basically was a flag officer's job. But apparently they didn't consider that it was appropriate to attach a flag officer for a rotating command. Normally a flag officer is assigned to a static unit rather than jumping from one to another, so in other words they saw no reason why the squadron commander shouldn't have the responsibility. Again, I was more or less independent, as I had been in the Mediterranean with my single ship over there.

Q: All of that appealed to you greatly.

Adm. T.: I am a loner, I love to be on my own. The commander of Seventh Fleet at that time was Jocko Clark. At any rate, he spent almost all of his time at Taipei, in the AGC, the Amphibious Force with an amphibious type flagship that he used. Of course later on, they changed to a cruiser as flagship for the Seventh Fleet, but at that time he used an AGC. He rarely went anywhere else, He would make side trips to Hong Kong occasionally, and occasionally come up to Yokosuka. Of course the whole situation completely flip-flopped later on, not too much later either. It seemed to me the first order of business out there was to find out what the probabilities were for the future, along such lines let us say, as the evacuation of the Vietnamese had been, and of course, that situation had been taken care of. The next possibility was the evacuation of Quemoy and Matsu, the Nationalist offshore islands which are within spitting distance of the Chinese mainland, which are enormously heavily fortified and manned by some 60,000 or 70,000 Chinese troops plus X number of civilians, camp followers. So the possibility of course, was uppermost at that time that they might have to be evacuated, because there had been a constant fusillade (as you recall there had been a huge exchange of pamphlets, shells, recriminations and so forth) to try to dislodge the Nationalists from those islands, which were in highly strategic spots, one of them right off the entrance to Amoy Harbor, one of the principal China ports. Of course, the only logical way to get those people back on Taiwan would be to land them over the beaches. None of the ports were suitable for large numbers of ships to get in in a hurry, or if they could have gotten in at all, all of the harbor entrances were narrow. The entrance to Taipei is a narrow gate. So I made it my business first to take my flagship

down to Taiwan and case the place. I first called on the
commander of the Seventh Fleet and his staff and enquired
as to what information they had on the beaches, so in case
I had to land these people from the offshore islands back
on Taiwan and I had to land over the beaches. What were
they like, the configuration, the reefs there and the tides
and all that. They had no idea; they had no information on
that. So I took my staff over there and arranged a presentation on our capabilitites and proposals, if we had to
carry out an evacuation and what we needed to know. Then
they said the next best bet for you to do was to go over
to the MAAG outfit on Taiwan. They ought to know. They have
a Marine colonel there who is supposed to know everything
about amphibious warfare. So I toddled over to the MAAG
outfit and the colonel was sitting there with his feet on
the desk and I posed the same questions I had tried on the
commander of Seventh Fleet staff. "No," he didn't know anything about the beaches. He knew all about the Chinese
beaches, but the Taiwanese were not about to tell him anything about their own beaches. "Go see the Naval Attaché.
Maybe he knew something." So I went to see the Naval Attaché,
a very nice guy. He spoke Chinese. He was a Chinese language
student. But "No," he didn't know anything about the beaches.
Go see the Seventh Fleet staff. He was sure they had all
the info. Of course, when the smoke cleared away, it became
obvious that none of them had the foggiest idea as to what
the others had as to information, what they did or didn't

know or how to get it.

Q: Who had raised the question of possible evacuation?

Adm. T.: I did. They were being bombarded, there was no telling--the Chinese Nationalist naval forces at that time were laughable (I don't know whether they are any better now), they had a collection of old American destroyers and a few small craft and I am sure they would have been of no conceivable value in making an evacuation or even of supporting one. So it became obvious that if something had to be done I was the guy who had to do it. Without background knowledge, I would have been wholly culpable had I made no attempt to find out. I never did find out. There was nobody who knew and the Chinese wouldn't talk. They would tell you all you wanted to know about the Chinese mainland but nothing about Taiwan.

Q: Not even if you could convince them it was to their benefit?

Adm. T.: They derided and decried and were aghast at the mere suggestion that any such thing as the evacuation of Quemoy and Matsu would ever have to be taken and under such circumstances, when you have that factor of misplaced pride and what you figure your capabilitites you can't get an answer, if they knew themselves, which is highly doubtful. Having spent a rather frustrating week as far as any useful purpose was concerned, I at least had a good look at Taiwan, which I discovered looked very much like Japan; a beautiful place; hot, everybody busy. I became great friends with the mayor of Taipei and, of course, I was invited out after my official call, to several dinner parties in the Chinese style and was literally slugged with maotai and samshu and these various first cousins to shellac that the Chinese consider delectable wine. Samshu is a relatively mild wine, I guess derived from rice. Maotai is about 120 proof and you really think you have been hit by a stroke of lightning. It is positively awful stuff, embalming fluid I guess. When I left, I had explained to the Chinese when they were out aboard ship that I was awfully sorry we couldn't serve booze on board but that was a rule of the US Navy, and they said they understood that. When it was time to leave, a large package came out to the ship and on it was a letter addressed to my grandmother, "Dear Madam," (I had told them I had a grandmother that I was very fond of; actually she had been long dead) "Enclosed is a package that I am sure you will enjoy. As my dear friend, your grandson, has explained, you are particularly accustomed to something of this nature to set you off on a good day." I opened it up and it was a half gallon of maotai. A typical way of the Chinese to circumvent the rules.

During that cruise again, I was allowed to go wherever I wanted. So we went down to Hong Kong and stayed a while and I was very much reminded of my earlier days there aboard the gunboat MINDANAO. My commodore was a four-stripe captain.

We would make a call on the British commanding general and the British commanding general would either ignore the call completely as far as a return was concerned, or send his flag lieutenant down. Not his chief of staff, which he should have done, but his flag lieutenant or some such aide. This time the British commander of the Far Eastern Fleet was a vice admiral. So I called on him; buckled on sword and pinned on medals and the like, uniform and all that, and chugged over to the British flagship, which was a sloop about half the size of my flagship and his fleet I think was about half of the size of my squadron. I went in and shook hands and we had about a ten-minute chat. I was never invited to sit down. We both stood up and of course, I didn't dare sit down as long as he stood up, and he reached out and said, "Thanks very much for the call, goodbye", and that's the last I ever saw of him or any of his party. No return call at all, which I thought was rather odd.

Then I went down to the Philippines and had the usual marvelous trip up to Baguio and went out to my old haunts where I had lived as a three to five-year-old at Fort McKinley, and found that my house was still standing and was one of the very few left. The rest had all been smashed during the war. Then, back up to Japan. They were looking for somebody to represent the US Navy at the Shimoda Festival. Shimoda was Perry's home port. It is a gorgeous, little, sort of horn shaped bay, stuck in the pocket of mountains, hardly big enough to get a modern ship in and it contains an old graveyard where some of Perry's sailors were buried back in 1860-'70; somewhere along there. And strangely enough, alongside are some Russian sailors, where Count (Admiral) Putiatin's ships also used to visit, because that was the only open port at that time.

It is an interesting commentary on Count Putiatin, at the time that Perry went out to Japan. Of course, there was a certain rivalry among all the great powers--Russia and the United States and particularly the British and the French, to get into Japan. The British were already pre-eminent on the mainland, China, and the French pretty well too, although much farther down south. The Russians were doing their best although, their installation was still pretty primitive on the Siberian Coast. Vladivostok was just a mud village, more or less, but they had a fleet out there. The Russians were wholly pragmatic about the thing. They perfectly well knew that they couldn't single-handedly cope with the British, but they felt the Americans were in the same spot, so perhaps the two of them together would make a more equal match against the British. It is interesting to recall that when the foreign emissaries were going up the river to Tientsin to carry out the protocols that had been tentatively signed before, to close out the hostilities between the foreign powers and the Chinese, I guess it was in 1870, Admiral Putiatin and the American High Commissioner in China rode up in a Russian ship flying both the Russian and the American flags and the name of the ship was AMERIKA. On the other hand, the British and the French emissaries went up in the same British ship flying their twin flags. So although Putiatin and Perry were competitors, they were friendly competitors. They were both trying for the same thing and Putiatin was set back ever so slightly by the fact that his logistics out there were delicate and to make them ever more so and dependent upon the Americans, Perry had had the foresight to buy up all the coal available in Shanghai. So if Putiatin wanted any, he would have to get it from the Americans. Thereafter however, apparently they were very friendly, and as I say, the Russian bodies and those of the American lie side by side in this very well tended little graveyard, next to the temple where Townsend Harris, the first American consul lived, the American who really set American/Japanese relations on the road in the first place.

This Shimoda Festival had been something that had been developed since the war and, of course, it was a propaganda measure to enhance American/Japanese co-prosperity. The Russians would have loved to have come, and proposed that they send a cruiser. But by the usual Japanese ability to say "No," when you think they are saying "Yes," the Russians never got their foot in. I volunteered myself to go down and represent the US and, of course, that established my real love for Japan. When I first came over there it was with mixed emotions. I had desperately hated the Japanese during the war, because before the war I had been so abused on every occasion where I had to do anything with the Japanese. Let us say if I were riding a horse, nothing a Japanese soldier loved more than to buzz the horse with his motorcycle, scare the horse and throw me off. They had tried it a half dozen times. There was something about a Japanese soldier, prewar, that made him a quite different creature. One time on a trans-Siberian, the Manchurian part of it, there was a group of Japanese station guards and I was looking out the window and here these soldiers with big hobnailed boots were crushing a little puppy that had playfully come out to yap around their feet and one of them put his big hobnailed boots on top of the puppy and rolled it in the dirt like you would a hamburger and it was just a bloody mess. Basically the Japanese soldier was something converted from an ordinary country peasant boy into a fighting machine that had absolutely no compunction about shedding blood, his own or somebody else's. When I got out to Japan I discovered that the whole attitude had changed, it was a completely different ball game; the more I saw it the better I liked it, particularly after this Shimoda episode.

Basically the whole cruise out there was an eye-opener in many respects as far as our own capabilitites were concerned and our own readiness. About the Japanese, of course, I didn't see any Chinese. We couldn't go there except Hong Kong.

Q: What about your own personal arrangements, your family arrangements?

Adm. T.: Vlada had met somebody in San Diego, Mrs. Ray, married to a classmate of mine, who said, "By all means go down to Mexico. It's cheap, it's delightful. You'll love it, and the people are great." So we stored the furniture, bundled the two kids up; they were then about four and six, and down Vlada went to Mexico and discovered (first of all she moved into a boarding house, a sort of super hotel with boarding house arrangements, and it was largely populated by American widows and divorcees who were down there living on the cheap) they were chiefly interested in playing bridge, getting drunk and commiserating and crying into their drinks about their hard life and the duplicity of mankind. Vlada didn't care much for that, so she answered an ad in the paper for an apartment in a private house. She discovered this was a large mansion, a beautifully appointed thing, belonging to the wife of the former Mexican Foreign Minister, who had also been Ambassador to China at one time, and of course she knew all the diplomatic colony. Amongst the diplomats she knew was Edwardo Espinosa who had been the Mexican ambassador in Moscow and was a dear friend of Vlada's. So to sum up the thing, during the six months Vlada was there, she was feted and everything the Mexican diplomatic corps put on in the way of receptions for the foreign embassies Vlada went to. She went to the Soviet Embassy, and Czech Embassy, the British Embassy; you name it she was there, except one--she never got her foot in the American Embassy. She was never invited and never went there. I inquired of the naval attaché if I might direct my mail to him, and he said it wasn't customary and very awkward and he suggested I send it directly to the address concerned.

To get back to Japan again, we had an exercise there with an Army regiment that was stationed on Okinawa. Before I had ever gone out to the Far East with this squadron, while I was still in San Diego, I had heard there was a group of Chinese training over at the amphibious training base which was commanded at that time by Rear Admiral A. E. Jarrell. I like Chinese in general and I thought, well I'll go over and see if I can make myself useful. I met the Chinese Rear Admiral Benjamin Huang and he was voluble in English and Chinese, very jolly and in general sort of looked like a Chinese Santa Claus without the whiskers. I entertained these people at our house and got to be great friends. And, when I went over and deployed with the squadron, I naturally enough looked up Benny. Purely by accident it happened that Benny had been invited to come up and watch this Army exercise. So here I was in Okinawa and along comes Benny and the major general of the Chinese Marines, one of the toughest looking hombres I have ever seen in any Army, and about four captains and a commander or two, up to observe the exercise. While I had been down in Taipei, I had gotten in touch with the Chinese Air Force. I had known this operation was coming off and I also knew that it was almost impossible to get the US Air Force on Okinawa to cooperate in any landing exercise. It had been tried before and the answer was always no.

They were too busy, or their airplanes were down or it didn't fit in with their schedule or something. So I thought we ought to have some airplanes and if we had to do anything at Matsu and Quemoy it will be Chinese airplanes most likely, as ours will be busy elsewhere. So I said, "How about sending some Chinese aircraft up here for this exercise?" "Sure, we will send you our crack squadron." They had an outfit of four airplanes that were, you might say, a copy of the Blue Angels. They were great flat-hatters and stunters and they had hot airplanes and they were hot pilots. So they were up for the exercise, and strangely enough my operations officer, a lieutenant, was a classmate at the Naval Academy of the operations officer of the Air Force unit (US) on Okinawa. They had been roommates at the Naval Academy and classmates. Much to everybody's astonishment, especially that of Admiral Settle, who was commander of the Amphibious Force, when he heard about it back in the States, this guy set up US Air Force cooperation as well, so we had about 15 or 20 US Air Force airplanes in the operation and the Army regiment on board. It was a very successful operation. We took the regiment to sea for about two days and they all got sick naturally enough. We came back in and made a very successful landing. The Chinese airplanes flew like mad all over the place, the US Air Force planes flew all over the place, it was just absolutely a flying circus, it was great.

The only other thing that we did that was notable was to carry Marines, maybe a regiment, but it was a lot of people, from one of their bases on the Inland Sea down to Okinawa. We were gradually phasing out land forces in Japan. Here they were established in what I suppose you would call Marine simplicity. Their barracks were rather Spartan, but they had a very nice club, lots of booze, very cheap, so they put on a grand farewell party to take care of the excess ship's service profits and entertainment money they had in the club. I must say I have rarely been to anything more unusual. I guess that would cover all aspects of it. Of course they were out there without their families, so some of them had become rather friendly, I believe the word is "fraternize", sisterize I guess is what it really means, with some of the Japanese and one or two of the rather senior officers turned up with pretty handsome gals. I think the commanding colonel was rather embarrassed that I was there to observe some of this stuff. Anyway, on it went, including a lot of topless dancers and I hadn't realized that the Japanese were so well endowed, because normally they are rather modest in the way they strap themselves up. It was rather a grand and glorious farewell to Japan as far as that group was concerned. So we hauled them down to Okinawa and that was that.

The time I had left in Japan, of course my chief desire was to come back again. So when the squadron re-deployed to the United States my time was about up. I had had an unusually long tour, a year and a half, which meant that I had had almost six years continuous sea duty and most of it in command.

So I certainly had nothing to complain about. Meanwhile my friendship with Admiral Jarrell had paid off in that, when I discovered that he was about to go out and take command of the Naval Base which went under the conglomerate name of Commander Fleet Activities, Yokosuka, I applied to him to take me out as his Chief of Staff, because I had about three years left of active duty and the chances of being selected at that time for flag rank were not too good. So rather than be drafted to some Naval District as the base dead-end proprietor or some such, I thought nothing could be better than to go out to Japan. Admiral Jarrell was delighted, said, "Sure, I'll take you."

Q: Perhaps we had better stop at this point and say what really turned you around as far as the Japanese were concerned and what had made you like them so much that you wanted to go back.

Adm. T.: I had never really known any Japanese before other than strictly part of the passing scene. Most of the Japanese that I had known were what generally turns out to be the seamier side or the less attractive side and that would be the ones living in China. The same is true in many cases with Americans or any foreigners. They are people that first of all are there because they feel their prospects are better, or that possibly they couldn't make it as well at home, which is highly likely. Small people generally when they are given a little power, a little authority, are overset by it to the point that they become arrogant far beyond the parameters of whatever their authority really is, and they become obnoxious and ill mannered and in general not the type of people that you would feel to be truly representative of the ones you would find back home. I didn't know that in China. I rather suspected that this must be a fair sample of all Japanese. Of course the Japanese military was extremely obnoxious. As I said before, the Japanese Army-- they are the ones who had the military police in Tsingtao and any place I ever went in China where they had control. We rarely made contact with the Japanese Navy, and of course, unfortunately there was this almost insuperable language barrier. Practically none of the Japanese naval officers with whom we came in contact, and that was not often, spoke any English at all and none of us spoke any Japanese. So there was no contact at all with normal Japanese. So when we went to Japan and went to Shimoda and met the mayor and some of the citizens and the townspeople and the traders and so forth, we got a completely different idea. Such things for example, as giving you the wrong change and then running after you for two blocks to give you back two cents. Or the ability to be able to lay something down and not have it stolen. For example, a Navy lieutenant and his Navy nurse friend were out driving in one of the back environs of Yokosuka in a not particularly attractive part of it, and they apparently had a quarrel and the nurse somehow got her escort's wallet and threw the contents thereof out the window. It included a fair amount of money. Of course the lieutenant brought the car to a screeching halt straightaway and almost instantly the crowd of little kids that had rallied around had gathered up all the money and returned it to the lieutenant as if that was the regulation procedure. Now I would hesitate to suggest that such a thing would happen in Harlem or in South Baltimore or any place else I can think of in the United States. Such little instances as that sort of endeared you to these guys, especially when you saw the workmen who came aboard when some of our ships went in for minor overhaul jobs in the yard. These Japanese workmen were something the like of which I hadn't seen since the Philippines, pre-war, where they did an honest day's work, more than what I considered an honest day's work. They were never idle, never leaning on their shovels. The whole picture of it that you saw gave you the impression that they were honest, industrious, sincere, friendly although shy. You would have to take the initiative. They weren't pushy. The sort of people I would like to know more about. I liked the food and I liked the saki, these mild drinks that they went for. Certain aspects of the country were so beautiful that it was breathtaking, although there was a lot of dirt and squalor too. The interior of a Japanese home gave you the idea of such simplicity, such appreciation of art and line, just a universal idea of basic and intrinsic beauty in everything that they all appreciated, universal good taste in things that surrounded them. The whole scenario struck me as being a highly desirable one to know more about and to take part in. So I was delighted when Admiral Jarrell said, "Sure, let's go," and he went on out. He preceded us by about two months and he was pretty well established by the time I got there. The chief of staff had already been there with Admiral Jarrell's predecessor and had served only a year in the job and obviously enough had expected to continue. It was equally obvious that he was very much upset that he was to be displaced. Then he went back to Hawaii. After we had been there for about five months, I guess, Admiral Jarrell was hijacked to go over to Korea. They quickly needed a flag officer over there and he was available in the sense that he was geographically close by. He was sent over on temporary duty and I was upped, temporarily of course, to Commander Fleet Activities. I might add here that this was a tremendous complex; our budget was 25 million dollars a year and the complex involved a supply depot with a captain in command. All these various branches had captains in command except the ordnance depot which had a commander. We had a huge magazine area, some of which still had Japanese munitions in but they had enormous supplies of American munitions out there to support a war. The Korean War had not been over too long, so these supplies were still on hand. There was a shipyard as big as any in the United States almost. They could build ships. They could repair ships. They had a drydock there which was a thousand feet long and could take the biggest ship in the world at that time. They had a Naval Hospital of large proportions and a dental clinic. The housekeeping alone on the base required 2500 American sailors and Marines just for the maintenance of the base itself and supervision of the 15,000 Japanese employees. You can see it was a big organization, it was a big job. In addition to that of course we were constant hosts to the various ships of the Seventh Fleet. There was generally an aircraft carrier or a cruiser or 3 or 4 destroyers or some auxiliary ships in port, sometimes in drydock sometimes in for overhaul. The Asiatic Fleet ships were on a rotating basis, like my amphibious squadron had been. It wasn't until almost the time I left that they started homeporting ships out there, due to the shortage of quarters and facilities for the families. All of the repairs were done out there and much more cheaply than they could be done in Honolulu or Pearl or back in the States.

Q: Was there any resentment on the part of our people due to the fact that the repairs were accomplished out there?

Adm. T.: I was never in a position to know whether there was any resentment back in our own yards, but it certainly was the practice, as far as possible, that any ships deploying out there to defer any repairs they had to make or any alterations and wait until they got to Japan. Not only was it far cheaper, but it was far better done. The yard had a tremendous reputation throughout the Asiatic and throughout the Pacific Fleet because, as I say, most of the ships that operated out there were part of the Pacific Fleet on a temporary basis.

Admiral Jarrell stayed longer and longer and then it became clear that it was more or less a permanent affair. So after about 8 months of that, Commander Naval Forces Far East, Vice Admiral Roscoe Good, with whom I had served when he was a lieutenant and I was an ensign on the CANOPUS in 1932, and thus we had been long and old friends, approved of the way I was running things and particularly the fact that I had gotten on so well with the Japanese. As I say, my love affair with the Japanese had progressed to the point where I had to give speeches to a Japanese audience and I did it in Japanese. That sounds pretty expansive under the circumstances, because Japanese and Chinese both are languages that almost require the precaution of having been born in the country; or at least two or three years of intensive study. But the trick was (by the way, Admiral Jarrell started me on this), he desperately tried to do what he could to learn Japanese and I had a little advantage on him because if you learn one or two languages the third, fourth and fifth come easier. I had a civil service employee with rank equivalent to a commander I guess. He was a naturalized American born in Japan and he spoke impeccable English. He gave me my one hour a day Japanese lesson and would write my speeches for me in Japanese, but in latin letters, so I would actually read it, making the Japanese sounds but reading it from the English text; which of course was perfectly acceptable, because all Japanese read their speeches anyway. I have never yet seen any Japanese make an extemporaneous speech.

Q: Then Japanese lends itself to that technique.

Adm. T.: It does, because it has no inflections and no accent. It is sort of a straight line affair, which, if you speak any Spanish, is not too difficult to pronounce. The pronunciation is not too far off Spanish. As a result of my growing attachments to Japan in general, and the fact that I had made awfully good friends with the mayor and my opposite number, the vice admiral across the creek who was the commandant of the Yokosuka Regional Disitrict of the Maritime Self Defense Force, Admiral Good said there is no reason why you shouldn't be Fleet Activity, you are doing all that is supposed to be done anyway, so he sent back to Washington and made the necessary arrangements and I became Commander Fleet Activities, de facto.

Q: Did you get increased rank then?

Adm. T.: No, no increased rank, but it was a flag billet, as Commander Amphibious Force Western Pacific had been which also was a flag job. That's the way I finished my career out there and as I have mentioned before, I became increasingly aware of the fine qualities of the Japanese. Now I don't mean to say by any means that they are universally so, there were charlatans, there were rascally politicians, and I got to know some of them and understood precisely their shortcomings and rascality. And, not everybody was honest but there were some things you had to learn. For example my wife had a piece of jewelry fixed and very shortly it fell apart. So she took it back to the jeweler and complained, and he said, "Miss you never say Fix number One, you just say Fix," so there are degrees to everything you do and it is pro-rated on a payment basis that way.

Q: She came out, your family was there?

Adm. T.: Oh yes. Of course there are American schools on the base, taught by American teachers. The older one went to the American school, started in the first grade there. The younger one, who was only fourteen months younger--her nose was desperately out of joint because she thought anything her sister could do she could do too. Well, she couldn't go into first grade because it was illegal. So we sent her to a Japanese kindergarten just outside the gate run by the Japanese Catholic sisters. She was the only foreigner in the crowd. She couldn't speak Japanese and none of them could speak any English but she stuck it out. I must say she was a determined little cuss and she stayed there a year by which time she had decided that what she wanted for lunch in her little tin lunch box to take to school was a cold fried egg on a slab of cold mashed potato, just like her Japanese schoolmates had, with a little cold rice on the side with a pickle on it. That year, of course, was a real test in more ways than one. To begin with, I had to walk her out to the main gate and then she would walk from there about a block to the school, or maybe the maid would walk her out, somebody in the family. Then one fine day she turned up after school without anybody having gone out to get her. She had squeezed through the gate, one of the gates that was normally locked except in emergencies. She squeezed through about a six inch crack between the gate and the fence and when the Marines found out about that, they were aghast. They said, "You shouldn't do that! That's illegal. You mustn't do that." The Marines being a regulation lot. That's the way she got her start. They had their adventures too. The older one got hit by a Japanese taxi. We had base taxis; she was riding her bike and one of them bumped into her, not too high speed, threw her on the cowling of the car. It was pitiful almost, the anguish of this taxi driver. I suppose it was partly due to the fact that he had hit the base commander's kid. But the other fact was that they just had that compassion about anything like that. If you hit a drunk, for example, in Japan you are responsible, not the drunk. You are supposed to look out for drunks, for people who can't take care of themselves; the same for kids. They have a desperate fondness for kids. They are desperately spoiled, and allowed to do almost anything they want to at the age of 3, 4 or 5, males or females. So this poor devil went out and bought an enormous doll. I am sure it must have cost him half a month's wages and came around and insisted that we take it for the little girl that he had hit.

Q: The Japanese by this time had begun to reconstruct their country, had they not?

Adm. T.: Japan was a rapidly growing concern. The only thing that I deeply regret is that I didn't invest some money in Japanese stocks around that time. In fact, if I had invested in the stocks like some Americans did out there in 1954 when I first got out there, they increased in value about 20 times. Such things as Sony, which is now a familiar household word in the United States, or three or four electronics outfits, or Mitsubishi, the shipbuilding outfit, or Tokyo Electric, Tokyo Shibara; any one of a hundred stocks, I could be rich now, if I had had a little money to start with. But that of course, is water under the bridge.

Q: Tell me a little about the social life when you were in command of the base.

Adm. T.: Well, as the man at the top of the pole, I was invited to everything, and as a result, that meant Japanese parties too. I would say that in the average week, we would be at home for dinner one time at the most, we rarely had dinner at home and of course the kids never saw us except when they came home from school for a little while and when they shoved off in the morning, which was a bad thing. On weekends we sometimes went out to the beach with the kids but they were pretty well, I imagine, in the same groove that so many really wealthy families in this country are guilty of and their kids grow up more or less orphans. But, this was for a relatively short time so they managed to weather it.

The parties were of an enormous variety. They had the biggest club in the United States, when I say United States I mean under the supervision of Americans, in Yokosuka and it was enormously rich. The booze was, of course, duty free out there. A bottle of gin cost sixty cents and a bottle of whiskey a dollar and a half, so the cocktails were all a quarter apiece. In order not to gyp the poor character who was drinking martinis versus scotch, they served the martinis in champagne glasses. When visiting groups of skippers would come into the Brass Hat Bar (that was a separate bar for commanders and above) there would be rounds of drinks rolled for and roller A would drink whiskey and soda, roller B would drink a martini and then it would come time to roll again. There wasn't anything much else to do except chat and roll for drinks and pretty soon the martini customer would be pretty well ready to be carried out, drinking these martinis in the champagne glasses versus the whiskey drinker with the usual one ounce. You saw some funny things in there. The visiting ship, of course, they weren't too aware of what the real state of affairs was, but some reacted pretty rapidly. I recall one remarkable fellow of the Class of '28. He had been married and re-married several times. He played the piano beautifully; he painted;

in fact he painted so well he had completely papered, in effect not only the walls but the overhead in his stateroom of the CHAUMONT when he was on duty there. He had come out to Japan in command of a destroyer squadron and I went in there one day to say hello. I always liked to check in and see who was on board, if they were having a good time, and was there anything wrong, and so forth, and this gentleman had a shoe box on his lap and I thought, "What have you bought, Joe." He opened it up and it looked like a horse's tail, which I remarked on, and he said, "That's not a horse's tail, that's a Japanese girl's hair, she was so disappointed when I left that she cut off all her hair and put it into this shoe box and gave it to me." He was a fast worker. He had been in town only about a week. One of the rather odd duties I had was to adjudicate in marriages. They did all they could to discourage inter-racial marriages there, for two reasons. One was they felt it was on the spur of the moment, and the second that they might not work back home, and thirdly the Japanese didn't like it because it was an utter disaster for the Japanese family for their offspring to marry a foreigner. They consider us, discreetly of course, because they don't say so openly, but they consider us a lower form of human life; the Chinese even more so. The Chinese consider the Japanese distinctly down the human scale from them. They call them wojen (dwarf), a deprecatory term. In order for an American service man to marry over there, they have to go through as tough a rigamarole as could legally and logically be devised in the hopes that maybe the guy would have a change of heart, or that the girl would drop dead or he would be ordered home or that something would turn up that would turn off the heat. Among these things was first of all, sending home to the girl's village. Most of the girls that they met, sailors at any rate, were cabaret girls and Yokosuka had street after street of cabarets all sizes, all qualities, and they were populated largely by farm girls who were sending the much needed money home. What actual bargain was arrived at I don't know, when they are actually in effect sold (in the old days they actually used to sell their daughters for cash money), in any case here they were, mostly country bumpkins, some of them extremely pretty and some of them not so very, but females in any case and that, frequently, after five or six drinks was all that mattered as far as the guy on liberty was concerned. They would strike up an attachment and then they would find that for a relatively modest sum they could set up housekeeping ashore. Of course, in the case of the people attached to the base, the 2,500 sailors on the base, that was easy. Now a lot of those were married too. We had married enlisted men's quarters and there were lots of married families there, but a lot of them weren't, particularly the Marines. They seemed to be more on the loose than most of them. There were 250 Marines stationed there as perimeter guards. Of course, the ships coming in and out were in a less favorable position to push romance but some managed to do it, and then they would have to send home to the girl's village to get the family register and they would send copies of it down, which is a very laborious thing as obviously there were no Xerox machines, from some Japanese mountain village so it would all have to be transcribed by hand, five or ten pages reaching back sometimes, so help me, four or five hundred years. They would send the whole thing down, a copy of the family tree for four or five hundred years back. Then they would have a long session with the padre, then they would have a long session with their division officer, then they would be counselled by a Japanese priest, to be sure both sides understood the gravity of what they were about to get into. Well, there was a six months' waiting period, but after all this phoopheraw was gone through there was still quite a number of them. The last time I checked; I was writing an article on the subject, in about 1967, there were upward of 75,000 Japanese war brides which had come over since about 1948. Up until that time there was no fraternization. They weren't even allowed to go around and hold hands with the Japanese if they could catch them at it. After that, the ball started rolling and there was a constant stream. I must say that once the die was cast, everybody cooperated to the utmost. The enlisted men's wives, the Naval officers' wives, all did their damndest to try to make these kids feel at home. Lots of them hadn't the foggiest idea how to change a diaper, they don't use diapers in Japan in the sense that we do. How to fry an egg; they didn't fry an egg the way we do. Everything that could be construed as American housekeeping they knew nothing about. How to make a bed; they didn't sleep in beds, they slept on the deck. How to iron a shirt; they didn't wear shirts, they wore kimonos in that sense. So the Navy housewives would take these kids into their homes and run courses for them, how to make custard pie and a few other things and then they would have a big graduation. The graduation would take place in the equivalent of a town meeting hall. It actually was the parish house. I would make a speech half in Japanese and half in English, while these gals could barely speak the language. The romance must have been carried on in a purely physical sense. All the happy brides would rally around and I would shake hands with them and we would drink tea and eat cookies and they would be off on their way to the States. I was very curious to find out how this whole schmozzle came out, so I wrote to the American Red Cross in Washington and asked them to look into it, because after all, I was in a position to throw my weight either this way or that as far as the marriages were concerned. They wrote back and said that they were highly successful, that they were very few retrogressions, that practically none of the gals had turned to prostitution, which in effect some of them were when they started. At least, they had rather loose morals, which the Japanese basically have anyway. Very few of them wanted to go back to Japan. They more or less gravitated to the big cities like Chicago, New York, Baltimore, San Francisco and so forth, where the men found people in similar circumstances, so they were sort of grouped together in mutual support, so to speak. There is a colony here in Baltimore. They have a Doll Festival every year and I go down there and look at the dolls and eat Japanese cakes and see the husbands and the wives and see that everything is going fine. Of course by this time some of them have their children, some of them are little beauties, and as far as I know they have never caused any trouble legally or in any respect. They have been highly successful. That was one aspect of it.

The other was attempting to arrange some sort of a reasonable liberty town where temptations were great, prices were low, people were far away from home and controls were tenuous. We had to be awfully careful, because the Japanese are extremely touchy about any human contact or damage to an individual. If for example, a sailor would get drunk and beat up a Japanese, that was no laughing matter. It is not just like a couple of bums getting into a street fight. The Shore Patrol might arrest the guy, but the Japanese would demand custody, and he would be tried by a Japanese jury or a Japanese court and in certain cases these guys with a really serious crime would wind up in a Japanese prison, which is no Hilton Hotel.

Q: There was one rather notable case, was there not?

Adm. T.: There have been cases of murder and mayhem and rape and things like that and some of these birds have been sentenced to eight, ten, fifteen, twenty years or life in Japanese prisons and there they stayed. They are far better off than the Japanese prisoners. I have gone to inspect the prison where our people are kept. They have a little cell, and a desk. They live singly in cells but they bow from the waist when the jailor comes in, they wear Japanese clothes, eat Japanese food and smoke Japanese cigarettes when they can get them; it is not a jolly life. First of all, we had to try to keep the sailors themselves from committing mayhem on each other and particularly for them not to try the same on the Japanese. In order to do that we had probably the toughest Shore Patrol in the United States Armed Services. When they found some sailor who looked like he was about to get out of hand, he was leaned against the wall with his hands up on the wall and spread eagled out from it so he couldn't resist and he was patted from top to bottom to see what he had in the way of weapons. He was pretty roughly handled; the word got around and you didn't treat the patrol lightly. Time and again I had skippers come up and complain saying, "This is ridiculous the way your people man-handle our men. They've been out on a long cruise." Some of the submarine cruises would come across half the way under water and operate off the Soviet coast for two or three weeks and then come down to Yokosuka and they wanted to hit the beach and hit it hard. All I had to do was to show them "Chamber of Horrors", which is an exhibit as big as a screen, 4 x 10 feet, completely covered by weapons taken from the sailors. They would start off of course with the usual jack-knife or the flip out knife that the Italian gangsters are reputed to use. They would roll a piece of lifeline chain in their neckkerchief and put it around their neck. They would bury a razor blade with only about 1/8 of an inch showing out of a potato and put it in their sock and with that they would take a swipe across somebody's back and it would cut through the jumper and just the outer part of the skin and leave a huge, awfully bloody but not too serious, gash, and it would just absolutely horrify the guy who would think he was bleeding to death. They had brass knuckles. They would put five or six copper pennies in the end of the fingers of each glove and slap somebody across the face with it. The inventions they would cook up to defend themselves, which was the original purpose they thought, but which inevitably got into action when they got into a simple scrap. This meant that the hospital on the weekends absolutely looked like there had been a disaster. My younger daughter, Nina, had a nosebleed one night at three o'clock in the morning. It was so bad we couldn't do anything about it, so we took her over to the hospital. She was surprised but I was dumbfounded. I didn't realize such things happened. Here in the receiving room were about ten or twelve bodies. That's all you could say, Bodies. They looked like corpses.

Bloody, dirty, torn clothes, a wreck. Poor little Nina said, "Daddy, what happened?" I asked the same thing. They said, "This goes on every Saturday night." So I started to get statistics and totted up man hours lost, what ships were involved, where had they been and under what circumstances and how long they had been out of port; what did these guys do to get in this shape? Where did they get the booze and in what places and so forth? So we finally arrived at some pretty good statistics after which we started to control this business. Again, here I was at the top of the pile and didn't realize what was going on. I had never gone to the hospital at three o'clock in the morning to find out, and it was just by accident that I did that. The first thing we did, we had a package store at the huge enlisted men's club, one of the biggest I am sure in the Armed Services, seven stories, with every conceivable thing in there. We had a package store where any sailor could go over and buy a bottle of booze, gin for 60¢, a bottle of whiskey for $1.50 and so forth. So Mr. Seaman Second Class would go over and buy himself a quart and tuck it under his arm and go off to the various cabarets, because the Japanese hard liquor was very expensive. A bottle of whiskey in Japan cost $7.00. Any hard liquor, gin, whiskey, anything you liked, 7 or 8 dollars. So mixed drinks were expensive. Normally the sailors would only drink beer. They wouldn't attempt to get foreign liquor unless they bought it in the package store and carried it out. So what happens? Here is a young sailor, 18 or 19 years old with a whole bottle of booze. What is he going to do? He doesn't want to throw it away, so he tries to drink it all, and it floors him, knocks him out. He is a casualty, either by the booze or getting into a fight and getting laid low before he gets to drink it all. That sort of thing happened. So we chopped off the package store for anybody except married enlisted men. There was a frightful howl, letters to the <u>Navy Times</u>, letters to this and that, letters to Congressmen, discriminating against the unmarried man. So I had to reply to all that stuff and we finally got it back on the rails and everybody realized, especially the bo'sn's mates who had to deal with all these hangovers the next morning, they were all delighted that all these clamps were put on. Then we had the control of the various cabarets. We had an inspection team, which, of course, we had to change the character of about once every three weeks, because any oriental is marvelous at the old bribe game, and as soon and they got into a job like that the temptations were terrific.

Q: This was Sanitary Inspection?

Adm. T.: We had a Sanitary Inspection Team that would go out and look in the kitchens and go upstairs and look around where the girls were and so forth, where the cabaret girls all lived, over the top of the cabaret. They weren't houses of prostitution in that sense although some of them were such places; usually they would take the girl some place else. Go to a cheap hotel, if they could manage to do that.

So each one of these houses that passed inspection we gave a sign that said "Registered # so and so, in bounds". If they didn't have this sign, a sailor couldn't go in there. Or if he did, on the way out he would get nabbed by the Shore Patrol and they would end his fun right there but quick, and back to the base he would go with his liberty card in escrow. That word soon got around. Strangely enough there were some Japanese establishments that didn't want the "In Bounds" sign. They were delighted with this thing because the last thing they wanted was some drunken sailor barging in and demanding a bottle of beer or whiskey, whereas this was simply a sushi parlor where they served saki and raw fish. They didn't want Americans in there scaring the bejesus out of their regular customers. On the other hand, there were always infractions. There was a bunch of gangsters involved in these places and to keep tabs on this stuff, I felt, after I had been over there about a year, I agreed we couldn't trust anybody. The damndest things went on. For example, refrigerators were extremely highly valued. We could get a thousand dollars for a new refrigerator in Japan because they weren't allowed to be imported. The exchange control was on. So we discovered that civilians and employees of the Ship's Service would order X number of refrigerators to be sent out for the Ship's Service to the United States on special order. You could order anything out there, including an automobile. They would add on a few for themselves and those would go out the back door of the warehouse and of course, this was a growing concern. That sort of stuff you simply had to do personally. You couldn't trust anybody. In order to do this I strictly forbade my picture ever being taken and my picture was never taken, though lots of people would have loved to be shown with the commander shaking hands, or the boss inspecting the troops and all that. My picture never appeared anywhere and I would go out there personally and go through these cabarets, go out to the Ship's Service place and go in the back door. They had one section of Yokosuka which was known as the "Heavenly Kingdom" and was only for black sailors and white sailors went in there at their own risk. Basically they stayed clear of it. It had a gate, and it had a big flowery decoration in neon lights over top of it and only black boys went through there, excepting the Shore Patrol. But they didn't go in there very much, they policed their own area. Well, I thought I would go down there one night. So I started out in my civilian clothes and told the Shore Patrol where I was going and they said, "Sir, don't go down there, don't even dare," and I said, "Why not?" They said, "It's just plain dangerous, we'll go with you," and I said, "Don't come close, I don't want these guys to think I'm going down there on an armed guard tour or anything like that." I walked in one of these places, all black, Japanese gals of course, and I was greeted not by a handshake but a reach for the crotch, they would reach for your crotch and give it a good shake, sort of jingle it, so to speak. Apparently that was the password. I went in and looked around, everybody looked me over, nothing happened and I walked out and the Shore Patrol said, "Come on, let's get out of here, that's enough." And then there were all sorts of fast-buck operators and it worked the other way too. There was a Japanese, an amazing fellow who had been in Shanghai when I was there in 1934 except he was on duty on the other side of the street so to speak. He spoke perfect English, as he had been to college in the United States, and he was then with one of the big shipbuilding companies as sort of a liaison man with the Naval Base. We did a lot of business with the Japanese shipbuilding companies, because we had the only really big drydocks in the whole area and they would hire our drydocks to complete ships.

Q: The big tankers were coming in then?

Adm. T.: They would come in there, after their standardization trials and whatnot, to get certain alterations made. They didn't come in for overhaul. It was mostly with new ships. So, they all have liaison officers. This guy was baldheaded, so we couldn't tell whether he had kinky hair or not, and he looked like a negro. George Misoda was his name. He and I got to be great friends. He loved martinis and I would get him a bottle of gin now and then and pour three or four drops of vermouth in it and he would take home a bottle of martinis, which was the way he liked them. I took George out on a tour one night and went into several of these cabarets and every one that I went into in the white section said, "Get that nigger out of here." He was a Japanese but he looked like a black boy and they didn't want him in the white section.

Q: That was quite a job, playing father to that whole outfit.

Adm. T.: One of the extraordinary aspects with the Japanese was the vast difference between the civilian Japanese and the Japanese Self Defense Force, most of whom, the older ones at any rate, my contemporaries, were ex-Japanese Imperial Navy and I felt perfectly at home with them. Most of them spoke a fair degree of English but, for example I am of the Class of '29 at the Naval Academy and there were enough '29ers from the Japanese Naval Academy to make up a dinner party. Whenever Vlada would go on a trip, down to Kobe or someplace, I would have a bachelor party in my quarters for the Japanese Classmates of '29, and we'd have a marvelous time. We would bring over waitresses from the club to act. They all sang and they were very personable, very pretty, beautiful kimonos, and for about 50¢ apiece for the evening (we would pay the club for their services over there), they would come over and be, in effect, informal geisha at our party. We saw eye to eye and got along famously. Now civilians would come over there under similar circumstances; some of the shipping people who used to entertain me, or some of the town politicians and whatnot, and there was a subtle but very noticeable difference in our ability to get along socially.

There was always a gap between us and the Japanese civilians. It could have been my own reaction.

I guess one of the most unusual opportunities I had there was to pick the brains and pump the memories of the Imperial Japanese officers who had had important places in the war. For example, my opposite number across the creek was for a while, an ex-flier in the Imperial Japanese Navy and he had quite a row of ribbons. He was the one who was so receptive to my idea for the restoration of the MIKASA. When I first went out there in 1954 with the squadron the MIKASA was a shapeless hulk. Of course, it was the old Imperial HIJMS MIKASA which had been Togo's flagship at Tsushima when they beat the Russians. When Nimitz had come out there he had spotted the thing and he, like I, had contacts with the Japanese before the war. But he was far more fortunate in his contacts in that he had been CO of the flagship cruiser AUGUSTA in '36-'37 along there, and had made several visits to Japan and they had been so charmed with the place that Mrs. Nimitz, instead of living in China like most of the wives, had stayed in Japan for the time, because the flagship moved around so much it really wasn't worthwhile to try to settle any place definite in China. The ships went down to Manila in the wintertime. But in the summer they were all over the place. So they had a great affinity with Japan. They lived in the country. They knew the common people, the poor people, not the military. So when Nimitz saw the frightful state the MIKASA was in--

they had torn it to pieces for scrap, souvenirs and what-have-you, it was just completely neglected. He put a guard on it and forbade any further demolition. Shortly after that, her guns had been removed largely under the influence of the Russians, who of course, were very keen that she be completely demolished and obliterated because it was a very gruesome memory as far as they were concerned.

Q: Even though it was Imperial Navy?

Adm. T.: It didn't matter, Russians are Russians, by that time it wasn't the second Imperialist War any more it was the Great Patriotic War. They had brought back shoulder boards and the Orthodox Archbishop and all that stuff, they had dusted off a lot of the old Imperial traditions which they had never really lost. Of course, MacArthur very astutely saw the handwriting on the wall; if the Russians should ever occupy Hokkaido, which they desperately wanted to do, it would be part of Russia right now if they had. He was so repressive in his treatment of the Soviet representatives in Tokyo that they finally pulled out and left, rather than to lose face under the circumstances. The Russian Control Mission departed. MIKASA minus her guns, which at least that far the Russians had got, lay there as a hulk. They built a dancehall on top of it and the thing was absolutely disreputable. So after Admiral Nimitz retired, he wrote a little article for a Japanese periodical, pushing the idea of restoring the MIKASA as a national memorial.

At that stage of the game, 1956 or '57, along in there, the Japanese people in general thought that the military was so discredited that anything to do with the military--the hell with it. They weren't interested. At least Admiral Nimitz got them off to a minor start by contributing the money that he had got from the article to this fledgling society for the reconstitution of the MIKASA. This was mostly an organization of ex-Imperial Navy people. Of course, they were having a hard time even getting off the ground. They made a collection which I sponsored on the base amongst the enlisted men and the officers and the ships in port. It ran to about three thousand dollars, which wasn't an inconsiderable sum, when you consider it was for something in which they had absolutely no basic interest. They had scraped up about another three thousand from the Japanese MSDF personnel (Maritime Self Defense Force) and they were, of course, living on a shoestring too, so it didn't look like it was getting very far. We had an LST hulk lying there in the base, which originally had been the property of the Army down in Okinawa and it was on nobody's books. It had been brought up to Yokosuka and during the Korean War had been used for excess barracks space. Of course that was 6 or 7 years previous, Meanwhile, it was more or less being held together by layers of paint, rust underneath. So the thought struck me "Why not contribute this LST which is not signed up to anybody as far as I could determine, contribute it to the MIKASA fund? They could sell it for scrap and get them off the ground."

So I went over to see Admiral Freddie Withington, my next door boss and he said, "Great, that's all right with me."

My tour had been extended and I had to come back to Washington. I was supposed to leave Japan after three years, in January of 1959. I was to retire in June of 1959, so what would I do with six months? In order to prepare my Ma for the blow, (She was pretty old by them and feeble) I got permission to take a couple of weeks leave and fly back and prepare her for it and also to polish off a few items in Washington. They had a building ways, an overhead building crane in a building ways on which they had built some of these earlier Japanese battleships in Yokosuka, which was then the Imperial Japanese Navy Yard. It was in bad repair and something had to be done to it. It cost money to paint it. We were merely custodians of Yokosuka. In other words, we were sort of renters without rent. We were holding the place in trust and eventually everybody knew we would give it back to the Japanese, ten years, a hundred years, who knew? Why hold on to and pay the repairs on parts that we did not need and the Japanese would desperately like to have? The thing to do there was to turn back this building ways and about five acres of contiguous territory. So I flew back to Washington: a - to straighten my Ma out and b - to work on this building ways thing and c - to try to push the MIKASA thing through, this LST deal. Well, just exactly as the Japanese had predicted when I offered the thing to them, they said, "there is going to be

one hell of a lot of red tape on your side and my side."
There was, but after I had been relieved, the Navy Department
said, "Okay, give it to the MIKASA Fund." They sold it for
twenty million yen, about 67 thousand bucks, which was about
one-third of the total cost to rehabilitate the MIKASA,
which of course endeared me deeply with the Japanese.
Incidentally, I managed also to get an Okay, which was a purely
pragmatic thing and to our advantage--to give this building
ways back. They gave that back too, and the Japanese thought
that was magnificient; they thought that was the most wondrous
thing ever. Probably that was why I got a Japanese decoration
when I left, complete with band ceremony and a parade and
all that.

Q: You did want to say something about the Soviet contact.

Adm. T.: I will get to that but one thing I would like to
add in here, at this atage of the game the Japanese Maritime
Self Defense Force was absolutely scraping the bottom of
the barrel, moneywise.

Q: They were not favorites with the Japanese public, were they?

Adm. T.: None of the military were favorites. They had been
wholly discredited, because they had lost the war. But, the
other aspect of it was: they were on our side, something
had to be done about it. We had to support them in our own
best interest, at least to a point. The Japanese JMSDF
of course was very much afraid that the various advantages

of having the yard, like the building ways, the drydocks, this and that, all of which commercial Japanese were desperately keen to get, would fall into commercial hands and then, if and when they ever reached a little higher spot on the totem pole it would be too late. In other words, we were the custodians for the JMSDF in the era to come.

Q: Until such time as public opinion turned?

Adm. T.: Right. Here I was stuck on dead center. If I gave it back to the civilians, I would be doing a big favor to the civilian economy of Japan, the shipbuilders and all these people who were trying to get foreign currency; mind you they weren't as rich then as they are now, even though it was only fifteen years ago. If I gave back too much, then I knew the Japanese Military Self Defense Force would never get it back, so I had to walk a tight line between. For example, Admiral Withington lived in what used to be the residence of the senior admiral of that whole region, and Yokosuka was the top of the Japanese Imperial pile-naval and it was an enormous, beautiful residence, largely in Japanese style but with a Western end on it and it was about a mile out from town. This was an anachronism in some respects, in that here was our senior admiral living a mile away from the base, whereas on the base there were two very nice admirals' quarters, sets of quarters. The Japanese civilians, the mayor, was desperately keen to get that residence back for the mayor's house. He was living in some unpretentious little two by four up on the hill. The Japanese Navy said, "For God's sake don't give it back, because we'll never see it again and one day we hope our own admiral will be living in there." That's the sort of thing we had to contend with.

Q: Tell me about your Soviet contact.

Adm. T.: I first bumped into this guy in a destroyer that we made a little cruise on, which incidentally is an interesting vignette in Japanese Navy current reactions. This was a brand new destroyer escort. This was before Admiral Jarrell left, and they invited Admiral Jarrell and of course, I went along as chief of staff. Also, some of the naval attachés, including the Soviet, to take a ride on this new ship. Out we went into Tokyo Bay. It was cold and foggy and we were up on the bridge watching everything go by. Then back to Yokosuka into the Japanese side of the Naval Base. They had a small enclave over there for their ships. Here we were, steaming along, coasting along about 8 or 10 knots and here came a junk, right across the bow. Like in China the junks figured that the best way to cut devils off their tail is to go as close as they can to somebody else and then the devils would perforce get stuck aboard the guy that cut across his wake. Whether that was his intention or not I don't know but instead of giving a slight change of course to the right, this Japanese skipper, a lieutenant commander with all this brass aboard, a Japanese

vice admiral, an American rear admiral, a whole clutch
of naval attachés and stuff, he froze. He just froze on
the bridge and we just stood there gripping the rails until
we said to ourselves "For God's sake, do something!", inwardly.
We couldn't say anything outwardly. Nobody on the bridge
said a word, as far as the Japs were concerned and "BANG"
into this fishing junk they went. It slid off the portside
down the side, scraped the paint, a few dents here and there.
Without a word, the Japanese admiral's chief of staff,
Etichi Sugie, Classmate, '29, Etajima and a dear friend of
mine and still is, without so much as a word (like saying
"I take command," or "stand clear", or anything like that) he
took charge of the situation (he was a captain then). And
I said, "That guy is going to make it big", just like I
said years ago that H. Page Smith was going to make it big.
Of course, Etichi Sugie wound up first as Chief of the
Maritime Self Defense Force staff and then Chief of the
Joint Chiefs of Staff, like Tom Moorer is. There you have
the two kids: the lieutenant commander who froze, who
did nothing and in a crisis became utterly useless; this
other guy who reacted automatically and took control of the
situation and brought it off. Whatever happened to the
lieutenant commander I don't know, I am sure nothing good.
Along with this crowd was a colonel in the Soviet Army and
a lieutenant commander in the Soviet Navy. The colonel was
dressed up in something that any bellhop in New York hotels
would be flabbergasted to see, red piping, green piping,

purple pants and a red hatband. Honestly, it was the most fantastic galaxy of color you ever saw. Ridiculous. Just plain ridiculous. But that was his idea of a dress uniform.

Q: Is the Russian at liberty to choose his own?

Adm. T.: No, that was the official Russian dress uniform of that day and he absolutely looked like a clown. The commander was in an ordinary blue Navy uniform a lot like ours and obviously he was the working member. I found out later he had a beautiful wife and they had insinuated themselves into the foreign society and were asking all sorts of penetrating questions and doing very well. But the colonel in the Army was obviously an old sergeant who came up the hard way.

We got back in again and I forgot all about it. I had gone up and said, "Hello" and "How are you enjoying the cruise" and all that, but then I forgot about those guys. Well, then an Indian cruiser came in. I think its name was NEW DEHLI, the only cruiser in the Indian Navy. It was a beautiful thing. They had taken over the traditions that of course were originally British. Gorgeous red and white striped awning, and they had a huge cocktail party on the fantail, the after deck, and all the dignitaries of Tokyo were invited. Of course, they had some Indian cadets aboard and some of these guys wore turbans, which of course indicated that they were Moslems. Some were bareheaded because the whole show was under cover. In many similar situations you will find midshipmen for example, all grouped together and the hell with guests. The guests will make their own way. But these Indians were absolutely the very model of wonderful hosts and they were going around mixing with the guests and offering drinks and all speaking perfectly good English and I saw over there on one side a Soviet rear admiral. I walked over, along with Vlada. He was surrounded by two or three Indians. I introduced myself in Russian and about that time an Indian cadet with a turban on came up and stuck out his hand and the Soviet rear admiral completely ignored him. This, as far as I could determine, was not an unusual gesture on the part of a race or nationality that is exceedingly rank conscious. I had noticed that in the Soviet Union, for example, when a three striper pulled out a cigarette about six lieutenants were there instantly with a match. When somebody invited a senior officer to a party and also invited someone that they considered too far down the totem pole, a clerk let us say, the senior officer wouldn't come when he found out about this. It didn't surprise me at all to see rather an air of disdain on the part of the Soviet rear admiral when he failed to be chummy with the Indian cadet. I didn't take offense at it. That was his business and not mine.

Q: As a footnote, how does this stack up in a Communist society?

Adm. T.: It stacks up absolutely 100% because there is no

place in the world where the pecking order is more distant than in the Soviet Union, both in the political order and in the military order. When a Soviet officer comes onto a streetcar and there is a Soviet soldier sitting down, the soldier gets up and offers the officer the seat and he takes it. The same is true in almost all aspects of Soviet life. There are all sorts of special prerogatives and it doesn't just extend to military rank. For example, there are other aspects of it. A pregnant woman gets on the front end of the streetcar instead of the back end, or, widows of old bolsheviks get a special ID card which allows them to go to the head of the line and buy many things at half price-- theatre tickets, train rides and things of that nature. So it is a country of privileged classes far more than we are. There is no democracy in the real sense in which we understand it--that all people are created equal and remain equal. It will never happen there.

To get back to this Soviet, he turned out to be an exceedingly nice guy. He had a set of stainless steel teeth from ear to ear, and obviously a very plebian background. Just how he got to be a naval attaché nobody here will ever know, but in any case, he was probably thoroughly reliable. Otherwise, he would never have been sent out of the country, particularly since he had his wife along with him. But his children were still in the Soviet Union, as hostages in effect. We tentatively agreed to meet again and he said, "I suppose you wouldn't care to come to my house, so I would be very happy to take you to lunch in a restaurant some place." and I said, "We would be delighted to come to your house." Obviously he thought perhaps we would be embarrased or we might be followed; that the American secret police might report on us if we came to his house or the Japanese secret police, or something. Anyway we did eventually go to his house for lunch and had a delightful time. Of course foundered with food and learned a little about his background and it was really a comedy in some respects. His wife looked to be the real boss of the show. She was a real female "Sandow the wrestler", also pretty well equipped with stainless steel teeth. They were delighted to see us. They said that they had very few contacts in Tokyo, that the Japanese didn't like them and they didn't like the Japanese and the only company they had was their own embassy pals and they pretty soon wore thin. They had an enormous dog; one of the biggest dogs I ever saw, a prestige item I guess, because dogs are pretty rare in the Soviet Union; they were then. After we had chatted for about ten or twelve minutes he said, "Well, its time to crack a bottle," so off we went to this groaning board, absolutely loaded with sakousa of all kinds, bottles of wine, vodka all over the place and he said, "I've got high blood pressure and why not, look at this." Of course all Soviet officials have high blood pressure. It is endemic amongst them, due to the worry and the pressures on them. After the dinner was over the comrade admiral took his shoes off and they turned on the radio and got Moscow somehow and it was playing a high speed tune. They loved loud, fast music; he took his shoes off and danced around on the floor with Vlada and had a marvelous time. Later when I came back to Japan in 1961 on temporary duty, called back to active duty, he was still there and still very friendly and he recalled the occasion when I had invited him down to my quarters on Yokosuka. In return for this dinner at his house I said, "Why not come down to Yokosuka?" And he said, "I couldn't do that, the Japanese won't allow it. I'm not supposed to stir outside of Tokyo without special permission." And I said, "Get special permission, it's not all that difficult. If it's embarrassing to you, I will meet you outside the Navy Yard gate in my car (and I described it to him) and you come down there at such and such a time and you can jump out of your car and into mine." I learned later that he came down there about an hour early, having gotten official permission to visit Yokosuka and had circled around all over the place for about an hour, casing the joint so to speak, and then had come over and he and his wife had hopped out of their car into mine and left his outside, and then came inside and to his utter astonishment I took him on a tour of the base, not down to where the ships were, but I am sure it would have been all right to do that, and then he came (still with his jaw hung down) with his wife over to the house (which we had bugged for sound, by the way, to be sure we didn't miss anything) and he was very easy on the vodka.

He didn't drink nearly as much as he did at home. During the course of the conversation I said, "Well Comrade Admiral," [I like to try this on these guys, they don't respond generally. I have been called Comrade myself very infrequently by the Soviets,] "Comrade Admiral, you know we were allies once before during the war between you and the Germans and we were in there on your side. Maybe we will be allies again, this time against the Chinese." Of course at that stage of the game-- this was before the big break-up, but the first cracks in the dike were already appearing in 1956, but this was in 1958 and the real breach had not yet occurred. He got all red in the face and he said, "What about Korea?" apropos of nothing at all. He was backed into a corner and obviously he was very much upset about the whole thing and it took some little time to get the conversation back on a reasonable track again in a friendly fashion. When I came back in 1961 I was invited to the US Naval attache's house for dinner and Ouspensky was invited too. His wife had meanwhile gone home. I said, "Comrade Admiral, do you remember that occasion three or four years ago when I mentioned the fact that you and I might be allies against the Chinese?" and he said, "Comrade Admiral (this time he said Comrade) I remember it very well, you were right and I was wrong." By that time, of course, the crack was wide open.

You have probably heard from time to time that there have been Japanese demonstrations against atomic armed ships coming in, atomic submarines, but it goes farther than that, aircraft carriers with, presumably, atomic bombs on too. Everybody had been mum about this. The governments of both countries have played it in a low key and the thing has died away. When I was there, with all these carriers coming in, I knew perfectly well they had atomic arms aboard. That was standard armament and equipment for ships in that area. I said nothing about it. Didn't get into the business at all. If they transferred the stuff ashore for storage or for repairs or back out again, that was none of my business and I found out that was a very wise course. Some years after I had come back to the States, I have kept in pretty close contact with some of my old friends and staff officers out there and they said, "You know, Admiral, I shouldn't tell you this I guess, but we were instructed by a high authority, way around the corner, not to tell you anything about transfer of atomic equipment in Yokosuka because then if you were asked or if anything came up you could honestly say, 'I don't know a thing about it.' It went on at a working level and you were not supposed to know and that is why you weren't informed. But I think you ought to know about it now."

Q: Didn't we have a policy however, in terms of the atomic submarines, getting permission from the government to come in? We did in China and in the Philippines.

Adm. T.: Off-hand I can't remember whether the submarines that came out there at that time were atomic propelled or not,

I'm inclined to believe they weren't. Maybe they were, but it wasn't so much the atomic propulsion that the Japs were worried about, it was the atomic armament, the fact that they carried the bombs on board. Everybody pretty well knew that the atomic propulsion thing was absolutely safe, but somehow or other, bombs were different. They were the offensive aspect of it. After all, the atomic propulsion of the submarines was just a matter of a means of getting from here to there. The bomb was something that you could throw against anybody--them, the Chinese. They were anti-bomb, period. Not necessarily atomic propulsion, that was quite a different question.

An example of some of the real skull-crackers that come along when you have a job like that, was the case of the Naval Academy Stadium Gate. There had been a terrific contest between the commanders Sixth Fleet and Seventh Fleet as to who should raise the most money for a gate at the new Navy Stadium in Annapolis. I don't know what the procedure was for the Sixth Fleet, but in the Seventh Fleet, their staff and commander had in effect carried on a shake-down campaign amongst the tailors and the various cabarets and places that served sailors in Hong Kong and Manila and places like that--if you contribute nicely we have a little plaque that we will put in the window to suggest that here is the place to patronize. This in effect, was a quiet sort of shake-down which was more or less the name of the game in the Far East. Everybody does it from the general right on down to the next to the lowest rank and he kicks the dog, the guy at the bottom; that's all he can do. When they got up to Yokosuka they sent ashore to me and said we would like to have a list of all of the cabarets frequented by the enlisted men in Yokosuka. "We want to gently prod them for a slight contribution to the Seventh Fleet Gate." And they said, "We'll give them a nice plaque for their window to encourage people to go to that particular place." Of course by that time, I was at the pinnacle of my career and they couldn't do a hell of a lot to me. I was ready to bow out gracefully any time and they could have the whole show. The admiral himself came over and sat in the office of the Commander of Naval Forces of Japan, which at that time was occupied by an interim commander waiting for Admiral Freddie Withington to come out. This was a junior rear admiral who was the incumbent, and of course, the commander of the Seventh Fleet was a vice admiral, so he said nothing. But, my Japanese adviser and I went over there, and I said, "Sir, we simply can't do this. First of all this is not in the samurai tradition that we go around shaking people down, which in effect this is. Secondly, you cannot take Japanese currency out of Japan, which you would be doing because they would give you yen and you would convert the yen to dollars through the paymaster and you would be taking the yen out of Japan, it is illegal." The man blew up.

Q: The CinC did?

Adm. T.: Yes, the CinC was very, very put out about the whole thing. He was an explosive type anyway. He insisted on doing it and he said, "If you won't cooperate we will do it ourselves, and if you won't give us the names we will simply go out there and take the whole thing ourselves." So, this left me absolutely no recourse. Through private sources I had to report it to the Ambassador. I wasn't about to have the Navy's name dragged in the dirt for such a piece of chicanery, over something of that sort; I like the Navy Athletic Association like a brother but not in a dishonorable way. Well, he got a gentle hint from Ambassador Douglas MacArthur to cease and desist and that was the end of that.

Q: That the CinC should desist?

Adm. T.: That the CinC should desist in his effort to squeeze the money.

Q: When your time for retirement arrived, the Japanese wanted you to stay on, did they not?

Adm. T.: The mayor brought a delegation out with a long document of beautiful Japanese characters to present to Admiral Fred Withington to let me stay on. Of course, there was a precedent for it. My predecessor about three times removed had stayed on. In fact two had done this. Benny Decker had been retained and another who had been a classmate of the Chief of Staff of the Commander Naval Forces Far East, which made things a little easier and they had stayed on. So they thought there was a precedent for it. But in this case the Navy thought otherwise, so back home I came.

I guess in addition to the seemingly fine qualities of the Japanese that I appreciated so much and the general good atmosphere that pertained throughout; I remarked about the ComSeventhFlt a while back, specifically the relationships between the fleet and the base were absolutely first class. The ships would come in, and they would call on me, I would call on them and talk over any problems and it was a big, happy family. Of course, enhancing all this was the fact that the first Commander Naval Forces Far East that I had worked under was Admiral Roscoe Good, who was one of the outstanding logisticians in the Navy and rather a cold man in some respects, a little humorless, he didn't have an easy, jolly way of breaking the ice, he was all business but he was extremely fair and extremely intelligent and he understood the Japanese and of course, his sense of humor and his austerity were precisely down the Japanese alley. The Japanese are not a joking race. Their sense of humor is contrived. I recall packing a suitcase out there one time and the hotel manager, as usual, was always on hand for anybody who was 'VIP' like I was, and a necktie was sticking out the end of the suitcase; in Japanese I told the boy who was supposed to carry the thing down "Bring a pair of scissors so we can cut this off," so the Japanese boy dashed off to get a pair of scissors and the manager called out, "No, no, joke is, joke is." That is a typical manifestation of the Japanese in what is such an obvious absurdity. You can see that anybody like Roscoe might not have gone to get the scissors, nor would he have ever proposed cutting off the necktie as a joke. Now, Fred Withington came along under slightly new auspices. When Roscoe left, he was a vice admiral and he was Commander of Naval Forces Far East which meant everything out there west of the 180th meridian. They had re-examined the bidding by the time Admiral Withington relieved and he came out as a rear admiral with command of Naval Forces Japan, which included all the naval air forces out there and such naval aspects as Sasebo and Yokosuka and so forth, that actually were on the islands of Japan. It had nothing to do with Korea or Taiwan. It possibly suggests the unfortunate situation that arose when our spy-ship was captured by the Koreans out there, the PUEBLO. Obviously when that happened there was an inability to act in concert. There was divided authority. Nobody was in the driver's seat. Everybody was in the back seat. Nobody took action. In fact, they weren't prepared for action. Nobody, in the days of Naval Forces Far East, when Korea and all the rest of it was cranked into it, had conceivably foreseen such a thing. And of course, that is a great abberation when it comes to any Naval command. You have got to foresee every casualty, every possible enemy contingency and so forth. If you don't and it happens, your lag in reaction is fatal.

Well nobody had this covered obviously enough, because the command situation didn't provide for it. That's where they went wrong. They should have never evolved this Command of Naval Forces Far East to supply Naval forces in Japan with nothing to bridge the gap between the various forces. In other words, everybody was waiting for "George" to do it and who was George? Who knew?

Q: You came back to the States to retire from the Navy.

Adm. T.: Correct.

Q: This was in June, the end of June 1959 - June 30. What were your plans at that point?

Adm. T.: My plans at that point were to rehabilitate this house, which through many years, more or less stood on its own, genteelly deteriorated and it needed a lot of additions and changes and things to make it more attractive and habitable. So I felt that my time would be more valuable spent as a carpenter and a plumber and an electrician and a painter, than in any conceivable civilian occupation that an old, broken down sailor, saturated with no outside industrial contacts or expertise in anything other than sailing ships and what goes on in the Navy, could possibly find outside the parameters of my little old farm.

Q: Did you contemplate writing at all?

Adm. T.: I retired in 1959 and in about 1961 or 1962,

somewhere along in there, a Japanese admiral whom I had
known well wrote an article in the Naval Institute Proceedings
bringing out the fact that the United States Navy had
suffered more casualties through its own incompetence than
it had through the efforts of the Japanese, through collisions,
explosions, drowning, just plain accidents, in most cases
preventable. The moral of the story, I suppose, was to
shape up. I thoroughly agreed with him, because when I had
had Amphibious Squadron 5, I had had a series of the most
stupid accidents. For example, people would paint a tank,
come up, put the manhole cover on and forget to screw the
nuts down, so the next time the LSD in this case, pumped
ballast into the tank the unsecured hatch cover popped off.
Sea water would drown out the motors and it would cost about
five or six thousand dollars to fry the salt water out of the
steering motors. Or, one ship would be towing another and
they would both lie to, so the guys down in the engine room
would say, "Well, we'd better jack the engine over every three
or four minutes to keep the cylinders warm or the turbines
warm,' and they would forget to warn the jaspers up on the
bridge that they were doing so and of course in about thirty
minutes they would find that they had 14 or 15 turns of
huge wire hawser around the propeller. Such absolutely
stupid things like that which were easily preventable. That
article, I think, was my first venture into journalism. It
brought all these silly things out, a whole series of them.
And I said that Admiral Nakayama was right, that we are our

own worst enemy. One thing led to another and I wrote some more and I thought, 'well I had all these, in some cases, unique adventures, why not share these with the public and maybe make a few bucks.' Then it got to be almost a part-time profession.

Q: That's when you set up your writing studio over here?

Adm. T.: No, that's something I dreamed about since I was a little boy.

Q: In 1961 you did come back briefly on a tour of duty for the Navy.

Adm. T.: Again, this is one of the extraordinary fine characteristics of the Japanese. They show gratitude and they remember things. So when it came time to commission the MIKASA in a reconstitution ceremony so to speak, they felt that it was only fitting that the people who had been closely connected with it should come out. Admiral Nimitz was invited and Admiral Withington, who had been the turner overer of the LST (I had since left Japan and Admiral Withington was still there) and he officiated at the turnover of the LST to Admiral Terai, who was then the regional district commander; (and still a dear friend by the way and we had a wonderful reunion in Tokyo in 1973 with Vlada and me). About that time President Eisenhower had been all set to go to Japan, and there had been student riots in opposition thereto, so the thing had been cancelled. Admiral Nimitz felt that he was so well known that had he gone over there and any such untoward incidents had occurred it would be not only of great embarrassment to the Japanese government but a severe loss of face for him. In other words, it would be an unfortunate thing all around. So he refused. Admiral Withington had personal reasons. He couldn't go, so I was it. I communicated with Admiral Nimitz. I meanwhile had taken a course as Convoy Commodore down in Norfolk and I was then put back on the Ready List as a retired officer ready to be recalled--after 30 years you can't be recalled against your own request or against your own wishes. But in this case, I volunteered to go to the Commodore Convoy School in Norfolk which made me eligible until age 62 to be recalled to service as Convoy Commodore. While I was down there, I communicated with Admiral Nimitz and I said "I am going out there. I know you have been invited and you can't go or you don't want to go. Is there any message I could give?" Well there was. "Stop in and see me on the way out." Meanwhile I had gotten in communication with Smedberg, who was then Chief of Naval Personnel and I said, "Maybe Arleigh Burke or Secretary Connolly would like to send greetings. After all, this is a big event for the Japanese. We might as well lay it on as thick as we can." "Fine." They both had messages for me to take out. I went out and Admiral Nimitz was then living in Berkeley. That was before he had gone back into Quarters One at Treasure Island. So just to show you his remarkable nature, he had a big framed photograph of himself which he had signed and he said, "Tolley, what do you think I should put on here?" knowing damn well what he intended to put on it.

Q: Was that the photograph of him signing on the MISSOURI?

Adm. T.: No, no, this was just a big portrait of him, very nice. It looked like a lithograph sort of; about two by three feet, and he knew perfectly well what he intended to put on it. But he, I suppose, in his inimitable way knowing that it would flatter me and make me feel good if my opinion were asked. Maybe he would have taken some suggestion that I made, but basically that's the kind of man he was. He made you feel a part of everything, that you were not just a flunky. Well, he gave me a message to be delivered, which I took out along with Burke's and Connolly's and it was marvelous to be received. I was guest of the city, put up at the best hotel, the Commander of Fleet Activities gave me a personal car and we had absolutely the place at our disposal, more or less. Admiral Yeomans, who was then Commander Naval Forces, Japan, was most hospitable.

Q: Did Vlada go with you?

Adm. T.: Yes, she went too. At the convocation or whatever you want to call it, I delivered the messages (I didn't make any speech myself.) I thought it would be rather forward on my part when I was delivering messages from three such super individuals as Secretary of the Navy, and CNO, and

Admiral Nimitz, I simply delivered their greetings, in
Japanese, which had been translated out there for me by
my old friend Matsumoto, my former assistant. One thing
rather amused me at the time. Of course Don Griffin
was there as ComSeventh Fleet, and while we were there, we
were invited by the Japanese Secretary of Defense. (He was
called the Director of the Defense Agency) to a formal
banquet in Tokyo and we were the guests of honor, and the
Joint Chiefs of Staff, the Chief of the Joint Chiefs and
all of the Joint Chiefs were there of the Navy, the Army,
and the Air Force, quite a show and Don Griffin was there
too. It was perfectly obvious: 'What the hell is this
guy Tolley doing to deserve all this stuff?' I don't
think he was hurt but he was curious. He didn't know the
background and I didn't feel it was my part to go up and
explain it. I tell you all this merely as an indication
of the degree of gratitude the Japanese show. A lot of
people wouldn't give a damn and the whole thing would be
laughed off and forgotten. I am sure that any action like
that on the part of an American in this country would be
too, for a Japanese. This extended even to 1976 when the
ball is very beautifully and gently returned to our side
of the court when this same MIKASA Association which re-
established the ship as a memorial, has collected much more
money than we contributed, in fact $86,000, to build a
memorial park at the Nimitz Center in Fredericksburg, Texas
and they sent over an expert gardener and six or seven

Japanese laborers and most of the raw material in the form of stones and bridges and stone lanterns and a replica of Togo's study after he retired and set the whole thing up behind the Nimitz Museum in Fredericksburg. Well, I was invited, and it's been a long time ago since I was in Japan; in 1961 the last time, but it was 1976 and they still remember. They invited me down there to be at the dedication. Here I am a nobody. I have no notoriety at all. I could see why they would invite Tom Moorer and Arleigh Burke but I am nobody in the public view but I was invited.

Q: You came back on active duty again in 1967. Tell me about that.

Adm. T.: 1967 was the period of the Vietnam War and it was more or less at its height then and my younger daughter greeted me one day when I came home, she said, "Daddy, somebody called up from Washington and they wanted to know if you wanted to go back on active duty and go out toward Vietnam, and I told him 'Sure he would'."

Q: Your daughter said this?

Adm. T.: Yes, that's what my daughter told him (or her), so I said, "You said precisely the right word, young lady." So, in very short order I was on an airplane headed for San Diego.

Q: Did they verify that before they gave you orders?

Adm. T.: I immediately called up and said, "What my daughter said is right on the ball." So I went to San Diego for ten days to an Anti-submarine School and Destroyer Tactics with a group of about 25 or 30, about 10 of whom were enlisted men and the rest were reserve officers. What they do or did, was to periodically call in teams of Convoy Commodore staffs, which consisted of 4 officers and usually 3 or 4 enlisted men. They would be assigned either training duties or the lucky ones picked for convoys, would continue their active duty for another two weeks and in my case, I was made the Convoy Commander of an amphibious squadron and by a strange coincidence the same one I had commanded some years before, Amphibious Squadron 5. And what a vast difference in flagship! They had a new flagship, the CLEVELAND, a gorgeous thing, all electronically equipped, air conditioned, mess halls painted in pastel colors, hot and cold running practically everything, and of course 22 knots. I might say that I had never worked with reserves before, the ones that are activated from time to time. Of course during WW2 there were reserves all over the place, but that was a different situation. These guys are businessmen, salesmen and every conceivable thing, bank clerks and whatnot. Then for two weeks to a month each year they get out there and put on a blue suit and do what comes naturally for a sailor. I couldn't imagine what these guys would be like in active Naval service. I soon found out. This four I had--there was one lieutenant commander whose normal capacity was setting up shopping centers. He would go out and case the place and find out if it was suitable as a location and then carry on from there. Another one was involved in a bank, I forget off-hand what the other two did. But they were really superior people, and they were so eager and so sharp to do the right thing. What particularly impressed me was the fact that, on those occasions going out of San Diego and coming into Pearl on the other end, my little staff of four people plus three enlisted men, always were the ones to sight the submarine periscope. Where the hell the ship's company was I don't know, but I was rather let down by the performance of the ship's company in general. First of all, I was probably put off a little bit by the rather cavalier reception with which we were received. The idea was, basically of course, that we were a bug in the ointment, that we would be excess baggage and we would slow up their training. Everybody thinks they need a lot of training and anything that interferes with that is a nuisance to be avoided, if possible. It would create the wrong reaction from the signalman because the convoy signals were a completely new bag. You have a bunch of colored lights on the masthead and you turn these things off and on. You use whistle signals. You use all sorts of different types of maneuvering signals that are applicable and useful only for a bunch of dumb merchant skippers. I don't say dumb in the sense that they are stupid, but they are not accustomed to Naval tactics and usage.

When the cruise was over, they had completely changed their minds. The skipper said, "You know this is a pretty valuable thing, because it has made us conscious of the fact that this is not our only job, conveying troops and running warships." I think we proved a valuable point in getting that across. We also proved the point that if war came along we would be in a hell of a spot to try to provide the equipment necessary to run these convoys. I could have sworn that the convoy lights that we patched and tenderly nursed and repaired, which went bad on us from time to time, was precisely the same string of lights that the Convoy Commodore had used who had ridden with me when I had deployed to the Far East twelve years before and there were four sets of them in the whole area of San Diego. This of course is absurd. We needed six sets for the ships we had and we had to jury rig the others.

I spent a very pleasant four days in Pearl, casing the place out there, touring around the island and whatnot, checking up on the Naval Base to see if I had a classmate there and to see how it was going. I came back to San Francisco to make the report and the Commander of the Western Sea Frontier and Commander of the Fourteenth Naval District was on hand to listen, along with his staff. I said, "It is a real thrill you know, to get out there and smell that salt water again and see that magnificent ship and see the Russian trawler that we passed and know that all these things were being checked up on and so forth."

He said, "Russian trawler? What Russian trawler?" Nobody had reported it.

Q: How long were you out?

Adm. T.: We left San Diego about 7 or 8 o'clock in the morning and we had an exit exercise wherein you're supposed to try to cut your way through submarines, trying to hack you up on the way out and we had a group of San Diego based destroyers, 7 or 8, I guess, in a scouting line. We got out. We didn't get plugged on the way. It gave practice to everybody, gave practice to me in maneuvering the convoy and when it was time to change the venue so to speak, I was the commander of the unit.

Q: You were taking troops?

Adm. T.: There were a few troops aboard, but actually it was just a deployment of the ships. They were going out to replace ships which were coming back. So the whole thing then transmuted itself, in the imagination, into a merchant convoy, using wholly merchant procedure. Of course the destroyers were out bird-dogging on the perimeter to try to pick up subs. They picked up all the ones that tried to plug us on the way out of San Diego. We had an entirely new group when we got over to Pearl or the approaches to Pearl, and not only did we get "sunk," but after I got back here on inactive duty again, I got some beautiful pictures taken through the submarine periscope from the submarine skippers. They said, "I thought you would like to have these," with the big, old fat USS CLEVELAND framed in a periscope just like a picture, with the cross-hairs right in the middle.

Q: Tell me why the Navy would call you back to active duty for one mission like that?

Adm. T.: This was the middle of the Vietnam War. They didn't know whether the Chinese were coming back into it in force. They were hanging on the fringes and nobody knew what would be next. The mining of Haiphong had been strongly considered. Would that bring the Russians in or not? So maybe this would break out into a full-scale war. So that is merely as I reconstruct the situation.

Q: So it was a training thing?

Adm. T.: It was strictly to dust me off and make me available and up to the minute on the latest tactics, which that two weeks in San Diego did. I found out about the capabilities of enemy ships, submarines, torpedoes, capabilities of our own and as far as convoy tactics were concerned, they hadn't changed in the slightest since WW1, even in the signals. As far as the capabilities of the enemy and our own side was concerned, of course it was absolutely a new deal, a new world, things I hadn't even dreamed of before. But, I felt perfectly capable after that going back out. Now, of course, as you possibly know, a retired officer, by Navy regulations, can never take command of anything. He is merely in an advisory capacity. So if I went out there as the Convoy Commodore I could order the convoy but they don't have to obey the order. Nobody is going to court martial the skipper of a merchant ship if they don't do what I say, turn left, turn right, stop, go. As far as the convoy escort is concerned he can command me. He might be a lieutenant junior grade and I am a rear admiral and if he says the convoy will go east, or the convoy will go west, and I go east or west as he says. I could only advise.

Q: Well since that event in 1967 you have taken off your suit?

Adm. T.: No, no, when I became 62 years old, which was some time after that, I got a very nice letter from the Secretary of the Navy and he said, "We certainly appreciate your patriotic motives in allowing yourself to remain on the mobilization rolls and we feel now that it is time for you to retire to your laurels," or something to that effect. In other words, you are 62, "So long".

Q: Well that hasn't deterred you, because you have another career.

Adm. T.: I don't have another career, I simply have a continuing career in many fields.

Q: I was referring to your writing ability.

Adm. T.: Well, that is in no sense a career, especially as

far, I hope, as the Internal Revenue is concerned, or the Sociable Security. It keeps the brain alert, all these things. You find new processes, new things to do outside, new crops to grow, new ways to husband fish, new type of paint, predicting the strange vagaries of the weather, manufacturing your own odds and ends of parts and things, keeping your motor cars in repair, doing your own plumbing repairs, some of these things possibly against the building code but the building codes are only to protect the insurance companies, I guess. Otherwise you are not bothered.
And, writing; the main thing is this tremendous correspondence that this writing generates. I buy my printed US government stamped envelopes 500 at a time because it is cheaper that way. You get them wholesale. That, of course, reflects certain other clever economies that I have been able to perpetrate or perhaps exercise. One time when I had Amphibious Squadron 5, I used to take these various reserve groups out and amongst those present one time was a lieutenant colonel who in real life worked for National Distillers, or one of those booze departments. So he taught me how to make booze. He said, "You know it's the same in this distilling outfit as it is in Standard Oil, where they start you out cranking the gas pump. When you start in the distilling business you are in there shovelling grain into a vat and you take it from there and finally you wind up at the top of the pile, maybe as the president of the company with a free bottle of whiskey every other day. In the course of all this stuff, I have

learned how to do all of this and if you are interested I'll be delighted to tell you. That's the only thing I know other than doing what comes naturally to a Marine and this stuff I am trying to do now." So he told me all about how to make booze and I experimented on that, that is one thing. I put that aside, tried something else. Another time, another Marine lieutenant colonel was in the construction business so I told him about this house back here, that some day I would be sticking some more boards on it and nailing some shingles on the roof and he said, "I hope you are not going to do it retail," and I inquired into that and he said, "Why, you incorporate yourself. In a very modest way, you simply get yourself a title, get some billheads printed and you're in business. All these wholesalers are interested in is protecting their rear against a bunch of angry retailers who feel that you are a nincompoop circumventing their proper rules. But there are no rules. It's every man for himself. That's the way business operates." My flag captain, Freddy Hilles, was on hand at the time so Freddy said,"I've got the answer to that one. Why don't you call it, "Tolley Hobby Craft?" That covers the field. You can pretend you can do everything." So now I have billheads printed in Japan at very lost cost, Tolley Hobby Craft, and everything comes wholesale.

So when you add all these things together, and photography for example. When I was in Moscow, I had taken some lousy Brownie camera pictures before, but here in Moscow they had a very valuable camera and they simply handed it to me and said, "You are the intelligence officer, so learn how to take pictures." So step by step and by the help of Navy experts, photographers' mates aboard ship in one place or another I have become a photographer. The same thing aboard the VERMILION. You know the wretched gray steel furniture they have on the Navy warships? Well, we had a magnificent carpenter shop, and a lot of mahogany which was to be used for boat repair for the landing craft, and three or four unemployed, so to speak, carpenters' mates took me under their wing and told me how to carpenter. So now I am an expert cabinet maker. And when I see some of my classmates say, "Well I've got to leave lunch now, I've got to go play bridge," and they have nothing to talk about, they have no ulterior motives or exterior thoughts. All they think about is bridge during the afternoon and golf some other time when they can rake up a partner. It is really very sad. No outside interest. They are vegetating. They are dying on their feet, dead already.

Q: That can never be said of you. Thank you very much.

Index to
Reminiscences of
Rear Admiral Kemp Tolley
U.S. Navy (Retired)

Volume II

Adair, Lieutenant Commander Charles, USN (USNA, 1926)
Officer who relieved Tolley as skipper of the schooner *Lanikai* in 1942 greatly interested in news of the Pearl Harbor attack and Roosevelt's attempts to spy on the Japanese, p. 518.

Air Force, U.S.
Inferior educational background of students at the Armed Forces Staff College and service policy on in the 1950s, pp. 759-760; cooperation with U.S. Navy during amphibious exercise at Okinawa in the mid-1950s, pp. 793-794.

Amphibious Group 2
Make-up of staff, p. 767; discussion of commanding officers, pp. 767-771; international operations, pp. 774-779; participation in the Korean War, pp. 779-780.

Amphibious Squadron 5
Units comprising squadron, p. 782; reorganization in the mid-1950s, p. 783; as commanding officer Tolley explores possible mission of evacuating Taiwan, pp. 784-786; Tolley recalled to active duty as convoy commander in 1967, p. 847.

Amphibious warfare
Status of equipment in the 1950s, pp. 776-774, 782; ship characteristics of attack transport ship tested en route to Korean War, p. 780; during World War II, p. 781; see LST Squadron 2; Amphibious Group 2; Amphibious Squadron 5; Exercises, international.

Armed Forces Staff College; Norfolk, Virginia
Rotation of command among services, pp. 753-754; mission, p. 754; Tolley heads intelligence division between 1949 and 1952, pp. 754-757, 762; make-up of faculty and student body, pp. 758-760; social life, p. 761.

Army, U.S.
Enlargement of U.S. military strength in Russia during World War II, p. 654; emphasis on professional schools for officers, p. 759.

Atomic weapons
Notice prior to 1945 bomb droppings given to U.S. ships in the Pacific, pp. 681, 683; dissension within Japan regarding atomic armaments on U.S. ships in the late 1950s and their use of Japanese ports, pp. 833-835.

Australia
Condition of the Asiatic Fleet and military in 1942, pp. 501-502; see *Lanikai*, USS.

Battle fatigue
North Carolina takes load of officers being returned home on way to repairs at Okinawa in the mid-1940s, pp. 692-693.

Battleships
　Discussion of division chain of command and flagships during World War II, pp. 690-692.

Boyd, Captain Alston M., Jr., USN (USNA, 1930)
　Tolley's predecessor as commander of LST Squadron 2 sets up signal for deciding upon best lunch being served in squadron, p. 750.

Bradley, Major General Follett, USAAF (USNA, 1910)
　As administrator of U.S. lend-lease aircraft provided to Russia upset by casual remark made by Tolley at a party, pp. 525, 542-543, 592, 594-595.

Britain
　In early December, 1941 Roosevelt hedges on assurance of aid via Lord Halifax pending materialization of Japanese attack, pp. 492-493; Tolley's opinion of Bundles for Britain, p. 503; presence in Iraq in 1942, pp. 509-511; relations with Russia in the early 1940s, pp. 551, 589-594, 597-598; code clerk at U.S. embassy trying to prove Roosevelt was making secret deals with Churchill arrested by British government, pp. 562, 564-566; Rainbow 5/ABC 1 plan, p. 566; cooperation with U.S. intelligence after World War II, p. 703; interest in Trieste in 1947, pp. 722, 727; way of dealing with temporary nature of U.S. Navy officer ranks in World War I, p. 728; Royal Navy in the Mediterranean in the late 1940s, pp. 731-732; poor quality of hospitality to Americans in Hong Kong in the mid-1950s, p. 788.

Bullitt, William
　Treatment as ambassador to Russia in the 1940s, pp. 539-540, 558; reaction to Tolley's bleak assessment of conditions in China in the early 1940s, pp. 555-557; as ambassador to France in the 1930s, pp. 557-558, 562, 567-569.

Canada
　Games played by army unit in Halifax hosting Tolley's LST squadron during training exercise in late 1940s, pp. 747-749; navy commodore entertains Tolley in Lunenburg, p. 749; course offered in cold weather tactics at McGill University in the 1950s, p. 764; handling of border customs versus U.S. methods, pp. 764-765; French-English animosities, p. 765.

Carrier Operations
　Third Fleet in 1944-1945, pp. 662, 672.

Chiang Kai-Shek
　Dealings with communists in China in World War II, pp. 556-557.

Churchill, Sir Winston
　Dealings with President Roosevelt prior to U.S. entry into World War II, pp. 562-563, 567, 597; relations with Stalin, pp. 589-594, 597-598.

Cicala, HMS
Tolley surprised by the presence of this Yangtze River gunboat in Iran in 1942, pp. 510-511.

Clark, Vice Admiral Joseph J. "Jocko", USN (USNA, 1918)
As Commander, Seventh Fleet in the early 1950s spent most of his time in Taiwan, pp. 783-784.

Clarke, Colonel Carter W., USA
Embittered intelligence officer demoted from brigadier general after expressing negative opinion of Roosevelt administration handling of Pearl Harbor intelligence, p. 700.

Cleveland, USS (LPD-7)
As Tolley's flagship as convoy commander of Amphibious Squadron 5 in the mid-1960s, p. 847.

Codes
Japanese message intercepted the morning of the Pearl Harbor attack, and subsequent knowledge of message by those in U.S. intelligence, pp. 494, 500, 701; Roosevelt and Churchill communicate in easily deciphered gray code prior to U.S. entry into World War II, pp. 562-563; Russian access to code rooms at U.S. embassy in the Soviet Union during the war, pp. 586, 588-589; introduction of cipher machines vastly helped integrity of messages, p. 589; U.S. Army and Navy cooperation and competition for credit, pp. 595, 700, 702; problem of too many people decoding messages meant for others, pp. 688-689; controversy over role of intelligence versus operations when working with codes, pp. 755-756.

Colclough, Captain Oswald S., USN (USNA, 1921)
Tolley's assessment of as commanding officer of the battleship North Carolina (BB-55) in the 1940s, pp. 663-664, 667; hosts Tolley at impromptu Officers' Club for flag officers at Ulithi during World War II, p. 685.

Convoy training
In the Pacific during the Vietnam War, pp. 848-852.

Cooley, Rear Admiral Thomas R., Jr., USN (USNA, 1917)
As tactical and administrative commander of a battleship division in World War II, Tolley felt Cooley had nothing to do because he was subordinate to the air admiral commanding the task group, p. 691.

Correspondents, War
Their accuracy in World War II, pp. 527, 671-672.

Creighton, Commander John M., USN (USNA, 1914)
Friend of Tolley's from Office of Naval Intelligence duty in Singapore who helped Tolley get back to language/intelligence duties in Russia in 1941, pp. 502, 508.

Crete
  Tolley and other officers on a picnic mistakenly captured by Cretians in 1947, pp. 733-736.

Currie, Laughlin
  As Roosevelt's advisor on China in 1940s and a communist, pp. 560, 653.

Dall, Curtis
  President Franklin Roosevelt's son-in-law tells his lawyer about the president's prior knowledge of Pearl Harbor attack, pp. 486-488, 492.

Deane, Major General John R., USA
  In charge of military mission in Russia under Ambassador Harriman who dispelled intelligence gathering as divisive to war effort, pp. 584-587, 653.

DeMetropolis, Commander George, USN (USNA, 1931)
  Tolley's assessment of colorful officer he met in Athens in the late 1940s, pp. 739-740.

Duncan, Captain Jack H., USN (USNA, 1918)
  As William Standley's aide as ambassador to Russia in the 1940s, pp. 528-533, 543, 545-546, 592, 595, 646; incident at banquet with Churchill and Stalin, pp. 593-594.

Education
  Greater emphasis in Army than Navy or Air Force on professional schools, p. 759; see Armed Forces Staff College.

Eggers, Captain Fremont B., USN (USNA, 1925)
  As former commanding officer of USS Vermilion (AKA-107) praised by Tolley for excellent condition in which he turned over the ship in 1947, p. 716.

Exercises, International
  Amphibious Group 2 with North Atlantic Treaty Organization (NATO) members in the North Sea in 1951, pp. 774-779; Amphibious Group 2 with NATO members in the Mediterranean in the early 1950s, pp. 777-779; Chinese Air Force participates in amphibious exercise on Okinawa with U.S. Navy and Air Force in the mid-1950s, pp. 793-794.

Fahrion, Rear Admiral Frank G., USN (USNA, 1917)
  As commanding officer of the battleship North Carolina (BB-55) in the mid-1940s was the first flag officer to have a ship command, pp. 664, 669.

Faymonville, Brigadier General Philip R., USA (USMA, 1912)
  As pro-communist White House aide and military attache to Russia in the 1930s, pp. 522-523, 528-529, 541-543, 584.

Fleet Operations
   Third Fleet during 1944-1945, pp. 660-696; see Seventh Fleet.

France
   Commanding officer of Jean Bart, French battleship that fired on American ships in World War II, invites Tolley to lunch in Algiers, pp. 730-731; while commander of NATO exercise in the early 1950s, Commander Amphibious Group 2 surreptitiously passed command at various times to a senior French admiral to smooth ruffled feathers, pp. 777-778.

Franklin, USS (CV-13)
   Attacked by kamikazes as Tolley watched from the battleship North Carolina in 1945, pp. 675-678.

Germany
   Presence in Iraq in 1942, p. 509; occupation of Russia in the 1940s, p. 530; alliance with Russia, pp. 567, 569-570.

Glassford, Vice Admiral William A., Jr., USN (USNA, 1906)
   As Commander, U.S. Naval Forces, Southwest Pacific in Australia in 1942, pp. 502, 518; description of, p. 511.

Good, Vice Admiral Roscoe F., USN (USNA, 1920)
   As Commander Naval Forces, Far East approved Tolley's remaining as Commander Fleet Activities, Yokosuka in 1958, pp. 801-802, 838-839.

Greece
   Hospitality to U.S. Fleet in the late 1940s, pp. 723-725, 736-737, 741; situation with Rhodes in 1947, p. 736; incident of U.S. sailor hitting local in Rhodes, pp. 738-739; tense atmosphere in the late 1940s, pp. 740-741; tension with Turks, p. 739; participation in NATO amphibious operation in 1951, pp. 778-779; see Crete.

Griffin Vice Admiral Charles D., USN (USNA, 1927)
   As Commander, Seventh Fleet in the early 1960s confused by attention shown Tolley by the Japanese at the Mikasa dedication, p. 845.

Halifax, Earl of (Edward F.L. Wood)
   British ambassador to U.S. during the early 1940s requests support from United States through President Roosevelt prior to Japanese attack on Pearl Harbor, pp. 492-493.

Hall, Vice Admiral John L., Jr., USN (USNA, 1913)
   As Commandant of the Armed Forces Staff College while Tolley taught there in the early 1950s admired by Tolley and characterized as a forward thinker, pp. 754, 757, 763.

Halsey, Admiral William F., Jr., USN (USNA, 1904)
   Tolley's assessment of, p. 661, 691; leads ships into typhoon in 1945, pp. 673, 674; defends General MacArthur to other Navy flag officers at Officers' Club at Ulithi, p. 685.

Hanson, George
  As American Consul General in Moscow was removed from duties after giving American merchants too honest assessment of Russians, and later commits suicide after rapid shuffling to other posts, pp. 641-643.

Harriman, W. Averell
  As U.S. ambassador to Russia in the 1940s, pp. 525, 528, 584, 587, 590, 594, 646.

Henderson, Loy
  State Department chief in Eastern Europe section reassigned by Roosevelt after disparaging comments on Russian character contrary to the President's beliefs, pp. 521, 523, 634-635; as minister to Iraq in the early 1940s, pp. 523-525, 594, 634-635, 638-640.

Hilles, Captain Frederick V., USN (USNA, 1930)
  As a division commander in Tolley's Amphibious Group, Western Pacific in the mid-1950s suggests title for business when Tolley decides to incorporate, p. 854.

Iceland
  Tolley discovers unpopularity of American servicemen during visit in 1951, pp. 775-777.

Indian Navy
  Cocktail party on Indian cruiser off Tokyo in the late 1950s, pp. 828-829.

Ingersoll, Rear Admiral Royal E., USN (USNA, 1905)
  As Assistant Chief of Naval Operations for Admiral Stark in the early 1940s, fielded oral directive from President Roosevelt, making sure it could not be attributed to anyone else, p. 496; Tolley views as most truthful witness at Pearl Harbor investigation, p. 496; dealings with war plans and Office of Naval Intelligence during World War II, p. 649.

Intelligence
  See Naval Intelligence.

Inter-service relationships
  Regarding education in the 1950s, pp. 758-760; poor state during World War II, pp. 761-762.

Iraq
  Tolley arrives at Abadan in May, 1942 to find upheaval caused by German infiltrators, pp. 509-512; Loy Henderson as U.S. minister to in the early 1940s, pp. 523-524.

Italian Navy
  Poor performance during North Atlantic Treaty Organization (NATO) amphibious exercise in 1951, pp. 778-779.

Italy
  Trouble with Yugoslavians over Trieste in 1947, pp. 722, 726-727; situation with Rhodes in 1947, p. 736.

Japan
  Air action during World War II, pp. 666, 676-677; conditions during last year of World War II, pp. 670-671, 682; submarine menace, pp. 666, 678, 684; kamikazes, pp. 676-679, 693; Tolley represents U.S. at Shimoda Festival in the mid-1950s, pp. 788, 790; Tolley's thoughts towards Japanese, pp. 790-791, 796-798, 802-803, 816-821, 838, 842; U.S. Navy complex at Yokosuka, pp. 799-800, 806; resurgence in the 1950s, p. 805; Black Market, p. 816; shipbuilding with U.S. drydock, p. 818; Japanese Maritime Self Defense Force, pp. 819, 822, 824, 827; opposition to atomic armaments in the late 1950s, pp. 833-835, 842; see Okinawa; Yokosuka; dealings with the Russians, pp. 788-790, 821, 830-833.

Jarrell, Rear Admiral Albert E., USN (USNA, 1925)
  Friendship with Tolley while commanding amphibious training base in the Far East in the mid-1950s leads to Tolley's selection as his chief of staff as Commander Fleet Activities, pp. 793, 796.

Kamikazes
  See *Franklin*, USS (CV-13)

Kennan, George
  Credited as author of Marshall Plan, p. 488; as second secretary of U.S. embassy in Moscow in early 1940s, pp. 555, 571.

Kent, Tyler
  American code clerk in London embassy who sought to prove that President Roosevelt maneuvered U.S. into European war with incriminating messages, pp. 562, 564-566, 568-569.

Kimmel, Admiral Husband E., USN (USNA, 1904)
  Kimmel's lawyer attempts to prove President Roosevelt's prior knowledge of Pearl Harbor attack, pp. 486-488; sent message by Secretary of the Navy Knox warning of possible Japanese attack, but Knox's message was intercepted, pp. 494-495; Tolley feels judged less-than-impartially by Roberts Commission, pp. 499-500; Standley's opinion of Kimmel's treatment by Roberts Commission, p. 520.

King, Fleet Admiral Ernest J., USN (USNA, 1901)
  Established own intelligence office within his U.S. Fleet staff while simultaneously holding the position of Chief of Naval Operations in the mid-1940s, pp. 649, 696, 705-706.

Knox, Frank
  As Secretary of the Navy in the early 1940s, prior knowledge of the Pearl Harbor attack, pp. 490-491; sends Commander in Chief, Pacific Fleet Kimmel warning message which is not passed along, pp. 494-495.

Korea
  See Pueblo, USS (AGER-2)

Korean War
  Amphibious Group 2 participation in, pp. 779-780.

LST Squadron 2
  Position of commander in fleet chain of command, pp. 742-743; units comprising, pp. 743-744; operations in Atlantic in the 1950s, pp. 744-750; troubles with peddlers at home base in Norfolk, pp. 751-753.

Lanikai, USS (Schooner)
  Cruises Australian coast looking for Japanese infiltrators in 1941-1942, pp. 501, 508; layover in Indonesia before Japanese invasion during World War II, p. 517.

Lattimore, Owen
  Advisor who misinformed President Roosevelt on situation in China in the 1940s, pp. 560-561, 653.

Leahy, Admiral William D., USN (USNA, 1897)
  As President Franklin Roosevelt's chief of staff in the early 1940s, pp. 489, 599.

Lend-lease
  In Iraq in 1942, p. 510; in Russia in 1942, pp. 515-516, 526, 542, 653-655.

MacArthur, General Douglas, USA (USMA, 1903)
  Defended by Admiral Halsey at the Officers' Club at Ulithi during World War II, p. 685; astute summation of Russian intentions regarding Japan after World War II, p. 821.

MacArthur, Douglas, 2nd
  As ambassador to Japan in the late 1950s stops Seventh Fleet commander from shaking down local merchants to raise funds for a Naval Academy stadium gate, p. 837.

McWhinnie, Captain Charles J., USN (USNA, 1922)
  Sent with division from Amphibious Group 2 from Norfolk to Korea with men and supplies and tasked en route by RADM Wellings to test ship characteristics, p. 780.

Marshall, General George C., USA
  Tolley's assessment of, p. 488; dealings with President Roosevelt, pp. 488-489, 701; connection to Pearl Harbor attack, pp. 489-491, 494, 701.

Mediterranean Sea
  See Sixth Fleet, U.S.; Crete; Greece; Turkey.

Mexico
  Americans living there in the mid-1950s, p. 792; hostility of the U.S. embassy, pp. 792-793.

Mikasa, HIJMS
  Tolley continues Admiral Nimitz's interest in restoring Togo's flagship as a national memorial in the late 1950s, pp. 820-824; dedication ceremony in the early 1960s, pp. 842-845; Mikasa Association collects funds for memorial park at Nimitz Museum in Texas in 1976, pp. 845-846.

Molotov, Vyacheslav
  Ribbentrop-Molotov Agreement, p. 569; meets with Churchill and Harriman in 1943, p. 590.

NATO
  See North Atlantic Treaty Organization.

Naval Academy, U.S.
  Sixth and Seventh Fleets compete to raise funds for a gate at the new Navy-Marine Corps Stadium in the late 1950s, pp. 835-837.

Naval Intelligence
  Condition after World War II, pp. 648-650, 696; Chief of Naval Operations Ernest King's private intelligence department on his U.S. Fleet staff in the mid-1940s, pp. 649, 696, 700-701; Admiral Sherman's Map Room in the late 1940s, pp. 706-708.

Naval Reserves
  See Reserves, U.S. Navy.

Navigation
  Aboard USS North Carolina (BB-55) during World War II, pp. 664-665.

Nimitz, Fleet Admiral Chester W., USN (USNA, 1905)
  Faith in intelligence provided him in 1942, p. 706; affection for Japanese acquired prior to World War II, p. 820; interest in restoring Japanese ship Mikasa, pp. 820-822, 842-844.

Nimmer, Major David R., USMC
  As naval attache in Moscow in the late 1930s, pp. 539-540.

North Atlantic Treaty Organization (NATO)
  Amphibious Group 2 participates in exercise in 1951, pp. 777-781; language difficulties, p. 778.

North Carolina, USS (BB-55)
  Conditions on board during Tolley's tour in the mid-1940s, pp. 658-659, 664-665, 668-669, 685-687; duty with Third and Fifth Fleets in 1944-1945, pp. 659-663, 665-682, 687; as training ground for flag officers, pp. 664, 669-670, 690; in typhoon of 1945, p. 673; Japanese attack off Okinawa wounds Tolley, pp. 679-680, 692; part of occupation force landing on VJ Day, pp. 681-682, 694; relaxation for officers, pp. 684-685.

Norway
  Oslo popular for port visits during international amphibious exercise in 1951, pp. 775, 778.

O'Keefe, Captain George F., USN (USNA, 1925)
  Tolley's favorable assessment of O'Keefe as commanding officer of the tender Shenandoah (AD-26) traveling in company with Vermilion (AKA-107) in the late 1940s, pp. 732-733.

Pearl Harbor, Hawaiian Islands
  Tolley's speculation on President Roosevelt's prior knowledge of December, 1941 attack, pp. 485-500, 701; Congressional investigation of attack, pp. 487, 489-490, 496, 499-501, 520; Tolley learns the extent of the damage, p. 517.

Peddlers
  Tolley's troubles with at the Navy Amphibious Base, Norfolk in the late 1940s, pp. 751-753.

Perry, Commodore Matthew, USN
  Situation with Russians in Japan in the 1850s, pp. 788-790.

Personnel, U.S. Navy
  Officer recalls to active duty in the 1960s, pp. 846-847, 851-852; see Reserves, U.S. Navy.

Pittsburgh, USS (CA-72)
  Loses bow during Philippine Sea typhoon in 1945, p. 673.

Poland
  Precarious position prior to German invasion during World War II, pp. 561-562, 567, 569, 596.

Prisoners of war
  U.S. Navy attitude towards downed Japanese pilots during World War II, pp. 689-690.

Promotions
  Temporary nature in some officer billets in the 1940s, pp. 727-729.

Pueblo, USS (AGER-2)
  Tolley suggests that rearrangement of U.S. authority in the Korean area contributed to the confusion around the January, 1968 seizing of this ship, pp. 839-840.

Radar
  Tolley's introduction to aboard the battleship North Carolina (BB-55) during World War II, pp. 660, 670-671.

Ranks
  In the Soviet military, pp. 535-539, 543-547, 827-830; temporary nature of officer ranks in some billets in the U.S. Navy, pp. 727-729.

Reserves, U.S. Navy
   Tolley's favorable impression of dealing with during recall to active duty as convoy commander in 1967, pp. 847-848.

Richardson, Admiral James O., USN (USNA, 1902)
   Replaced as Commander in Chief, Pacific Fleet in 1941 after protesting to President Roosevelt the Fleet's vulnerability and telling him that the Navy had no confidence in the political leadership, pp. 493-494.

Roberts Commission
   Partisan committee headed by Justice Owen Roberts formed by President Roosevelt to investigate and lay blame after the Pearl Harbor attack, pp. 499-501, 520.

Roberts, Owen
   Loyal supporter chosen by President Roosevelt to investigate the Pearl Harbor attack, p. 499; see Roberts Commission.

Rochefort, Commander Joseph J., USN
   Provided high-quality intelligence to Nimitz prior to Battle of Midway, p. 706.

Roosevelt, Franklin D.
   Tolley's evidence of the President's prior knowledge of the Pearl Harbor attack, pp. 485-500; dedication to the Navy, pp. 492, 497-498; ulterior motive for backing the British, pp. 498-499; proclivity for oral versus written directives, pp. 495-496, 525, 560, 566-567; orders three small ships set off Indo-Chinese coast to spy on Japanese in late 1941, pp. 496-497, 517-518; attitude towards Russians and Stalin, pp. 521-525, 540-541, 586, 588-589, 596-599, 652; as a Liberal, pp. 540, 558, 596; attitude towards Jews, pp. 560, 639; dealings and relationship with Churchill, pp. 562-563, 567-568, 597-598.

Rose, Rear Admiral Rufus E., USN (USNA, 1924)
   As commander of Amphibious Group 2 in the 1950s characterized by Tolley as a better staff officer than commander, pp. 767-768, 775, 777.

Roullard, Lieutenant Commander George D., USN (USNA, 1933)
   Fellow assistant naval attache in Moscow in the early 1940s introduces Tolley to his future wife, pp. 514-516.

Russia
   See Soviet Union.

Sebald, Commander William J., USNR (USNA, 1922)
   Brief description of the career of this intelligence/language officer-turned-diplomat, pp. 696-700, 702.

Seventh Fleet, U.S.
   Commander in Chief Jocko Clark makes Taipei his headquarters in the mid-1950s, pp. 683-784; lack of knowledge on staff

about conditions in Taiwan, pp. 685-786; commander in chief attempts to shakedown Japanese merchants to fund U.S. Naval Academy stadium gate in the late 1950s until halted by Ambassador Douglas MacArthur, pp. 835-837.

Sheen, Captain Fulton J., CHC, USNR
Asset to Vermilion (AKA-107) during transit to special mission with the Pope in the late 1940s, pp. 717-718.

Sherman, Vice Admiral Forrest P., USN (USNA, 1918)
As Commander, Carrier Division One in the mid-1940s often treated rudely by Congressmen when justifying Navy positions, pp. 706-707; transfers Tolley from intelligence position in 1947, pp. 711, 722; Tolley's assessment of, pp. 715-716, 725-726; visit to Tunisia as Commander, U.S. Naval Forces, Mediterranean in 1947, pp. 720-723; excellent representative of U.S. in Greece in the late 1940s, pp. 723-724; sends complimentary message upon Tolley's departure from Sixth Fleet as commanding officer of the Vermilion (AKA-107), pp. 726, 742; gives Tolley complete freedom in scheduling port visits as CO of the Vermilion in the late 1940s, pp. 729, 732, 736.

Sixth Fleet, U.S.
Operations in the Mediterranean in the 1940s, pp. 716, 719-720, 723, 726, 729; port visits by units of the Sixth Fleet, pp. 720-721, 723, 729, 732-740.

Smedberg, Vice Admiral William R., III, USN (USNA, 1926)
As head of Chief of Naval Operations Ernest King's intelligence unit on his U.S. Fleet staff gives Tolley carte blanche to set up network of connections, pp. 696, 700; contacted Tolley as Chief of Naval Personnel in the early 1960s regarding the Mikasa dedication, p. 843.

Smith, Rear Admiral Harold Page, USN (USNA, 1924)
Assessed by Tolley as Commander, Amphibious Group 2 in the early 1950s, pp. 772-774.

Sorge, Richard
Brilliant Soviet spy during World War II eventually hanged by the Japanese, pp. 576-577.

Soviet Union
Presence of U.S. naval observer at Vladivostok in 1942 couched in diplomatic role, pp. 511-512; conditions for foreign diplomatic personnel in the mid-1940s, pp. 514, 528-536, 540, 606-616; pertinence of having U.S. military personnel as ambassadors, p. 519; Lend-lease, pp. 515-516, 526, 529-531, 653-655; military uniforms and rank, pp. 535-539, 543-547, 827-830; conditions in the 1940s, pp. 534-535, 559, 578-581, 600, 626, 647; relations with Britain in the early 1940s, pp. 551, 562, 571, 603; American Embassy in the 1940s, pp. 552-556; alliance with Germany, pp. 567, 569-570; Poltava Naval Base, pp. 570,

574-575, 584; reluctance to allow any foreign military into country, pp. 570-571, 573-576; characteristics of people, pp. 571-574, 600-604; defectors, pp. 578, 614-615; military inventions, pp. 581-584; Second Front, pp. 589-591; marriage and divorce, pp. 605-606, 609; attitude towards foreigners, pp. 572-573, 600-601, 611-614, 629-632, 648; social conditions for Russians, pp. 618-625; American disillusionment with and watchfulness of in the 1940s, pp. 683, 707-708; Georgians, p. 709; submarine spying on U.S. training operations in the Atlantic in the late 1940s, pp. 746-747; Tolley teaches Russian intelligence gathering techniques at the Armed Forces Staff College in the early 1950s, pp. 754-755; dealings with Matthew Perry in Japan in the 1850s, importance of foreign currency, p. 620; attitude towards Japan after World War II, p. 821; spies during World War II, pp. 576-577; Tolley's friendship with Russian attache in Tokyo in the late 1950s, pp. 830-833.

Stalin, Josef
  Demanded second front in World War II, pp. 589, 591; relationship with Churchill, pp. 589-594, 597-598; relationship with Franklin Roosevelt, pp. 597-598; decadent son, p. 624.

Standley, Admiral William H., USN (USNA, 1895)
  Selected by President Roosevelt for Roberts Committee because of dedication to the Navy, pp. 497-500; sent to view damage at Pearl Harbor, after which he wrote ignored minority opinion, pp. 500-501, 520; as ambassador to Russia in the mid-1940s, pp. 501, 513-514, 518-519, 521, 525, 543, 590, 592; interest in learning of the Lanikai's exploits in 1941 after being a member of Roberts Committee, pp. 516, 518.

Stark, Admiral Harold R. "Betty," USN (USNA, 1903)
  Compared to George Marshall, p. 489; prior knowledge of Pearl Harbor attack, pp. 491, 494; orally directed by President Roosevelt to send three ships off Indo-Chinese coast to watch the Japanese, p. 496; Standley's opinion of Stark's treatment after Pearl Harbor, p. 520; put into awkward position due to verbal versus written instruction from Roosevelt, p. 567; dealings with Kelly Turner regarding war plans and the Office of Naval Instelligence, p. 649.

State Department
  Reliance on U.S. Navy for supplies for personnel in Russia in the 1940s, pp. 607-609; transfer of personnel whose views differed from administration policy, pp. 521, 523, 634-635, 640, 642-644; communists in in the 1940s, pp. 702, 704-705; embassy in Mexico in the mid-1950s, pp. 792-793.

Strong, Anna Louise
  Known communist supporter given V.I.P. treatment by State Department after World War II to get her back to China, pp. 704-705.

Taiwan
  Commander, U.S. Seventh Fleet spends most of his time in Taipei in the mid-1950s, pp. 783-784; Tolley views as Commander, Amphibious Squadron 5 with an eye towards possible necessity of amphibious evacuation, and is appalled by the lack of knowledge about the area, pp. 784-786; state of naval forces in the mid-1950s, p. 786; hospitality offered to Tolley, p. 787

Thomas, Captain Frank P., USN (USNA, 1914)
  Only commanding officer of the battleship North Carolina (BB-55) during Tolley's duty aboard in World War II who did not make flag rank, pp. 664, 669-670.

Tolley, Rear Admiral Kemp, USN (USNA, 1929)
  Command of USS Lanikai from December, 1941 to April, 1942, pp. 485, 493, 501-508, 516-520; duty at the U.S. Naval Academy in 1940, pp. 502-506; assistant naval attache in Russia from 1942 to 1944, pp. 511-616; family, pp. 514, 605-607, 614-620, 659, 708-709, 761, 792, 803-804, 813-814, 819, 844; vacation trip in 1944 through Iran, India, Israel, and Morocco, pp. 626-638; navigation officer on battleship North Carolina (BB-55) in 1944 and 1945, pp. 655-693; intelligence officer on OpNav staff from 1945 to 1947, pp. 644-652, 700-716; commanding officer of USS Vermilion (AKA-107) in 1947 and 1948, pp. 716-741, 772, 780-781; Commander, LST Squadron 2 in 1948 and 1949, pp. 742-753; Director, Intelligence Division, Armed Forces Staff College from 1949 to 1952, pp. 753-763; operations officer, Commander, Amphibious Group 2 (1952-1954), pp. 767-780; Commander, Amphibious Squad/Group 5 in 1954 to 1956 in the Western Pacific, pp. 781-795, 841, 853; chief of staff and aide to Commander Fleet Activities from 1956 to 1958, pp. 799-800, 826-833; Commander Fleet Activities in 1958 and 1959, pp. 799, 801-826, 833-840; retirement from the U.S. Navy in June, 1959, pp. 840-842; brief recall to active duty in 1961, pp. 842-845; second recall in 1967 as convoy commander in the Pacific, pp. 846-852; retirement since 1967, pp. 852-855.

Training, Cold Weather
  In Atlantic in the late 1940s, pp. 744-745, 747; course in tactics vis-a-vis the Russians offered in Canada in the early 1950s, p. 764.

Transport Squadron 5
  See Amphibious Squadron 5.

Trieste
  Controversy over this land between Yugoslavians and Italians creates touchy situation for U.S. Navy units in the Mediterranean in 1947, p. 722.

Trinity, MV
  Tolley's cruise aboard enroute from Australia to Iraq in 1942, p. 509.

Tunisia
  Tolley visits Commander U.S. Naval Forces, Mediterranean Forrest Sherman at Sfax in 1947, pp. 720-722.

Turkey
  Tension with the Greeks during participation in NATO amphibious exercise in 1951, pp. 778-779.

Turner, Rear Admiral Richmond K., USN (USNA, 1908)
  Presses for greater intelligence capacity for War Plans Office during World War II, p. 649.

<u>Vermilion</u>, USS (AKA-107)
  Excellent condition of ship upon Tolley's assumption of command in 1947, pp. 716, 771-772; operates with the Sixth Fleet in the 1940s, p. 716, 719-720, 723, 726, 729; description and purpose, p. 717; port visits in the late 1940s, pp. 720-721, 723, 729, 732-740; ship characteristics, pp. 780-781.

VonHeimburg, Commander Ernest H., USN (USNA, 1919)
  While on duty at the Office of Naval Intelligence in 1941 refuses to back Tolley's request for duty in Russia, p. 504.

Weather problems
  Heavy seas encountered by Tolley's LST squadron off Canadian coast in the late 1940s, pp. 749-750; typhoon in the Philippine Sea in 1945, pp. 673-675.

Wellings, Rear Admiral Augustus J., USN (USNA, 1920)
  As Commander, Amphibious Group 2 characterized as a practical logistician by staff officer Tolley in the 1950s, pp. 768-771, 780.

White, Captain Thomas A., USAAF (USMA, 1934)
  Future Air Force Chief of Staff as private pilot to William Bullitt in Russia in the early 1940s, pp. 539-540.

Wiley, Major Andrew, USMCR
  As officer in charge of the Russian section in the Office of Naval Intelligence in the mid-1940s, pp. 650-652.

Withington, Rear Admiral Frederic S., USN (USNA, 1923)
  As Commander Naval Forces, Japan in the mid-1950s, pp. 823, 836, 839.

World War II
  Relations between Allied countries in the early 1940s, pp. 561-562, 568-569, 591, 595-596; VJ Day, p. 681; demobilization at the end of war, pp. 695-696; Unknown Soldier from North Africa campaign, pp. 729-730.

Wright, Rear Admiral Jerauld, USN (USNA, 1918)
As Commander, Atlantic Fleet Amphibious Force in the late 1940s surprised at commendation Tolley received from Admiral Sherman after Mediterranean cruise, p. 726; backs Tolley's decision to keep peddlers off Annex 3, Naval Amphibious Base, Norfolk in the late 1940s, p. 753.

Yokosuka, Japan
U.S. Navy complex in the 1950s, pp. 799-800, 806; marriages between Japanese women and Americans, pp. 807-811; handling of American troublemakers, pp. 811-816; building ways and small acreage returned to Japanese in the 1950s, pp. 823-824.

Yugoslavia
Feud with Italy over Trieste creates tense situation for U.S. Navy units in the Mediterranean in 1947, p. 722.

www.ingramcontent.com/pod-product-compliance
Lightning Source LLC
Chambersburg PA
CBHW080622170426
43209CB00007B/1492